This book provides the fullest contemporary treatment of an issue which is particularly pressing today; when the claims of the nearest (e.g. parents, children, spouses, friends) conflict with the claims of the neediest, as they constantly do, where should preference go? Professor Hallett focuses first on a specific, representative case, pitting the lesser need of a son against the greater need of starving strangers. He brings to bear on this single paradigm all the resources of theological and philosophical reflection – scriptures, patristic teaching, the Thomistic tradition, current debates; and from this single example he sheds light on a wide range of comparable cases both private and public. This distinctive strategy leads to distinctive and challenging results, and at the same time helps to clarify the traditional "order of charity" and the celebrated "preferential option for the poor."

NEW STUDIES IN CHRISTIAN ETHICS

PRIORITIES AND CHRISTIAN ETHICS

NEW STUDIES IN CHRISTIAN ETHICS

General editor: Robin Gill

Editorial board: Stephen R. L. Clark, Anthony O. Dyson,
Stanley Hauerwas and Robin W. Lovin

Christian ethics has increasingly assumed a central place within academic theology. At the same time the growing power and ambiguity of modern science and the rising dissatisfaction within the social sciences about claims to value-neutrality have prompted renewed interest in ethics within the secular academic world. There is, therefore, a need for studies in Christian ethics which, as well as being concerned with the relevance of Christian ethics to the present day secular debate, are well informed about parallel discussions in recent philosophy, science or social science. *New Studies in Christian Ethics* aims to provide books that do this at the highest intellectual level and demonstrate that Christian ethics can make a distinctive contribution to this debate – either in moral substance or in terms of underlying moral justifications.

Other titles published in the series

PRIORITIES AND CHRISTIAN ETHICS

GARTH L. HALLETT

Saint Louis University

CAMBRIDGE
UNIVERSITY PRESS

PUBLISHED BY THE PRESS SYNDICATE OF THE UNIVERSITY OF CAMBRIDGE
The Pitt Building, Trumpington Street, Cambridge CB2 1RP, United Kingdom

CAMBRIDGE UNIVERSITY PRESS
The Edinburgh Building, Cambridge CB2 2RU, United Kingdom
40 West 20th Street, New York, NY 10011–4211, USA
10 Stamford Road, Oakleigh, Melbourne 3166, Australia

First published 1998

Printed in the United Kingdom at the University Press, Cambridge

Typeset in Baskerville 11/12.5pt [CE]

A catalogue record for this book is available from the British Library

Library of Congress cataloguing in publication data
Hallett, Garth.
Priorities and Christian Ethics / Garth L. Hallett.
p.   cm. – (New Studies in Christian Ethics)
Includes bibliographical references and index.
ISBN 0 521 62351 0 (hardback)
1. Christian ethics.   2. Priority (Philosophy).
I. Title.   II. Series.
BJ1278.P73H35   1998
241–dc21   97–41080   CIP

ISBN 0 521 62351 0 hardback

Christians already know that they should love one another, although they would benefit from further reflection about what that means. But even with more insight into their most basic moral standard, Christians would continue to face difficult decisions about what love requires under various kinds of conflicts.

Joseph L. Allen, *Love and Conflict*

One special relation limits another, and indeed, there can be little doubt that much of the moral life involves various competing obligations of this sort.

Gilbert Meilaender, *Friendship*

We should all agree that each of us is bound to show kindness to his parents and spouse and children, and to other kinsmen in a less degree . . . And to all men with whom we may be brought into relation we are held to owe slight services, and such as may be rendered without inconvenience: but those who are in distress or urgent need have a claim on us for special kindness. These are generally recognised claims: but we find considerable difficulty and divergence, when we attempt to determine more precisely their extent and relative obligation.

Henry Sidgwick, *The Methods of Ethics*

The problem is not whether we should do more for those who are close to us. The problem is that we are likely to do too much. We are fearful not of excessive distance but of complicity in evil.

George P. Fletcher, *Loyalty*

Contents

General editor's preface

This book is the twelfth in the series New Studies in Christian Ethics. Like the previous book in the series, Stanley Rudman's *Concepts of Persons and Christian Ethics*, as well as the very first book, Kieran Cronin's well received *Rights and Christian Ethics*, this present book provides a reliable guide for Christian ethics through a complex area of philosophical discussion. All three books exemplify the two key aims of this series – firstly to engage centrally with the secular moral debate at the highest possible intellectual level and, secondly, to demonstrate that Christian ethics can make a distinctive contribution to this debate, either in moral substance or in terms of underlying moral justifications.

Using the philosopher A. C. Ewing's moral dilemma about whether to spend money on a son going to university or instead on the needs of many people threatened with famine, Hallett seeks to explore a classic dilemma in both Christian and secular morality. Which is finally to be preferred, the nearest in the form of the son or the neediest in the form of the starving strangers? He explores this dilemma with style and obvious commitment and is, indeed, exploring an issue which is of real interest within and beyond Christian ethics. Working from an admittedly narrow basis, he is able to show that important broad questions about our responsibilities towards our families, neighbours and fellow nationals are raised by this moral dilemma. The questions raised by *Priorities and Christian Ethics* turn out to be amongst some of the most crucial for moral and, indeed, Christian living.

In the first two chapters Garth Hallett sets out a variety of philosophical and theological ways in which Ewing's moral dilemma might be resolved, arguing that none is in the end very satisfactory. Next he examines the New Testament and then the early Church in relation to the same moral dilemma. In them he sees an emphasis upon the neediest rather than the nearest. However, the Thomist tradition, and much subsequent Christian wisdom, although not fully losing sight of the needy, tends to reverse the order of preferential options. Now it is often the nearest who are preferred rather than the neediest. Hallett believes that this later development is mistaken. In the final two chapters he sets out his own distinctively Christian position, arguing that it is relevant to a wide range of moral issues. For him "the contribution which Christian ethics makes is strong, both negatively and positively – that is, both in what it excludes and in what it includes and powerfully supports." Negatively, it disregards class distinctions, as such, and, in contrast to much recent secular ethics, shifts preference from self to others. Positively, it supports the equal worth of persons and the parity, other things being equal, of acts and omissions. These considerations, which determine the verdict in Ewing's difficult case, would figure prominently in countless comparable cases pitting the near against the needy.

This book makes an important and distinctive contribution to the series.

ROBIN GILL

Acknowledgments

To Victoria Carlson-Casaregola, I am indebted for fine stylistic editing; to Charles Bouchard, John Langan, Richard Peddicord, and especially Martin Palmer, for comments on individual chapters; and to Gerard Hughes, John Kavanaugh, Gene Outka, William Rehg, and Edward Vacek, for their encouragement and comments on the whole work. May their generosity be blessed by a richer reward than my sincere thanks.

CHAPTER I

A thorny question

Among Christians there has been general agreement that loving concern should extend to all, including enemies, and that love in the heart should manifest itself in deeds. Concerning what those deeds should be there has been much less agreement. Indeed, Christians' views have diverged at every level of moral discernment – with respect to all actions, general types of action, specific types of action, and individual actions. At the second, next-to-most-general level, on which this study will focus, various Christian preference-rules vie for recognition or jostle for precedence. With respect to self and others, competing rules have varied from self-preference at one extreme to denial of all self-seeking at the other. With respect to specific categories of others, there has been somewhat greater consensus. Christians have agreed, for example, both that preference should go to one's nearest and dearest, to some extent, and that preference should go to the neediest, to some extent. However, to what extent? Suppose these two preferences come into conflict, as they frequently do, and nearest vie with neediest. What then?

A TROUBLING VERDICT

Philosophers as well as theologians have grappled with this question; and society at large has had its own, less formulated views. Some decades ago, the Cambridge philosopher A. C. Ewing remarked: "It is clear that the money spent by a man in order to provide his son with a university education could save the lives of many people who were perishing of hunger in a famine, yet most people would rather blame than praise a man who should deprive his son of a university education on this account."[1] Both parts of Ewing's judgment sound plausible: the action might save many lives, and most people here or in Britain – including many Christians – would nonetheless condemn it. Indeed, as James Rachels has observed:

> Most people seem to believe that one has an obligation to provide the necessities of life for other children only after one has already provided a great range of luxuries for one's own. On this view, it is permissible to provide one's own children with virtually everything they need in order to have a good start in life – not only food and clothing, but, if possible, a good education, opportunities for travel, opportunities for enjoyable leisure, and so forth. In the United States children of affluent families often have TV sets, stereos, and new computers, all laid out in their own rooms. They drive their own cars to high school. Few people seem to think there is anything wrong with this – parents who are unable to provide their children with such luxuries nevertheless aspire to do so.[2]

The same attitude may be taken, notes Frank Sharp, "when the alternatives are the good of a friend and that of an acquaintance, a neighbor and a stranger, a fellow-countryman and a foreigner, a member of one's own race and a member of another race."[3] One should prefer the interests of the friend, neighbor, countryman, or member of the same race, even though less benefit results overall.

To have a convenient term, suggests Sharp, we may say that representatives of this viewpoint favor the *good of the nearer.* "'Nearer' here means nearer to the agent in the sense that he or she feels bound to the individual in question by ties of affection, friendship, blood, personal gratitude, or congeniality of tastes and interests."[4] Within the bounds thus amply drawn, Ewing's case pits the nearest of the near (one's own children) against the neediest of the needy (starving strangers).

Some ethicists favor one side,[5] some the other,[6] while still others confess their perplexity.[7] The issue Ewing poses is difficult, and troubling.

On the one hand, a verdict in favor of the starving might carry alarming implications. If parents should not finance

something as important as their children's higher education,
what of other, less intimate relationships, and what of other,
less important expenditures? "What about the children's music
lessons, the family camping trips? Hardly the necessities of
life"[8] – yet should they all go? Should nothing but strict
necessities – shoes, socks, soap, paper – surround the Christmas
tree? Should there even be a Christmas tree? Troubling question follows troubling question, not only for parents, children,
grandparents, cousins, friends, and others, faced with similar
options, but also for those affected by their decisions. If parents
should not finance their children's higher education, what
follows for people like myself? Should I teach in a university
that parents should not support? Should the admissions office
recruit their children or the university's development office
solicit their funds? Given the pressing needs of the destitute,
should there even be an institution such as Saint Louis
University? Common sense offers reassuring answers to these
and similar queries, or dismisses them as quixotic. However, is
common sense trustworthy?

Its verdict, favoring the son over the starving, prompts as
grave misgivings as does the contrary verdict – misgivings
about our culture and its "necessities,"[9] misgivings about the
"common sense" that renders such a judgment.[10] Our moral
perceptions, like our other perceptions, are subject to a law of
perspective: "Matters which are near to us, both psychically
and physically, loom large; we consider them more important.
And since our reactions reflect our assessment of the various
possible outcomes, our actions too typically reflect this bias to
what is near to us."[11] A cutting remark disturbs our sleep; a
distant disaster does not. Thus it appears, as Hume noted,
"that in the original frame of our mind, our strongest attention
is confin'd to ourselves; our next is extended to our relations
and acquaintance; and 'tis only the weakest which reaches to
strangers and indifferent persons. This partiality, then, and
unequal affection, must not only have an influence on our
behaviour and conduct in society, but even on our ideas of vice
and virtue."[12]

What inclination fosters, familiarity affirms. Our tendencies gain strength from our surroundings. Thus Peter Singer has observed:

> Given a society in which a wealthy man who gives 5 percent of his income to famine relief is regarded as most generous, it is not surprising that a proposal that we all ought to give away half our incomes will be thought to be absurdly unrealistic. In a society which held that no man should have more than enough while others have less than they need, such a proposal might seem narrow-minded. What it is possible for a man to do and what he is likely to do are both, I think, very greatly influenced by what people around him are doing and expecting him to do.[13]

And what the individual considers right and morally acceptable is strongly influenced by what others consider right and morally acceptable. So the majority opinion which Ewing cites in support of his verdict may also cast doubt on its validity.

Bias shows when Ewing argues:

> It still seems plain to me, and I am sure would seem so to almost everybody else that, if a man were to deprive his wife and children against their will of all comforts and purchasable pleasures, leaving them only bare necessaries, on the ground that he could use the money thus saved to preserve several families from a greater pain or loss of happiness than he inflicted on his own by giving it to a charitable organization he would be acting wrongly not rightly.[14]

Why "against their will"? Why thus load the dice? If the man's wife and children agreed, would the deed still be plainly wrong?

Ewing's choice of witnesses elicits still stronger misgivings. "Most people," he says, would agree with him; but what of the starving? Would they agree that they should die and the son should get his university education? If not, who would be the biased ones? Might not the destitute have a more realistic appreciation of what was at stake than Ewing or the rest of us ensconced in Western comfort? Might not the deprived have sharper mind-sight than we to spot our rationalizations?[15]

The great disadvantage, it seems, of the distant people whom we might save is their anonymity. To us, they have no names, no faces, no life histories, no goals, hopes, and aspirations, no loved ones dependent on them or distressed by their plight.

They are mere ciphers. What chance, then, do they stand in competition with our nearest and dearest, whom we know so intimately? How could a father possibly agree that he should assist such nonentities and leave his flesh and blood in the lurch?

Even the slaves whom their masters demoted from full humanity were more real than these remote wraiths. So were feudal serfs. So were the Indians whom Spaniards, Portuguese, and other colonizers despised and mistreated. So were the wives, mothers, and daughters who for so long occupied a secondary status. They at least had names and faces. Will distant, faceless strangers therefore be the last to join the human race? And do we, the well-to-do, now stand in their regard as masters, lords, colonizers, and husbands once stood with respect to slaves, serfs, natives, and wives? Is that why Ewing's verdict sounds so commonsensical? Will future generations view our common sense as one more instance of moral blindness, comparable to these prior instances?[16]

"Fifty years ago," comments Joseph Sneed, "it was at least tolerable to most people in developed nations that a good portion of the rest of the world's population lived at or near the starvation level for their entire, rather short lives. The number of people for whom this is a tolerable situation appears to be diminishing."[17] Are we then witnessing a phenomenon similar to the erosion of support for slavery? "Perhaps," surmises Susan James, "this neglect will look as outrageous to our descendants as slavery now seems to us and the justifications offered for it as self-serving and contradictory as the moral beliefs of plantation owners."[18]

Queries and misgivings multiply. How would we react if the starving acquired faces? What would our verdict be if the competing parties stood before us – the well-fed son on the left, hankering (perhaps) for a university education; a tottering grandfather, emaciated father, grieving mother, and skin-and-bones children on the right, pleading for minimal subsistence? How would we judge a parent who took from the son to assist such specific, desperately needy individuals? How *do* we regard such sharing?

In *The Starved and the Silent*, Aloysius Schwartz tells of visiting Mrs. Rhi, a Korean mother of six. Their shack, slapped together with canvas, tar paper, cardboard, and old lumber, had no plumbing, electricity, or sanitation. The family, supported by scavenging, had the bare minimum to stay alive. And yet, "Her children frequently would bring home orphan waifs and beggars picked up in the streets whom she would feed and clothe. As a matter of fact the whole family seemed to have inherited the mother's generous heart."[19]

Such generosity may be rare, but Schwartz's admiring reaction to it is not. At the turn of the century, Edward Westermarck reported:

Captain Hall holds an equally favourable opinion of those Eskimo with whom he came in contact. "As between themselves," he says, "there can be no people exceeding them in this virtue – kindness of heart. Take, for instance, times of great scarcity of food. If one family happens to have any provisions on hand, these are shared with all their neighbours. If one man is successful in capturing a seal, though his family may need it all to save them from the pangs of hunger, yet the whole of his people about, including the poor, the widow, the fatherless, are at once invited to a seal-feast."[20]

In these real-life instances, the lineup shifts. Multiple, hungry children – Mrs. Rhi's, the Eskimos' – replace the single, well-fed son; so the destitute have much stronger competition. Yet the reaction of Schwartz, Hall, Westermarck, and others – perhaps ourselves – is one of admiration, not condemnation, when these parents take from their nearest and dearest to share with still needier neighbors.[21]

The Eskimos were not Christians. Neither was Mrs. Rhi. Yet Schwartz speaks of her "Christ-like" attitude. Should Christians be less generous? Would it be wrong for them to do as she did? What does the much-touted "preferential option for the poor" amount to if it means denying the starving so that the well-fed may flourish?[22]

These queries are not arguments. They are only straws in the wind, blowing the other way, against Ewing's verdict and the dictates of "common sense." I find Ewing's case problematic, and I think other Christians should too. What light, then, can Christian ethics, assisting and assisted by moral philosophy, throw on this troubling sample and the dilemma it poses?

A PARADOX

Contemporary Christian ethics reveals this paradox: the issue of nearest versus neediest is much more pressing today than in earlier times, yet is much less closely studied now than then.

First, the issue is more pressing, for three reasons:[23]

(1) Thanks to modern means of production, the wealth of whole nations – indeed of whole regions – is unprecedented; yet their wealth contrasts starkly with the deprivation and misery of other nations and regions.[24] According to a recent estimate, approximately 786 million people – one in every five – in the developing world are chronically malnourished.[25] More than half the world's people go hungry every day.[26] "Today," declares an Oxfam America circular, "34,000 children will die as a result of hunger and malnutrition."

(2) Thanks to modern communications, this contrast is known, in general and in detail. "We are the first generation," wrote William Temple in 1977, "to hear the cry of the suffering expressed from every corner of the world, and knowledge brings responsibility."[27]

(3) Thanks to modern modes of transportation and social organization, we are now much better equipped to meet these global needs. "Until very recently," notes Earl Winkler, "it was only in what can be roughly characterized as emergency situations that any possibility existed of saving others through the sacrifice of the self, or a child, friend, etc."[28] Today, as Rachels observes, "with relief agencies ready to take our assistance all over the world, needing only sufficient resources to do so, it is almost as easy to provide food for a child in Africa as to provide for one's own. The same goes for providing basic medical care: International relief agencies carry medical assistance around the world on the same basis."[29]

Given these changes, most better-off people now face the

kind of dilemma Ewing described. The issue of nearest versus neediest cannot be avoided. Whoever might devote resources of money, time, or energy to a child, parent, spouse, friend, or neighbor might devote them instead to far needier people. And the alternative is constantly present, on a daily basis, as it was not earlier. A famine or plague might strike, and then it would pass. Beggars generally were not starving, and the alms they asked posed no great threat to one's nearest and dearest. Thus moral theologians of the past sometimes remarked how little application their treatment of nearest versus neediest had in real life – even as they studied the problem in sometimes lavish detail.[30]

Contemporary Christian ethics has no comparable treatment to offer.[31] Yet more than ever contemporary Christians need light on this vexing issue. How to account for this paradox? I can think of various likely reasons for contemporary neglect, and I shall mention some of them, so as to indicate more fully the need for the present study. Reasons for the neglect suggest reasons for remedying it.

(1) The new world situation not only makes the problem more pressing; it also makes it more troubling. Always difficult, the issue is now thornier than ever. Whoever grasps it firmly may be forced to painful conclusions. Whoever does not grasp it firmly should not bother to grasp it at all; better to remain silent than to waffle. So abstention is understandable. However, if the issue is not only pressing but also deeply troubling, this adds further reason to consider what light Christian ethics can shed on it.

(2) In the *Summa theologica*'s treatments of the order of charity and of almsgiving, Aquinas confronted the issue of nearest versus neediest more carefully and fully than his predecessors had. Cajetan and others elucidated Aquinas's teaching; Bañez, Suarez, Vasquez, de Lugo, de Soto, de Toledo, de Vitoria, and others amplified and nuanced it;[32] and manualists perpetuated it far into the present century. Accordingly, some recent ethicians may have seen no need for further discussion. The matter had received adequate attention.

For reasons chapter 5 will indicate, I do not share this

favorable judgment. In some respects the Thomistic tradition has been admirable. However, its treatment of nearest versus neediest has suffered from notable defects: its conflating the service of nearest with the service of self, its preferring self to others, its placing great weight on social status, its neglecting the considerations which figure most prominently in the present inquiry. A new treatment is needed.

(3) Protestant ethicians long looked askance at Catholic casuistry, and doubtless many today, Catholic and Protestant, harbor sentiments akin to those of William Sherlock:[33]

> Had God prescribed how much every man must give to the poor, they might have observed this proportion of giving without any charity, and then such gifts as these had been no acts of charity, when the gift and the charity was parted: but a charitable man will give in proportion to the degrees of his charity, and therefore charity and the increase of charity is the only proper object of command; for he will give liberally, who loves much; and the proportion of giving is commanded in the degrees of charity, and will observe a just proportion.[34]

In short, "Love, then do what you will."

There is something right about this Augustinian saying. Loving acts are subjectively admirable, and well-regulated love is objectively admirable. But what kind of love, precisely, is well regulated? Love, if genuine, desires to be well informed, lest its good intentions go for naught.[35] It follows, then, that genuine love will recognize the need for deliberation and discernment – especially when one valid love vies with another. What is the "just proportion" that Sherlock alludes to?

(4) Current antipathy to "charity" and "almsgiving" – "things that were shown to be out of date by the end of the Middle Ages"[36] – also deflects attention from Ewing's question. So does the conviction that individual charity does not suffice. "Can the rich churches of the north, vis-à-vis the poor of the south, rectify the situation simply by means of alms – a mechanism, now familiar, of exploitation and injustice?"[37] " 'Giving to charity' is like an aspirin to dull the pain, but does nothing to cure the illness."[38]

To start with this last grievance, it is true and important that individual giving cannot cure the systemic ills that permit or occasion massive suffering. But so long as these ills remain – hence for the foreseeable future – such assistance may make the difference between life and death, misery and a tolerable existence, for many people. As Schwartz observes, "Although individual charity may not be enough, at least it is a step, a start, a striking out in the right direction – and this is infinitely better than merely wringing one's hands or rending one's garments."[39]

Besides, the issue of nearest versus neediest reaches beyond giving and other forms of individual assistance. Practically any move toward social justice involves both the nearest on the one hand and the neediest on the other, vying for limited resources. "An option for the poor," writes Donal Dorr, "is a commitment to struggle against structural injustice. Those who make such an option are in solidarity with the victims of our society, and with them they set out to work for a more equitable sharing of power and resources in society and in the Church."[40] They do so at a cost not only to themselves, but also to their nearest and dearest. As Stephen Pope has noted, these and other special ties are frequently slighted. "Discussion of the preferential option too often tends to oversimplify our responsibility to the poor by effectively ignoring the multitude of other concrete responsibilities that comprise and shape our lives."[41]

(5) Recently, emphasis has fallen more on public than on private remedies. Ewing's concerns may therefore seem passé. The government should do what individuals cannot do, or cannot do as effectively. However, political endeavor, at whatever level, can be analyzed in terms either of social wholes or of the individuals who compose them. If it is viewed atomically, in terms of the actions of individual voters, legislators, or officeholders, then they have kin, friends, neighbors, clients, or compatriots who may be affected by their decisions. If, instead, political endeavor is viewed collectively, as carried out by social wholes (cities, counties, states, nations, corporations), then they may be subject to preference-rules analogous to those for individuals. Whether, how, and to what extent the considerations that apply in the private sector apply also in the public

sphere remains to be considered. Christian ethics has neglected this dimension of the nearest-neediest issue, and the deficiency should be remedied.

(6) Today, as in the past, with respect to private or public assistance, attention has centered on the cost to self more than on the cost to one's nearest and dearest.[42] At first glance, this emphasis looks realistic. The concerns of one's nearest and dearest often coincide with one's own, and concern for one's own interests competes more powerfully, overall, with the concerns of the neediest than does concern for one's nearest and dearest. So primacy belongs, it would seem, to the second step in the traditional order of charity rather than to the third – that is, to the confrontation between self and others rather than that between various others (e.g., nearest and neediest). Neglect of the nearest-neediest confrontation is therefore understandable.

Understandable, perhaps, but not warranted.[43] Psychologically, concern for nearest and dearest seriously challenges concern for self as the chief competitor with concern for the neediest, and therefore merits serious attention.[44] Ethically, concern for nearest and dearest outranks concern for self.[45] As I shall indicate shortly, the Christian credentials of family-preference, as of other-preference generally, are far stronger than those of self-preference. Herein lies the answer to a further obstacle.

(7) Why combine these particular preference-rules – one favoring the nearest, the other the neediest? Why not study them separately? As Henry Sidgwick observed, "the duties of affection are admittedly liable to come into competition with each other, and with other duties; and when this apparent conflict of duties occurs, we manifestly need as precise a definition as possible of the conflicting obligations, in order to make a reasonable choice among the alternatives of conduct presented to us."[46] However, competing duties are many and various, and we cannot be expected to pair them all, two by two, and exhaustively study the pairs. So why not study the duties one by one, as Sidgwick's words suggest, and assess their respective weights, then draw the appropriate verdicts in

individual conflicts? Why not attend, for example, to the claims of the neediest, and the claims of the nearest, then compare them to decide which way the father should opt, in favor of his son's university education or in favor of the starving?

Some ethicians have proceeded in this fashion, considering each duty by itself. On one page they may proclaim the duty to assist the needy. ("How wicked it would be, if a little girl were run over by a carriage, and I were to leave her to be trodden to death, because I did not owe her anything, and wished to mind my own business."[47]) On another page they may declare the duty of parents to nurture their children. ("I would remark, that the parent is under obligation . . . so far as it is in his power, to give a child such an education, as is suited to his peculiar bias and capabilities."[48]) Everyone may agree. I should assist the needy as much as I can; I should provide for my children as best I can. However, suppose I cannot both assist the starving and provide my child with an optimal education. What then? Separate treatments typically offer no guidance for concrete conflicts.

It is doubtful whether they could. By what absolute standard might the weight of parental duty be assessed, then the weight of duty to the starving, and the two then be compared? An alternative is to assess their comparative weights. It may be that on this occasion, as on others, "to state one obligation without its counterpart is to miss the full meaning of the obligation."[49] Do you really understand a claim's strength if you do not know its strength relative to that of its chief rival?

In any case, concern for nearest and dearest figures as the foremost competitor, ethically, with concern for the neediest;[50] and the reverse also holds. "Many defend their economic privileges on the ground that they are providing for families. The ethical question is how far the self-protection of each family is justified against the claims of all families. In the world today, with its mass hunger, the question of how much of the world's goods, food, and land should belong to any family, becomes very acute."[51] This matching of nearest and neediest, therefore, is not a random but a natural, necessary confrontation. Among Christian preference-rules, these are the two chief contenders. Self-preference may be stronger *de facto*, but not *de jure* (again, see below).

(8) The vogue of virtue-centered ethics among contemporary Christian ethicists also helps to explain current neglect of the issue here confronted. The issue concerns conduct (e.g., should the father provide his son with a university education or feed the starving?), whereas it is sometimes suggested, as William Frankena notes, "that morality should center on character, dispositions, virtues and vices, rather than on external conduct, rules, and oughts or ought nots."[52] Such a stance marginalizes Ewing's issue.

It also leaves it in the dark. To be sure, generosity is a virtue; but should the father be more generous toward his son or toward the starving? To be sure, charity is a virtue; but what preferences does charity dictate? Devotion to duty is commendable, but where does duty lie? Concern for one's own is admirable, and so is concern for the needy; but what light do these truisms shed on the father's quandary? Rarely in the present inquiry will considerations of "character, dispositions, virtues and vices" serve to clarify "external conduct, rules, and oughts or ought nots." Clarification of conduct requires attention to conduct.

(9) Nowadays, many Christian ethicians take a jaundiced view of focused, analytic inquiry; they are therefore likely to regard a study like this one as unfortunately narrow.[53] There is so much more to Christianity than morality, they may feel, so much more to morality than conduct, so much more to conduct than distribution, so much more to distribution than nearest versus neediest! How cramped, how myopic, to fasten one's attention on that single spot! Accordingly, I am not surprised to find the spot little studied by contemporary Christian ethicians.[54]

It is legitimate and necessary, I submit, to specify a focus for inquiry and to do so with all requisite precision. Thereafter, any time the inclination arises to resist the resultant narrowing, the response should be: will a broader focus illuminate the chosen area of investigation, or will it only perpetuate past obscurity and confusion? I recognize, however, that fidelity to my stated purpose will exact a price. I shall have to bypass, as irrelevant, a variety of interesting, important considerations.

(10) Reluctance to tackle the issue of nearest versus neediest has a further likely explanation: the issue's special difficulty. The question of self versus others is far easier to deal with. In real life (as opposed to philosophers' imaginings), the distinction between self and others is clear-cut: there is no problem as to who is "I" and who is not, nor any problem of degree (more or less I, more or less another). By contrast, neither nearness nor neediness is similarly definite. Nearness varies widely in kind and degree,[55] and so does neediness.[56]

Indeed, the very notion of need is unclear. If I want something badly enough,[57] or enough people have it,[58] do I need it? If lacking it would interfere with my plan of life, do I need it – regardless of what my plan is?[59] "Even for such a fundamental human need as nutrition," one writer comments, "those minimal requirements that on the basis of scientific evidence may be called necessities cannot be rigorously prescribed . . . When we turn to objects of expenditure like education, aesthetics, recreation, religion, or even children, the minimal requirements must be expressed mostly in terms of the psychical, emotional, or spiritual needs of men rather than in terms of physical requirements."[60]

Nearness is equally problematic. Mere spatial proximity, in itself, lacks moral relevance. ("The fact that a person is physically near to us, so that we have personal contact with him, may make it more likely that we *shall* assist him, but this does not show that we *ought* to help him rather than another who happens to be further away."[61]) If, however, I am tied more closely to one person by kinship and to another by affection, which of the two is "nearer" to me? Of my kin, who is nearer: cousin, nephew, uncle, aunt? Of my next-of-kin, who is nearest: father, mother, child, spouse? And what of other types of kindred?

Canon law, in condemning marriages between kinsfolk as incestuous, held a much more complex view of kinship. In addition to consanguinity, whether legitimate or otherwise, which it termed *natural kinship*, it took cognizance of *legal kinship*, created by adoption and deemed to

exist between the adopted person and the entire family of his foster-
father; *legitimate affinity*, which marriage caused to exist between each
of the spouses and the family of the other; *illegitimate affinity*, which
resulted from all illicit carnal relations; and, finally, *spiritual kinship*,
which united the baptized child and his parents with the godfathers
and godmothers and their close relatives, and even the confessor with
the penitent and the catechist with the catechumen.[62]

Genetic science tops these complications with its own:
"When new reproductive technologies are used, each child
can, in theory, have five different people with some role in
creation: the woman who provides the egg, the man who
provides the sperm, the woman who carried the fetus and the
woman and man who raise the child. What then does it mean
to be mother, father or sibling?"[63] Add colleagues, clients,
neighbors, friends, associates, acquaintances, compatriots, coreligionists – perhaps even pets[64] – and it becomes evident why
Christian ethicians might hesitate to enter such a morass.[65]
How can the question of nearest versus neediest be rendered
manageable and intelligible, let alone be answered? My solution to this problem will appear in chapter 2.

(11) Finally, a reason that occasioned my own delay may
conceivably have affected others' readiness to undertake this
inquiry,[66] and in any case requires fuller comment than the
preceding suggestions. I had to write two books before this one,
because two related inquiries had to prepare the way.

PRELIMINARIES

First, a specific query about nearest and neediest cannot
entirely prescind from the more general query: what makes any
action right or wrong? What general criterion, if any, governs
this and other areas of conduct? A utilitarian criterion might
yield a ready verdict in Ewing's case: aid to the starving would
bring greater utility than aid to the son; so Ewing is wrong.
However, do special relationships count for nothing? Can
results alone dictate moral verdicts? General questions like
these had first to be clarified, from a Christian point of view

(which is not to say, just for Christians), before the specific issue of nearest versus neediest could be addressed.

A previous work proposed and defended the following Christian criterion: "Within a prospective, objective focus, and in the sense thus specified, an action is right if and only if it promises to maximize value as fully, or nearly as fully, as any alternative action, with no restriction on the kind of value concerned, whether human or nonhuman, moral or nonmoral, consequential or nonconsequential."[67] I need not here elucidate this principle of Value-Maximization, for in the present inquiry it will have only negative import: I cannot take for granted any utilitarian or consequentialist restrictions, but neither can I assume the contrary. The principle leaves open whether, in any given instance, results alone suffice to determine right and wrong, better and worse. Specifically, in the present instance it does not determine whether the fact of being nearest or the fact of being neediest adds extra, nonconsequential weight to the preference for nearest or neediest. Chapter 2 will amplify this point.

Second, discussion of nearest versus neediest cannot prescind from the further question of self versus others, with which many treatments link it, normatively as well as psychologically. "Parents love their children because they love themselves,"[68] it is said, approvingly. "Here," we are told, "is the governing principle: Since the foundation or motive of our charity is their union with God and with ourselves, the degree of our charity towards any person should be in proportion to the degree of these two unions. We should have a greater love for those who are more closely united with God and with us."[69] Our nearest are "our own."[70] Their interests are our interests; benefit to them is benefit to us.[71] So if preference should go to self over others, as traditional moral theology maintained, preference should go to nearest over others; and the degree of preference for the nearest may derive directly from the degree of preference for oneself.[72] ("I am entitled to put the thumb on the moral scales on behalf of my own interests – but I extend this to my offspring, my parents, my closest friends, and so on."[73]) However, *should* preference go to self over others? Should the two questions – nearest versus others and self versus others – be thus linked?

I have argued against this connection. The Christian credentials of parity for self and others, from which similar inferences have been drawn,[74] are weak, and the credentials of self-preference are still weaker. Much stronger, indeed strongest of all, are those of the rival norm I have labeled Self-Subordination: "One may and should give independent consideration to one's own benefit, but only on the condition that maximum benefit to others is first assured (whether directly or indirectly, through benefit to oneself)."[75] This norm illustrates the kind of relational, nonconsequentialist considerations which Value-Maximization accommodates. However it, too, casts slight positive illumination on Ewing's case or on the general issue of nearest versus neediest. Self-Subordination just adds further vetoes: as a verdict via consequentialist theory is excluded, so too is a verdict via self-others parity or self-preference.

Since the norm of Self-Subordination will play only this negative role in what follows, I need not try to summarize the case previously made for it, from Scripture, tradition, and philosophical reflection, in preference to each of the five rival norms represented in Christian thinking. That would not be feasible. When, however, in chapter 5, the norm's negative import comes into play, I can there make a case against the specific rival norm – self-preference – that figures prominently in the Thomistic treatment of nearest versus neediest.

THE INQUIRY'S RATIONALE

The connections severed and solutions precluded by Value Maximization and Self-Subordination make the problem of nearest versus neediest look more tractable than it is. Its difficulty, now heightened, constitutes one of many reasons that have come to light for addressing the problem at length. As anticipated, reasons for neglect of the problem have revealed numerous reasons for remedying the neglect; and these reasons, with earlier ones, explain the present inquiry. In summary, the issue here addressed deserves extended treatment because:

- It is very general – broader, for example, than much-discussed questions such as abortion, euthanasia, contraception, and capital punishment.
- It carries weighty, life-or-death implications for multitudes of people.
- It elicits great perplexity and disagreement.
- It presses with special urgency in our day.
- Earlier treatments, which were fuller, leave much to be desired.
- Intuitive, unreflective love offers inadequate guidance.
- The issue reaches beyond "charity" and "alms."
- It also extends beyond individual action.
- Ethicians have largely neglected these wider ramifications.
- Such a question, concerning conduct, cannot be settled indirectly, by adverting to "character, dispositions, virtues and vices."
- Abstractive, focused study of such an issue is both legitimate and necessary.
- The problem is particularly difficult – more difficult, for example, than facile derivations from consequences or self-interest would suggest – and therefore demands protracted treatment.

Lengthy though it is, this list may still leave doubts. Contemporary philosophers – Robert Goodin, James Rachels, Peter Singer, and others – have written more on nearest and neediest than have contemporary theologians. Why duplicate their efforts? What can a Christian approach possibly add? That remains to be seen. The principle of Value-Maximization already demands a break with some philosophical treatments; so does the norm of Self-Subordination, which, so far as I can judge, is unknown to philosophical literature. Moreover, regardless of the outcome, what has been lacking till now is a thorough study of what Christian scripture, tradition, and theological reflection, aided by contemporary philosophical thought, have to say on this subject of great interest to Christians as to others.

CHAPTER 2

Finding a focus

Informed of this study's topic, people sometimes ask: "Which side do you favor – the nearest or the neediest?" I have to reply that I cannot answer a query so worded. If my child begs for a dune buggy and the starving beg for food, I should favor the neediest. If my child is starving and so is a stranger, I should favor the nearest. The question requires more careful, specific formulation.

The same need, of greater care and precision, has often been apparent. Simple formulations have yielded simple solutions – too simple to be useful – on one side and the other.

A SAMPLING

On the side of the neediest, Domingo de Soto advised: "Where there is doubt, judgment should go for the poor rather than against them."[1] Apparently, then, in Ewing's case judgment should favor the starving rather than the son – provided there is doubt. But is there doubt? Should there be? Does poverty automatically trump all competing considerations? If not, how are we to explain or justify de Soto's judgment for the poor in all doubtful cases? Perhaps it echoes St. Louis's counsel to his son: "Always side with the poor rather than with the rich, until you are certain of the truth"[2] – that is, until you are sure about the facts. However, in cases of the kind that concern us – cases like Ewing's – if the facts are as stated or supposed, the doubt remains. The facts are the source of the doubt.

In *The Nature and Measure of Charity*, Sherlock more amply expressed a similar view:

Thus, as for proportions, a charitable mind sets no other bounds to its charity, but only ability; that the only question is, whether we can spare any thing from our selves and families? And what we can spare? Now when charity is the judge of this, it is always a favourable judge on the side of the poor and miserable, and always the more favourable judge, the greater the charity is. It will teach us to think, that we want less, and consequently can spare more, when we consider how much others want.[3]

Will charity teach the father, then, that his son can do without a university education? That he and his son can do without a home? That they can do without daily nourishment? "Can" is an elastic term. People are physically capable of sacrificing their lives for the starving, of reducing themselves and their families to misery for the sake of the miserable; but should they? Where does Sherlock draw the line, and why? The need for clarification becomes doubly evident in view of his earlier statement:

The great controversy then is between our love to ourselves, our wives and children, and charity to the poor. Now there is no dispute, but the first must have the preference; but yet charity to the poor must have its place also. And then the only question is, in what proportion this must be? And that is a very hard question, if you put it in arithmetick [*sic*], for I can name no proportion, nor has our Saviour thought fit to name any.[4]

What does this "indisputable" preference signify, if, as previously alleged, charity "is always a favourable judge on the side of the poor and miserable?" And what does the preference for ourselves and our loved ones amount to if Sherlock can state no proportion? What is the father in Ewing's case to do? Flip a coin?

John Wesley states the same preference in classic and somewhat fuller fashion:

If you desire to be a faithful and a wise steward, out of that portion of your Lord's goods which he has for the present lodged in your hands, but with the right of resuming whenever it pleases him, first, provide things needful for yourself – food to eat, raiment to put on, whatever nature moderately requires for preserving the body in health and strength. Secondly, provide these for your wife, your children, your servants, or any others who pertain to your household. If when this is done there be an overplus left, then "do good to them that are of the household of faith." If there be an overplus still, "as you have opportunity, do good unto all men."[5]

This ordering appears lexical: only when all previous claims have been met should one attend to subsequent claimants. Even the direst need cannot break in before its allotted moment – if that moment ever arrives. Mrs. Rhi, for example, should not share her family's minimal fare with starving children until she and her children have been reasonably clothed, fed, and sheltered. Is this Wesley's meaning? Would such be his verdict? One suspects that he here ignored such possible situations and, having ignored them, offered no clue to their resolution. Nearest won over neediest by default.

Stephen Pope inverts Wesley's priorities. "Rather," he writes, "than simply extend charity universally in an outward radiating series of concentric circles, the *preferential* option reverses the usual order of priorities whereby the nearest are given priority and needs of the most distant are secondary. Special devotion and priority is given to those to whom we are least bound by ties of affection, blood, class, etc."[6] This suggests that if my children are starving and others' children are starving, I should feed their children first, since I am less bound to them by ties of affection and blood. From one extreme, the pendulum swings to the other. I suspect that Pope might wish to revise his pronouncements rather than accept such a far-out inference. But how can a just balance be struck? Where does the happy mean lie?

"I would like to see theorists of Christian love take the familial sphere seriously – even as primary," writes Stephen Post.[7] In his view, proximities grounded in the familial sphere have a special weight and therefore create unique obligations. These obligations do not require extensive and strained justi-fication over against what we owe strangers, however distant, but rather constitute "a unique God-given trust of high moral value."[8] Doubtless Post would concur that the needs of the destitute also have special weight and create their own obliga-tions.[9] In what sense, then, are familial obligations "primary"? In a case like Ewing's, do the claims of the nearest automatically prevail over the claims of the neediest – regardless of what their respective claims are?

No doubt we should accord some weight to the claims of the nearest and some to those of the neediest, but how much weight? Familiar nostrums offer little guidance: "We need not impoverish ourselves to help the poor," we are told, "But we must do what we can."[10] "He defrauds the poor of their right, who detains from them beyond his own necessary, prudent, and convenient supplies."[11] "Let him ask himself, whether, in his own conscience, what he gives, bears any proportion to that love and charity to the poor and miserable which God requires."[12] "Justice demands that each one do what is in his power to relieve the wants of his fellow man."[13] In Ewing's case the father is *able* to feed the starving; he *can* deprive his son of a university education; but *should* he?

Lilian Brandt proposes a "pragmatic formula," according to which "A man can afford, and ought to contribute to philanthropic purposes such a part of his income as his informed intelligence, guided by a sincere concern for the common welfare, dictates; and this amount he can afford, and ought, to give, 'even though he be the poorest man in Israel.' "[14] To be sure, but what part of his income is that? What does an "informed intelligence" dictate, and how is it informed?

"Each individual, or each family," suggests Enrico Chiavacci, "should establish for itself a reasonable level of subsistence, while also anticipating foreseeable grave needs in the future, for which the state does not provide or does not provide adequately. Once this level is reached, the rest *should be given away*."[15] This advice, too, leaves us in the dark. Does a child's university education count as such a grave future need? Does it figure in a "reasonable level of subsistence"? "Can," "able," "informed," "prudent," "reasonable" – these are mere variables, blank checks, waiting to be filled with determinate content.

ALTERNATIVE APPROACHES

More definite guidance is needed than these samples reveal, but what form should it take? What form *can* it take? I shall here review some alternative approaches to the issue of nearest versus neediest, and thereby arrive at a focus for inquiry.

Single-factor proportionalism

Goodin's impressive work *Protecting the Vulnerable* focuses on "special responsibilities" which we have toward some people and not toward others. Quoting from Sidgwick, he catalogs these responsibilities as follows:

1. "Duties arising out of comparatively permanent relationships not voluntarily chosen, such as Kindred and in most cases Citizenship and Neighbourhood"
2. "Those of similar relationships voluntarily contracted," be they bilateral as in the cases of commercial contracts and friendship, or unilateral as in the cases of promises and the authorization of another to act on one's behalf
3. "Those that spring from special services received," such as duties of gratitude reciprocating a benefactor's past assistance, or analogously, reparation compensating victims for past wrongs
4. "Those that seem due to special need, or duties of Pity."[16]

Nearest and neediest appear in 1 and 4, along with other classes of persons. Thus Goodin's focus takes in more than mine. Yet he claims that a common thread runs through these many, varied obligations and accounts for them all: It is always vulnerability of one sort or another that gives rise to special obligations.[17] He writes:

What seems true for children in particular also seems to be true for other kin, neighbors, countrymen, and contractors. To some greater or lesser extent, they are all especially dependent upon you to do something for them; and your varying responsibilities toward each of them seem roughly proportional to the degree to which they are, in fact, dependent upon you (and you alone) to perform certain services.[18]

The proportion may be very rough, I suggest, if other factors besides vulnerability account for the responsibilities. In an approach such as Goodin's, it does not suffice to demonstrate, without excessive stretching, that the chosen denominator is indeed common to all the varied cases in question. It does not suffice to demonstrate that some competing account (e.g., contract theory) does require stretching, or cannot stretch far enough to cover all cases. It would also have to be shown – or be argued plausibly – that a uniform explanation for such varied duties and relationships is possible. It might be that vulnerability appears in all special obligations and helps to ground them all, but that other considerations also carry some weight in certain kinds of cases. If so, a simple proportion between duty and vulnerability would not hold throughout the cases Goodin cites.

A possible supplementary factor is the sort of agent-related weighting that appears in non-special relations and that perhaps may be found in special relations as well. Consider these sample rules:

Self-preference: in deciding between alternative lines of action, a person should take account of others' good but should give more weight to his or her own good than to the equal good, collective or individual, of others.

Parity: equal benefit, whether to oneself or another, should receive equal weight, and unequal benefit unequal weight, without preference either way.

Other-preference: in deciding between alternative courses of action, a person should take account of his or her own good but should give more weight to the equal good, collective or individual, of others.[19]

With respect to overall benefits, these three preference-rules yield the same total. The same amount of pleasure and nourishment may result if I get two-thirds of the proverbial pie and she gets a third (Self-Preference), or if I get a half and she gets a half (Parity), or if I get a third and she gets two-thirds (Other-Preference). These rules, however, are mutually incompatible, and they are not equally acceptable. Gospel altruism favors the third, and indeed takes a slightly stronger form – Self-Subordination.

The possibility cannot be excluded that something similar obtains in certain special relationships. It may be, for example, that I should show my child special preference not solely because, being my child, she is specially vulnerable to me, but also because she is my child – because she bears that relationship to me and I to her. Indeed, it may be that I should show her special preference not merely because she is my biological progeny but because she is my daughter Susan. Special relationships may be *very* special.[20] Goodin's common-denominator approach, proportioning obligation to a single pervasive factor, does scant justice to these possibilities.[21]

Rival rules

In Ewing's case, non-utilitarian, agent-related weighting might affect our responsibilities to the nearest or to the neediest or to both, and to varying degrees. Thus nearest-preference, for example, admits various interpretations, from minimal to maximal:[22] A sampling:

(1) Preference for the nearest, as for anyone, should be decided solely by prospective benefits. ("The standard of impartiality means that I ought to give as much weight to the interests of people in Chad or Cambodia as I do to the interests of my family or neighbors."[23])

(2) Since nearness itself counts for something, when benefits balance evenly preference should go to the nearest. In this view, "Other things being equal, those who are closest to us should be assisted first."[24] When benefits do not look equal, preference should be proportioned to prospective benefit. Thus, "it is better to give to the poor when the need of one's relatives is not equal to that of the poor who are not one's relatives."[25]

(3) Since their nearness counts for more than this minimum, the nearest *may*, to a point, be preferred even when preference to others would be more beneficial overall.[26]

(4) The nearest *should*, to a point, be preferred even when preference to others would be more beneficial.[27] ("This priority is not absolute," notes Derek Parfit. "We may not believe that I ought to save my child from some minor harm rather than saving a stranger's life. But I ought to protect my child rather than saving strangers from *somewhat* greater

harms. My duty to my child is not overridden whenever I could do somewhat greater good elsewhere."[28])

Parallel possibilities hold for the neediest, from weak preference (decided solely by prospective benefits) to strong preference (prescribing that the neediest be favored, to a point, even when favoring others would be more beneficial overall).Variously combined, these two sets of alternatives yield prescriptions such as the following for resolving conflicts between nearest and neediest:

(1) Preference should follow prospective benefit. Where that is equal, neither nearest nor neediest have a stronger claim.

(2) Where prospective benefit is equal, the nearest (neediest) should be preferred over the neediest (nearest). Otherwise, preference should go to those who stand to benefit more.

(3) Where prospective benefit is greater for the neediest (nearest), the nearest (neediest) may, to a point, be preferred (the point being determined by the degree of discrepancy in the prospective benefits).

(4) Where prospective benefit is greater for the neediest (nearest), the nearest (neediest) not only may but should be preferred, to the same point.

Such a set of rival rules might be tested by Scripture, Christian tradition, and contemporary thought, so as to weed out the weak rules and identify the strong; a winning candidate might then emerge by elimination. However, this procedure, which proved feasible in a previous, comparable inquiry, looks unpromising here.

I have already noted the problem of indefiniteness: in adjudicating between self and others there is no question who is I and who is other; but who, precisely, should count as nearest, and who as neediest? The degree of analyticity required by this approach poses a further hurdle. If someone as careful as Goodin slighted the distinctions that underlie these sample rules, it is not likely that Scriptural, patristic, and other Christian sources, which are less concerned with philosophical precision, have been more discriminating. And though philosophy may proceed more analytically, the prospects look dim that philosophical demonstration, resolving the issues which

Goodin did not address, could pinpoint the strongest of the rival rules.

Scripture offers some relevant evidence, as we shall see, but nothing definite enough to permit a verdict for one specific rule. The warning in 1 Timothy 5:8 ("whoever does not provide for relatives, and especially for family members, has denied the faith and is worse than an unbeliever") is as definite as New Testament sayings come, yet contradicts none of the rules I have catalogued. So it appears unlikely that in this instance a "pick-the-winner" strategy would work.

Even if it did, no decision might result for many a problematic case. Rules 3 and 4 permit or prescribe that preference be given "to a point," but they offer no hint as to where that point lies and on which side of it a case such as Ewing's would fall.

Rachels's single rule

James Rachels provides a simpler focus for inquiry. At the end of an admirable discussion in "Morality, Parents, and Children," he lists three contrasting views, each of which he finds implausible:

1. Extreme Bias ("On this view, parents may provide not only necessities but also luxuries for their own children, while other children starve, and yet be immune from moral criticism")
2. Complete Equality ("the view that all children are equal and that there is no difference at all between one's moral obligations toward one's own children and one's moral obligations toward other children")
3. The Most Common View ("Most people seem to believe that one has an obligation to provide the necessities of life for other children only after one has already provided a great range of luxuries for one's own").[29]

In preference to these three positions, to which most Christians would also take exception, Rachels proposes a fourth, Partial Bias: "We might say that, while we do have a substantial obligation to be concerned about the welfare of all children, our own nevertheless come first."[30] As he immediately notes:

This vague thought needs to be sharpened. One way of making it more precise is this. When considering similar needs, you may permissibly prefer to provide for the needs of your own children. For example, if you were faced with a choice between feeding your own children or contributing the money to provide food for other children, you could rightly choose to feed your own. But if the choice were between some relatively trivial thing for your own and necessities for other children, preference should be given to helping the others. Thus if the choice were between providing trendy toys for your own already well-fed children or feeding the starving, you should feed the starving.

Rachels can therefore claim that "even in a fairly weak form, this view would still require much greater concern for others than the view that is most common in our society."[31] Accordingly, a worthwhile inquiry might simply assess the Christian credentials of Rachels's rule. However, such an investigation would have limited interest. For one thing, its focus would be still narrower than that of the preceding approach, as that was narrower than Goodin's: the investigation would not cover all varieties of kinship, much less all varieties of nearness, much less all varieties of special relationships. Furthermore, even within its focus, it would leave a wide expanse of unclarity between its sharp extremes. Consider Ewing's case. On the one hand, the son and the starving do not have "similar needs," so perhaps the starving should be favored. On the other hand, a university education hardly qualifies as "a relatively trivial thing," so perhaps preference should go to the son. Rachels's rule offers no hint of a verdict.

Can Christian ethics do no better? Can it proffer no surer guidance for this and similar real-life quandaries?

Christian intuition

Christian ethicians have often appealed to prudence or the heart's intuition, rather than to rules. "It must be understood," wrote Aquinas,

that the obligation to do good first of all to those who are more closely connected with us comes with the proviso: other things being equal. But if of two persons, one is more closely connected with us and the other in greater want, it is not possible to decide by any general rule which of them we ought to help rather than the other, since there are varying degrees of want as well as of nearness: here the judgment of a prudent person is called for.[32]

Through the centuries, the same refrain recurs: "There is no great occasion to dispute proportions; let us learn to be charitable, and charity will teach us what to give."[33] "The important thing is the spirit of neighborliness."[34] "Here as elsewhere, the virtue of charity appears so ample and so nuanced, it enjoins spiritual attitudes of such delicacy, that it would be wrong to believe that our rational powers (especially as sin has left them) can suffice to direct us in its exercise. In this matter, nothing can replace the vital influence of the interior Master."[35] "Charity knows best to whom to extend alms and what amount, what to give and what to hold back."[36] Charity can best guide us – not reason, not rules, not any instructions that Christian ethicians might laboriously elaborate.[37]

"If you consider the disputes of moralists," writes Arthur Vermeersch, "you will be convinced that the positive precept of charity resists accurate definition."[38] In this indefiniteness he senses an advantage, a providential dispensation. The very obscurity of the precept tacitly instructs us to fulfill the law of love not from fear but from love, and to go far beyond strict requirements, out of filial love for God and fraternal love for our neighbor.[39] For "God loves a cheerful giver."[40]

Well and good, but to whom should we cheerfully give – to nearest or to neediest? What is the better, more Christian thing to do – feed the starving or finance the son's university education? In which direction do filial love for God and fraternal love for neighbor point? The starving are neighbors, and the son is a very special neighbor. Whom should we prefer? Perhaps no rule or set of rules can settle all such cases, but can nothing better be proffered than: "Be loving, be Christian, and the answer will surely come to you"?

Germain Grisez replies with a fuller version of the same basic approach:

No very specific norm can be articulated to guide choices in such cases. Rather, one should recall Jesus' teaching about wealth, including the lesson of the parable of Dives and Lazarus (Lk. 16.19–31 . . .); one should recall too how Jesus identifies with those in need, and the consequences for those who do not succor him in the poor: " 'Just as you did not do it to one of the least of these, you did not do it to me.' And these will go away into eternal punishment" (Mt. 25.45–46). One should bear in mind the universal destination of goods and the basic norm requiring owners to use their goods to meet not only their own and their dependents' needs but those of others. One should consider what others can do to meet their own needs, what is likely to be done by third parties, what one can do oneself, and all other relevant circumstances. Then one should apply the Golden Rule.[41]

This detailed advice appears to bring us back to where we started – to fraternal charity and its nebulous dictates. However, Grisez's instructions hint at an interesting possibility. At first glance, the recommended procedure looks daunting. In how many different directions should we look? What, precisely, will we discover in each of them and how relevant will it prove to be? How shall we correlate our varied findings so as to reach a verdict? How thoroughly or reliably can we be expected to conduct such a complex inquiry – each of us, person by person, case by case? Well, why not choose a single, representative case and do for it what Grisez suggests? Why not bring to bear on some single dilemma all the resources of Christian ethical reflection so as to elucidate not only that one case but others like it? Why not carry the process through fully, just once, so as to learn from that paradigm experience what considerations are most pertinent, and how, and why? Why not focus on this single point and let light radiate out from it?

A focal paradigm

Rachels's rule is regrettably indefinite, since it leaves us in the dark about Ewing's case and many others. Yet to ferret out a more definite rule, one that might render a verdict, does not seem feasible. Where, then, can we turn? The answer now emerges: if the rule is too indefinite, the definite case is not.

Take it as the focus of inquiry, and thereby learn things more definite than the rule could convey.

As a focal paradigm, casting light on others, Ewing's case may do as well as any, and a good deal better than most. True, there is more to caring than giving, and more to be given than money. However, as Schwartz has observed, "Nothing is so quickly given, so rapidly transferred, and represents such immediate power to transform hunger into contentment, sickness into health, ignorance into knowledge, and unemployment into jobs than that everyday, much-maligned, much-abused substance, money."[42] It is no drawback, then, if Ewing speaks of money. It may even make his case more representative.

Since references to Ewing's case (EC for short) will recur throughout the coming chapters, let me recall his words: "It is clear that the money spent by a man in order to provide his son with a university education could save the lives of many people who were perishing of hunger in a famine, yet most people would rather blame than praise a man who should deprive his son of a university education on this account." And let me note some advantages that recommend this particular paradigm.

EC is realistic, not a philosopher's fantasy. Granted, in the contemporary United States lack of parental support would often not rule out a university education; circumstances vary. Yet we repeatedly face such options. For example, we buy a nice new house for the family, or take them on a costly vacation. They need the house or the vacation, as the son needs a university education. Yet the money might assist the destitute. Should it?

For some readers, Ewing's formulation may betray a male propensity for sharp dichotomies. Why suppose that either the son or the starving must receive the entire sum? Might not half of the funds go to the son (who could cover remaining expenses with loans), and the other half go to the starving? Yes, but the same sort of perplexity would then return, only doubled. With respect to the partial funding and with respect to the loans, we would have to ask: should half the university education take precedence over half as many lives as are at stake in EC? Such "either-or" dilemmas as EC's do arise, and they sharpen the

general issue of nearest versus neediest in a way that other
choices do not.

EC, though realistic, is suitably abstract. Ewing does not mention
pertinent facts about the father and son; and the father does
not know many facts about the starving which, if known, might
merit consideration. For present purposes, this is as it should
be; the level of abstraction is about right, at least to initiate
discussion. If, for example, Ewing mentioned that the father
had promised his son a university education, attention would
be diverted from the kind of responsibility that concerns us,
based on nearness, to a different kind, based on promising. If
the father knew that those in need were all particularly holy, or
all depraved, or partially responsible for their own plight, that
information would importantly alter the case and needlessly
complicate matters. In ethics, abstraction is both permissible
and necessary, provided it is recognized and duly considered.
There need be no falsification in a verdict qualified by the
condition "other things being equal." In due course, however,
we shall have to examine a couple of key assumptions in EC –
the strong personal bond between father and son, and the
efficacy of the contemplated aid to the starving.

EC is truly problematic, not only in the sense that judgments on
it differ, but also in the sense that a verdict is not readily come
by. Theologically and philosophically, EC stands at the cutting
edge of inquiry. As subsequent discussion will attest, it is
genuinely difficult to determine which way the father's preference should go.

If my purpose were homiletic, I might replace EC with
Dickens's Mrs. Jellyby, and decry the neglect of one's children
for the sake of distant strangers; or I might replace it with a
millionaire's son cruising in luxury past wretched shores, and
deplore such callousness toward human misery. Clamorous
injustices cry out more urgently to heaven than any decision,
either way, in Ewing's case. However, the conduct that occasions most moral concern is not the conduct that most calls for
ethical clarification, nor the conduct which, once clarified,
illuminates the largest number of comparable cases. A verdict
against a yacht for one's son would permit no inferences about

EC or many in-between cases, whereas a verdict against the son's university education would permit a verdict not only on the yacht but also on all the cases between EC and that extreme. For theoretical purposes, EC is situated just right.

EC separates the nearest from the self. The university education is for the son, not the father, whereas the new house, the summer cottage, the motorboat, or the vacation is for the whole family. This difference in the paradigm simplifies analysis, and has an important advantage. Too often Christian ethicists have conflated self-preference and nearest-preference, despite their very different Christian standing (see chapter 1 and, more fully, chapter 5).

EC puts in proper perspective the kind of objections often urged against "almsgiving." Familiar complaints are the following: "(1) There is the tendency to regard almsgiving as a means of earning God's favor (as in Inter-Testamental Judaism, Islam, and medieval Christianity), (2) It easily leads to paternalistic feelings of the wealthy toward the poor (quite contrary to the Biblical perspective), (3) It may lead to professional begging and passive dependence."[43] In the face of famine, such warnings would appear mere trifling. The dangers cited may be real, but so too is the danger of giving charity a bad name because of such possibilities.

EC fits the focus of ethical discussion, which has centered chiefly on private rather than public conflicts between nearest and neediest. Collectively, Scripture, the Fathers, traditional moral theology, and contemporary moral philosophy have far more to say about the former than the latter. They speak more, for example, about the responsibilities of private individuals toward their dependents and destitute strangers than they do about the responsibilities of voters, legislators, and public officials toward fellow citizens and destitute foreigners. A purely philosophical inquiry might ignore some of these possible sources of enlightenment, but a theological inquiry cannot. Here, therefore, EC, which connects better with these sources, can better prepare discussion of public issues than a public paradigm could prepare discussion of private issues.

EC aptly represents both sides of the conflict. With respect to both nearness and neediness, Ewing's case has advantages as a paradigm rather than a rule, plus advantages as this particular paradigm.

If I proposed to test a specific rule concerning nearest and neediest, I would have to indicate clearly what kind of "nearness" and "neediness" I had in view. A paradigm, however, is not a rule, principle, or theory; it is an object of comparison. Thus, for present purposes, it suffices that in anybody's reckoning starving people count among the neediest and one's children among the nearest of the near. Aquinas asserted a certain priority of father over child, but not greater nearness. The father, he argued, is more closely joined to the child than the child to the father.[44]

Granted, for past moralists a starving pagan child needed baptism more than it needed food; baptism made the difference between eternal life and death, food the difference between temporal life and death. But Christian theologians now see things differently, and emphasis has shifted. It may still be true to say: "If you can free someone from *extreme spiritual necessity*, you should subordinate every other consideration and do so."[45] What has lessened is the conviction that you can surely save a person from extreme spiritual necessity – as surely as you can save a person from extreme physical necessity (for example, from starvation, as in EC).

Thus the advantages of this particular paradigm emerge. To pit a weak instance of nearness against a strong instance of neediness, or vice versa, would give no idea of the respective claims of nearness and neediness. Instead, EC pits a strong, clear instance of nearness (the son) against a strong, clear instance of neediness (the starving). Both claimants being at full strength, they worthily represent their respective constituencies.

EC represents countless cases. Though famines do not occur every day, in the 1980s the Director General of OXFAM could report: "Some 90,000 of our fellow human beings die every day from starvation or malnutrition."[46] In the 1990s, the same dire necessity persists, on a vast scale. Often, direct food assistance may not be the best remedy; attention now centers more on forestalling famine than on relieving it once it has occurred. However, famine does still occur. And whatever the measures adopted, whether preventive or remedial, they typically require financing. So long as governments do not provide adequate assistance, private efforts will be needed, of the kind Ewing envisaged. And for governments to do their share, individual citizens must be ready to do their share – whatever that may be. Nearest vie with neediest both publicly and privately.

The cases which EC represents it also illumines. This will appear in chapters to come – on Scripture, the Fathers, Thomistic tradition, and current discussion. Chapter by chapter, EC connects with considerations that apply to a great variety of other confrontations in which the near and the needy compete. Hence the paradigm succeeds in its purpose. Light can, and does, radiate out from this point.

A FOCAL QUESTION FOR THE FOCAL PARADIGM

Of Ewing's case, various questions might be asked: which option is permissible? Which is preferable? Which, perhaps, is obligatory? What does justice require, or charity? What rights can the competing parties claim? What inner dispositions should characterize the father's choice? As a guide to conduct, the most helpful query, I believe, is the second: which alternative – assisting the son or assisting the starving – is the better, preferable, more Christian thing to do? Less helpful are the following directions for inquiry:

"What is permissible?" This query has a minimalist ring, and it provides less guidance. The answer to it does not indicate the preferable course of action, which is what should interest Christians.

"What is obligatory?" This query, too, sounds minimalist; and it, too, provides less guidance. It might be that neither alternative is obligatory, in which case it would still be necessary to determine which is preferable; whereas if neither alternative is preferable, then neither is obligatory. Furthermore, determining what is obligatory is, I believe, both less needful and less possible than is frequently supposed.[47] Within the perspec-

tive of Value-Maximization (see chapter 1), the slightly better merges without break into the noticeably better and the noticeably better into the slightly obligatory and the slightly obligatory into the seriously obligatory. No Platonic marker pinpoints the transition from preferable to obligatory, as none marks the transition from slightly preferable to noticeably preferable or from slightly obligatory to seriously obligatory.

The position thus stated strikes a mean between Christian extremes: a sharp counsel-precept dichotomy on one side, and denial of any difference on the other.[48] Within Catholic tradition, a chasm has divided the merely preferable from the obligatory. And yet, not all obligations are equally weighty. Some are slight, and no gulf separates the slightly obligatory from the highly preferable. In Ewing's case as in others, I would say, all a Christian needs to know is which alternative is better and by how much. To then attach the label "obligatory," "slightly obligatory," or "seriously obligatory" may convey this assessment but adds to it nothing of practical moment.

"What does justice, as distinct from (mere) charity, require?" This query, too, has slight practical significance. In an instance like EC, labeling an option "just" might do one of two things. It might classify the option – that is, it might locate it within the broader realm of charity or morality[49] – in which case the labeling would have purely conceptual interest.[50] Or it might express a strong moral verdict – stronger than "better" or "preferable" – in which case the term "obligatory" could serve the same purpose, and serve it better. Too often, the justice-charity distinction reflects the unchristian view that charity does not oblige – that the greatest commandment is not a commandment at all.[51]

"Which party has a right – or the stronger right – to assistance?" The language of "rights," like the language of "justice", rhetorically insists: "This is really serious – unlike mere mercy, compassion, or charity." A Christian who takes charity seriously, communicating with others who also take it seriously, has no need of such language, with its adversarial tone.[52] As Brian Barry has remarked, the practice of asserting a "right" corresponding to each moral demand "seems to have very little to contribute to

rational discourse. In my view all it can be taken as claiming is that there is some valid reason for meeting the demand, but it does nothing to explain what that reason is."[53]

"For whom should the father feel more affection – his son or the starving?" For the son, no doubt. And love in act, it might be thought, should flow from love in the heart. Inner and outer should agree. From such a correlation it would follow, though, that however slight the son's need and however great the need of others, affection for the son should prevail, since it is greater. For instance, the father should not momentarily deprive the son of his company so as to save a drowning stranger. First things first! The next question in this series suggests a further difficulty: affection has – or should have – a rival not only in the head but also in the heart.

"For whom should the father feel more compassion – his son or the starving?" Doubtless for the starving, since they suffer greater misery. From this inner verdict, it might be suggested, the outer verdict follows. There is no need of quibbling about preference-rules. Quiet noisy reason! Let the heart speak! However, if the heart speaks as it should, with strong affection for the son and strong compassion for the starving, which strong feeling should prevail? If, more likely, the heart speaks strongly – perhaps too strongly – for one and too weakly for the other, it becomes still more evident that feelings alone offer inadequate guidance. Affection or compassion is excessive when it makes excessive claims – as judged by something other, or at least something more, than the promptings of the heart.

"With what motive should the father act?" According to Hume, "'tis evident, that when we praise any actions, we regard only the motives that produced them."[54] Not true. We readily say, for example, that somebody did the right thing with a bad motive or the wrong thing with a good motive. Such judgments make clear that knowledge of the motive's goodness or badness does not indicate an action's rightness or wrongness. So if we wish to determine whether the father should provide for the son or for the starving, or which would be preferable, we not only may but must prescind from the father's motives – past,

present, or future. He might deny his son out of spite, after a squabble, or deny the starving out of prejudice.

With these queries set aside, inquiry will be simplified. To illumine the issue of nearest versus neediest, we can focus on EC and ask which solution Christian reflection recommends: aid to the son or aid to the starving. Scripture, the basic Christian source, speaks somewhat to this question; the Fathers become more explicit; the Thomistic tradition waxes fuller; and recent discussion introduces new, important considerations. These, then, are the steps inquiry will follow in chapters 3 to 6, before turning from this one case to other, comparable cases and from the private to the public sphere (chapter 7).

CHAPTER 3

New Testament intimations

The Old Testament takes family claims for granted and stresses the claims of the needy, but as far as I can ascertain, it sheds no light on the respective strength of these claims. On this issue the New Testament, a surer source of Christian belief, looks more interesting. True, with the possible exception of a single text, which I shall examine below, the New Testament does not directly address our problem. No author or text considers the weight to accord preference for the nearest versus preference for the neediest, much less takes sides in Ewing's specific case. Nonetheless, interpretations have been advanced which, if valid, would enlist the New Testament more or less decisively on the side of the neediest; and other indications point in the same direction, albeit less decisively. I shall start with the interpretations.

THE NEW SOLIDARITY

No work of scriptural interpretation I have encountered has as much to say about the issue that concerns us as does Albert Nolan's *Jesus Before Christianity*, especially a chapter entitled "The Kingdom and Solidarity."[1] "Solidarity," Nolan acknowledges, "is not a Biblical word but it expresses better than any other word I know one of the most fundamental concepts in the Bible – the concept frequently referred to by scholars as the Hebrew notion of collectivity."[2] The corresponding reality pervaded Hebrew society. In particular,

The basic unit that lived together as one corporate being was the family – the extended family including all one's relatives. Ties of

39

blood (one's own flesh and blood) and of marriage (one flesh) were taken very seriously indeed. Not only were all members of the family regarded as brothers, sisters, mothers and fathers to one another but they identified themselves with one another . . . In the time of Jesus it was not only the extended family that lived together as one corporate entity. Solidarity was also experienced with one's friends, one's fellow-tradesmen, one's social group and within the confines of an elitist "sect" like the Pharisees or the Essenes. "Individualism," as Derrett points out, "was unknown except in the world of prayer."[3]

These traditional loyalties Nolan contrasts with the new solidarity which Jesus preached. In this contrast, as Nolan roughly draws it, three successively stronger claims can be discerned. The first asserts universal human solidarity, the second accords it precedence, and the third makes it exclusive – as follows:

(1) "The kingdom of Satan differs from the kingdom of God not because they are two different forms of group solidarity but because Satan's kingdom is based upon the exclusive and selfish solidarity of groups whereas God's kingdom is based upon the all-inclusive solidarity of the human race. 'You have learnt how it was said: you must love your neighbour and hate your enemy. But I say to you: love your enemies' (Mt. 5:43–44)."[4] Jesus' injunction is striking, its message unmistakable. "He could not have found a more effective way of shocking his audience into the realisation that he wished to include all men in this solidarity of love."[5] Though it bans group exclusivity, the contrast Nolan here draws between exclusive and inclusive solidarity does not clearly preclude competing loyalties. Specifically, while all should be loved, kith and kin might still be favored over others.

(2) "Solidarity with mankind is the basic attitude. It must take precedence over every other kind of love and every other kind of solidarity. 'If any man comes to me without *hating* his father, mother, wife, children, brothers, sisters, yes and his own life too, he cannot be my disciple' (Lk. 14:26)."[6] This looks stronger. Not only is there to be universal solidarity, but this solidarity is to take precedence over other solidarities. It is not clear, however, what this might signify in practice. In other

orderings, where children take precedence over parents, parents over siblings, siblings over cousins, or the like, the competing classes are distinct. But if everyone is a human being, who takes precedence over whom? The starving in EC are human beings, but so is the man's son. Though equal in this regard, they are not, however, equal with respect to kinship or to need; and Nolan's second thesis says nothing about these supposedly lesser priorities or their respective strength. It therefore throws no light on the issue of nearest versus neediest.

(3) "What Jesus is asking for is that the group solidarity of the family be replaced by a more basic solidarity with all mankind."[7] "A new universal solidarity must supersede all the old group solidarities,"[8] including "the artificial solidarity of the family."[9] Now there is no doubt; this thesis does make a difference. If human solidarity replaces kinship solidarity, the father in EC should look only to the common humanity of the starving and his son, and assist where the need is greater. He should not give any special weight to the fact that the one person is his own flesh and blood whereas the others are strangers.

So weak is the case for this third, most pertinent thesis that I might relegate Nolan's claim to a footnote were it not for the prevalence of similar views and the interest of the texts he cites. Given their general relevance, these texts demand attention. Yet the only way they might affect the verdict in EC would be by way of some exclusion such as Nolan asserts. So let us consider them from his perspective – for instance, Luke 12:51–53:

> "Do you suppose that I am here to bring peace on earth? No, I tell you, but rather division. For from now on a household of five will be divided:
> three against two and two against three;
> the father divided against the son,
> son against father,
> mother against daughter,
> daughter against mother,
> mother-in-law against daughter-in-law,
> daughter-in-law against mother-in-law."

"The second part of this passage," Nolan notes, "is a quotation from the prophet Micah, who deplores this breakdown in family solidarity as one of the sins of Israel in his time (Mic. 7:6). That Jesus can quote this as an inevitable result of his mission is one of the clearest indications of a radical change of values. A new universal solidarity must supersede all the old group solidarities."[10]

It is difficult to discern how this concluding inference might follow from the passage quoted, even when it is placed in its gospel context. As Abraham was ready to sacrifice his son, so Christians will be ready to sacrifice their closest family ties if the kingdom of God demands it. Yet, as Abraham's obedience does not show that family ties are superseded, so Christians' obedience will not show that family ties are superseded. Thus Joseph Fitzmyer remarks:

One is called to such "hatred" to the extent that such persons would be opposed to Jesus; the choice that the disciple has to make is between natural affection for kin and allegiance to Jesus. "In most cases these two are not incompatible, and to hate one's parents *as such* would be monstrous . . . But Christ's followers must be ready, if necessary, to act towards what is dearest to them as if it were an object of hatred."[11]

The most that might be inferred, then, from Luke 14:26, is that other, higher considerations may sometimes override the claims of kinship. This unsurprising conclusion relates to the first of Nolan's three theses, but it does not establish – or even suggest – the third.

Of Nolan's subsequent scriptural citations, only one shows a possible link with his strongest, most interesting claim:

Jesus was very seriously concerned that his love for his mother (or any other relative) should not be thought of as mere biological or family solidarity: "A woman in the crowd said: 'Blessed is the womb that bore you and the breasts you sucked!' But he said, 'Blessed rather are those who hear the word of God and keep it' " (Lk 11:27–28 RSV). Any particularly close and mutual solidarity between Jesus and his mother would have to be based upon the living out of God's will.[12]

Again, this inference goes beyond the text. Even so, it does not go as far as Nolan's third thesis, since it makes no reference to universal human solidarity and does not exclude a lesser degree of solidarity based on kinship.

The same holds for Mark 3:31–35 and Luke 8:19–20. When Jesus declares "My mother and my brothers are those who hear the word of God and do it," this does not mean, Leon Morris notes, "that family ties are unimportant or can be ignored: Jesus is not disowning his family. He thought of his mother even when he hung on the cross in the agony of achieving the world's redemption (Jn 19:26f). His meaning is that our duty to God takes precedence of all else."[13]

Clearly, Nolan's strongest thesis – the only one that has relevance for this inquiry – lacks scriptural backing. However, a parallel claim, carrying similar implications, has sometimes been advanced.

CHRISTIAN SOLIDARITY

The new *universal* solidarity which, in Nolan's view, supersedes all the old solidarities has a competitor – the new *Christian* solidarity which many texts suggest (e.g., 1 Cor. 6:8, Gal. 6:10). Thus, concerning 1 Thessalonians Wayne Meeks comments:

In a number of ways, some already mentioned, the rhetoric of this letter is so composed as to arouse the affection of the readers for one another, for the writers, and for Christian groups in other places with which they have had some direct or indirect connections. For example, Paul inserts a paragraph "On love of brothers" (4:9–12), a topic quite familiar in moral discourse of the day. Plutarch, for example, wrote a treatise with exactly this title. Plutarch's advice, however, concerned obligations between blood relatives, while in the Christian community every member was a brother or sister, for all were "children of God." More than a metaphor is involved here, for the Christians are evidently expected not only to cherish fellow members of the sect with the same care as they would natural siblings, but even to replace natural family ties by those of this new family of God, created by conversion and ritual initiation. That kind of deep resocialization was the norm not only in the Pauline mission circle but in other parts of the early Christian movement, too, as certain sayings of Jesus preserved in the Synoptic Gospels attest: "For I have come to set a man against his father, and a daughter against her

mother, and a daughter-in-law against her mother-in-law" (Matt.
10:35; cf. v. 37 = Luke 14:26; Mark 3:31–35 and parallels).[14]

Here the same New Testament evidence recurs, but in support
of another strong thesis, different from Nolan's. Christian
solidarity, not human solidarity, replaces familial loyalty. This
thesis, too, has evident relevance for EC and might tip the
verdict in the same direction by negating the son's claim to
special consideration.

Acts offers possible illustration and confirmation of the shift
Meeks alleges. The first believers, we there read, were all of
one heart and mind, holding all things in common and
distributing their resources "according as any had need" (Acts
2:44–45, 4:32–35). Though the Apostles and the brothers of
Jesus were married (1 Cor. 9:5), as no doubt were many other
Christians, nothing is said about any competing, familial
criterion for distributing resources. Where need is greatest,
assistance is greatest, regardless of blood ties. Such is the
impression given here, as also in Paul's instructions on the
collect for the Christians of Jerusalem: "I do not mean that
there should be relief for others and pressure on you, but it is a
question of a fair balance between your present abundance and
their need" (2 Cor. 8:13–14). Again, there is no question of
keeping a bit more for one's dependents, despite the greater
need of others. Need is the sole stated criterion. To be sure,
both *Acts* and Paul express an ideal, not what Christians are
"expected" to do. However, that ideal retains its relevance for
our issue, provided that the silence about family priorities is
read as Meeks's thesis suggests – that is, as an exclusion.

So the question is this: would Paul or the author of *Acts*
disagree or have difficulty with 1 Timothy 5:4 and 5:8, which
suggest familial solidarity: "If a widow has children or grand-
children, they should first learn their religious duty to their own
family . . . Whoever does not provide for relatives, and
especially for family members, has denied the faith and is worse
than an unbeliever"? If they did object, would their view
represent the Christian consensus, and would 1 Timothy
express an aberrant view? I find no reason, in the texts cited or

elsewhere, to favor an affirmative answer to these queries, and must therefore conclude that Meeks's exclusionary thesis, though somewhat more plausible than Nolan's, succeeds no better than his. However, one further New Testament reading, with similar significance, remains to be examined.

MATTHEW 25:31–46

Christians have adduced the judgment scene in Matthew 25 more frequently and strongly than any other text as a compelling reason for assisting the needy. "With a few words," writes S. Many, "Jesus Christ transported almsgiving into a new world, as it were, and, to bring his disciples to aid the poor, offered them a motive of prodigious elevation and efficacity: he declared that he would regard as done to himself whatever was done, for love of him, to the least of his own."[15] In the estimation of many, "What more sublime can be said about alms than that they are given to Christ the Lord?"[16]

As traditionally understood, this identification seems to trump any contrary consideration: if it is Jesus who is starving, then surely we should not refuse him, even if that means withholding support for a son's or daughter's college education. "Suppose Christ came to us in grave need," remarks Melchior Cano. "If he asked me for money and I didn't give it to him, who would say that I love Christ?"[17] With still more pointed relevance, Jerome admonishes Hedebia: "He did not say, 'Give to your children, your brothers, your kin' – if you had them, the Lord would rightly be preferred to them, too – but rather, 'Give to the poor,' give to Christ who is fed in the poor."[18] *A fortiori*, give to the starving, give to the starving Christ.

"The meaning is clear and unambiguous," declares Ronald Sider. "Jesus intends that his disciples imitate his own special concern for the poor and needy. Those who disobey will experience eternal damnation."[19] In truth, however, the meaning of Matthew 25:31–46 is far from clear; multiple uncertainties obscure the passage's significance for our inquiry. To be sure, its significance is only indirect. As noted at the start, no New Testament passage addresses the issue of nearest versus neediest, much less considers our specific illustration of the issue. This does not signify, though, that no passage can possibly illumine the issue or the illustration. As often read, the Matthean judgment scene does just that. Doubts about this reading focus on the following considerations: the scene's source, the identity of the "least," and the nature and extension of the identity with Jesus.

The source. Opinions differ about both the possibility and the importance of ascertaining Jesus' own words. I cannot here take a stand on these issues, but neither can I ignore them, since many have attached great significance to the provenance of gospel sayings, and many have sought to surmise it. In the present instance, "Some scholars consider this account of the judgment of the world as a direct discourse from the mouth of Jesus; others consider it wholly a Matthaean invention."[20] Many take an in-between position, attributing part to Jesus and part to the evangelist,[21] or one version to Jesus and another to the evangelist or the Christian community. In one account, Matthew "edited an original parable about the final judgment in which God as king would judge people on the basis of their treatment of the poor."[22] In another account, the sequence is reversed: "the church universalized [Jesus'] teaching in the ethical direction of all the poor."[23]

The "least." For some exegetes, Matthew identifies Jesus with persons who are suffering for whatever reason[24] – "with those who are hungry, thirsty, stranger, naked, sick, in prison, whoever these people might be."[25] For others, "the least of my brothers" refers primarily to "Christian disciples or missionaries (which for Matthew are virtually the same),"[26] or to "the lowliest and most insignificant of His disciples."[27] The first reading connects with the starving in EC; the second does not – or does not as clearly and strongly. It may be, as some propose, that the identification with Jesus is restricted but the lesson of compassion is not.[28] However, in that case the potentially decisive factor in favor of the destitute – identity with Jesus – has still been lost; the passage no more decides against the nearest than does, for example, the parable of the Good Samaritan.

The nature of the identity. The sayings of Jerome and Cano suggest strong identity with Jesus, as do more recent declarations. "How seriously," one commentator asks, "do we take the plain doctrine of this awful parable – that Christ, the eternal Son of God, the Judge of all nations, is literally incarnate in the most worthless tramp, the most ragged beggar, the vilest criminal? If for us this is only a dramatic metaphor, we cannot receive the deep redemptive thrust of it . . ."[29] Agreeing, another interpreter insists: "Our text goes further: it does not say 'as though.' "[30] What literal, non-metaphorical identity with Jesus might mean, we are not told (e.g., does Jesus have one body or millions?). Yet from Jerome and Cano we can sense the implications of such a metaphysical equation. If it is Jesus himself – literally, non-metaphorically – who is starving, then he should take precedence; he should be fed. Other readings, however, sound less conclusive.

It has been suggested that "the relationship which Christ claims to sustain with His brethren in this discourse is very similar to that of Jehovah and Israel in the Old Testament" – for example in Zechariah 2:8 ("Truly, one who touches you touches the apple of my eye").[31] Other texts elicit a different comparison:

In the Old Testament, in fact, the messenger was considered the mouth of the one who had sent him (cf. Jer 15:19); and according to Jewish tradition the emissary (*shaliah*) of a person is like the person himself. We can presume, therefore, that in using the words which have come down to us as "child" in Mark and "little ones" in Matthew, Jesus was referring to those he was sending out as his emissaries . . .[32]

For Théo Preiss, "there is something more here . . . We have in Mark 9:37 and Matt. 18:5, as well as in Matt. 25, a vast and profound juridical mysticism, which far transcends the limits of the rabbinical principle; the Son of Man has made himself one with all those who objectively need help, whatever be their subjective dispositions."[33] For Karl Rahner, this reading is likewise inadequate. The saying "that what is done to the least of his brethren is done to Jesus, [is] a saying which cannot be explained by an arbitrarily altruistic identification which, according to many commentators, Jesus himself undertakes as it were merely morally and juridically in a mere 'as if.' "[34] The identity is real. Jesus *is* the least, or *in* the least[35] – whatever that may mean. (There are standard criteria for the identity of individual persons, for instance of child and adult, and of individual physical objects, for instance of morning star and evening star, but none exist for the identity of one person with millions or billions of others.)

The extension of the identity. The uncertain nature of the identification weakens the case for the neediest vis-à-vis the nearest. So, too, does its uncertain scope. Suppose there is a strong identification. Suppose it to be with the neediest and with them alone.[36] Then, in EC, it might heavily favor the starving over the son. For the father's choice would then be between Jesus and his son, not between Jesus the starving and Jesus his son. However, on this question, too – on the identification's scope as well as its nature – opinions differ. It may be that here, or in the gospels generally,[37] Jesus identifies himself with all his brethren,[38] all people,[39] all those he loves,[40] and he uses this identification in Matthew 25 to stress the obligation to assist those in need. If so, nothing follows concerning the respective claims of the nearest or the neediest. Jesus identifies himself with the son, and he identifies himself with the starving. What is done for the son is done for him, and what is done for the starving is done for him. Which is the stronger obligation?

Individually, each of these uncertainties calls into question a verdict based on Matthew 25:31–46 that favors the starving over the son. Cumulatively, the uncertainties all but sever the connection. This is not to deny the passage's significance. It may still support a Christian preference for the neediest, and it probably does. But such a preference is this inquiry's starting point, not its terminus. To some extent, preference should go to the nearest; to some extent, preference should go to the neediest: on this Christians have agreed. But how strong is the one preference in comparison with the other? On this question the Matthean judgment scene throws little light, by itself. However, it does not stand alone.

NEAREST–NEEDIEST CONFRONTATIONS

In the New Testament, only one passage explicitly juxtaposes nearest and neediest and suggests a preference:

> He said also to the one who had invited him, "When you give a luncheon or a dinner, do not invite your friends or your brothers or your relatives or rich neighbors, in case they may invite you in return, and you would be repaid. But when you give a banquet, invite the poor, the crippled, the lame, and the blind. And you will be blessed, because they cannot repay you, for you will be repaid at the resurrection of the righteous." (Lk. 14:12–14)

"Obviously," Ronald Sider comments, "Jesus was employing hyperbole, a typical technique of Hebrew literature to emphasize his point. He did not mean to forbid parties with friends and relatives." Nonetheless, "he certainly did mean that we ought to entertain the poor and disadvantaged (who cannot reciprocate) at least as often – and perhaps a lot more often – than we entertain friends, relatives and 'successful' folk."[41] So read, the passage appears relevant to our inquiry. If generalized, Jesus' preference in this instance – for the poor, crippled, lame, and blind rather than friends, relatives, and rich neighbors – might suggest a similar preference, in EC, for starving strangers rather than the cherished son.

Such a reading could appear to miss the focus of Luke's tale. As Fitzmyer notes, in this second of two paired sayings "Jesus moves from self-seeking ambition to selfish recompense and tries to counteract this as well."[42] Thus, "Four affluent types of human beings, able to recompense, are contrasted with four unfortunate types, unable to do so."[43] Such, it might be urged, is the sole criterion for the choice of these contrasting types, not the nearness of the former or the neediness of the latter. This, however, would be a narrow reading. Fitzmyer's further remarks on the four classes of guests open larger perspectives:

> Three of the four ("the lame, the blind, the crippled") are mentioned (along with "one who has a permanent blemish in his flesh") as those to be excluded from the eschatological war of the "sons of light against the sons of darkness" in the Qumran *War Scroll* (1 QM 7:4) and also excluded from the common meal in Qsa 2:5–6 . . . By

contrast, the invitation of such persons by the Christian disciple will reveal his concern to relieve the need of fellow human beings.[44]

Thus, "The sayings of the Lucan Jesus in verses 12–14 fit into the general Lucan theme of the use of material possessions and of concern for the poor and unfortunate of this world."[45]

John Nolland adverts to a complementary perspective. "Apart from the inversion of the order of the last two terms," he notes, "the guest list is identical to that of verse 21, from where it has probably been borrowed. The link suggests that we are being directed to arrange our meal hospitality on the same basis as God does as he makes arrangements for the great eschatological banquet which he is convening."[46] If we do act as directed, "our hospitality will express true generosity of soul and will be like God's own generosity, extended to the most unlikely people."[47] The parallel can, perhaps, be carried farther, for the divine paradigm reveals a further aspect. Nolland's suggestion links one nearest-neediest contrast to another.

The divine generosity that we are asked to imitate is shown not only in bounty toward the evil as well as the good, the unrighteous as well as the righteous (Mt. 5:43–48), but in this: "God so loved the world that he gave his only Son, so that everyone who believes in him may not perish but may have eternal life" (Jn. 3:16). Other passages (e.g., Ro. 5:8, 8:3, 8:32; Gal. 4:4; 1 Jn. 4:10, 4:14) evoke the same perspective, but let us dwell on this formulation in John, with its succinct juxtaposition. On one side, "the world": "It is a distinctively Christian idea that God's love is wide enough to embrace all mankind."[48] On the other side, "his only Son": "His love is not a vaguely sentimental feeling, but a love that costs, God gave us what was most dear to Him."[49] In Paul's words, "He did not spare his own Son, but gave him up for the sake of all of us" (Ro. 8:32) – gave him up so that we "may not perish."

Does it follow, then, that the EC father, acting in imitation of the heavenly Father, should sacrifice his son's welfare so that the starving may not perish? Does it follow that such is the more perfect, more Christian course of action? No, to allege such an inference would be too strong; the paschal mystery provides at most a possible argument from analogy. Here, as in all such arguments, disanalogies are evident as well as analogies: the father is not related to his son as the Father is to the Son, nor is the father related to the starving as the Father is to perishing humanity; more are saved in one case than the other, and from a still direr fate; on the other hand, the son loses only a university education, not his life. Furthermore, as in most such arguments, it is difficult to determine just which analogies or disanalogies carry most weight. Nonetheless, despite the absence of any strict logical connection, arguments by analogy retain their own limited validity. This one, I believe, is at least suggestive.

A complementary perspective is that of the Son, who so loved the world that he left his Father (Jn. 16:28), impoverishing himself so that destitute humanity might thereby be enriched (2 Cor. 8:9). Also that of Mary's son, who left home and family for the same purpose, to be about his Father's redemptive business (Lk. 2:49). In these instances, too – in these possible paradigms for imitation – neediest take precedence over nearest. When the whole flock are lost in the desert, the Good Shepherd leaves Father and mother behind to seek out his straying sheep. Though these further analogies permit no pertinent inferences, they too are suggestive, in the same direction.

CUMULATIVE EMPHASIS

The overall imbalance of New Testament evidence is similarly suggestive. Insistent in Luke, vehement in James, recurrent elsewhere, New Testament concern for the needy far exceeds any expressed concern about assistance to one's kin. 1 Timothy's two passing remarks stand in lonely counterpoint.

I have already noted Matthew 25:31–46, Luke 14:12–14, Acts 2:44–45 and 4:32–35, as well as 2 Corinthians 8:13–14, one of many passages dealing with the collect for the needy brethren in Jerusalem (Acts 11:27–30, 24:17, Ro. 15:26–28, Gal. 2:10, 1 Cor. 16:1–4, 2 Cor. 8–9). Other indications, large and small, weigh on the same side of the scales. For example, in Luke 3:11, "the specific things that John recommends to his fellow Jews are intended by Luke to be recommendations for his Christian hearers as well."[50] Thus, "[e]ven the essentials of life, a tunic to wear and food to eat, are to be shared with one's less fortunate neighbors."[51] In Matthew 19:21, Mark 10:21, and 18:22, when Jesus instructs the inquirer to go, sell, give to the poor, then follow him, that third directive – giving the proceeds to the poor – may appear a secondary, inessential detail, yet it has its own significance. Jesus does not say, "Share the proceeds with your relatives." He does not leave the distribution to individual discretion. Again, in Luke 16: 19–26, the tale of the rich man and Lazarus may focus, for instance, on the reversal of fortunes in this life and the next, but there is no denying the connection between the rich man's insouciance and his later fate. Given Luke's general concerns, Fitzmyer can plausibly comment: "The description of the beggar is vivid and detailed to bring out the lack of concern for him on the part of the rich man."[52] In Luke 10:25–37 the tale of the Good Samaritan has still more evident relevance. "The point of the story is summed up in the lawyer's reaction, that a 'neighbor' is anyone in need with whom one comes into contact and to whom one can show pity and kindness, even beyond the bounds of one's own ethnic or religious group."[53] James, finally, picks the following illustration to show that faith has need of works: "If a brother or sister is naked and lacks daily food, and one of you says to them, 'Go in peace; keep warm and eat your fill,' and yet you do not supply their bodily needs, what is the good of that?" (Ja. 2:15–16). "Religion that is pure and undefiled before God, the Father, is this: to care for orphans and widows in their distress, and to keep oneself unstained by the world" (Ja. 1:27).

Jesus' example backs this doctrinal emphasis. In his self-description, "The Son of man came to seek out and to save the lost" (Luke 19:10). The lost, as the context and other passages (Mt. 9:12, Mk. 2:17, Lk. 5:31, 15:4) make clear, are sinners – "the outcasts, the irreligious, and the immoral";[54] but Jesus' concern extended farther: "The Spirit of the Lord is upon me, because he has anointed me to bring good news to the poor. He has sent me to proclaim release to the captives and recovery of sight to the blind, to let the oppressed go free, to proclaim the year of the Lord's favor" (Luke 4:18). This mission that inspired him, he lived, by showing compassion toward the hungry (Mt. 15:32, Mk. 8:2), the blind (Mt. 20:34), the leper (Mk. 1:41), the widow (Lk. 7:13), the crowds like sheep without a shepherd (Mt. 9:36, Mk. 6:34; cf. Mt. 14:14). "Go and tell John what you have seen and heard: the blind receive their sight, the lame walk, the lepers are cleansed, the deaf hear, the dead are raised, the poor have good news brought to them" (Lk. 7:22; cf. Mt. 11:5).

These allusions to "the deaf, dumb, blind, lame, poor, broken-hearted, captives and downtrodden," it has been said, "are simply different ways of referring to the poor and the oppressed."[55] It would be more natural and would require less forcing to say that all these classes of people experience special need – as do sinners, as does the man lying half-dead by the wayside (Lk. 10:30). Jesus' special solicitude centered on the neediest. With respect to the specific type and degree of need mentioned in EC, Nolan notes: "On the whole, the suffering of the poor was not destitution and starvation except during a war or a famine. They were sometimes hungry and thirsty, but, unlike millions today, they seldom starved."[56] There can be little doubt, though, how Jesus would have reacted had he encountered people who were starving and not merely hungry. "I have compassion for the crowd, because they have been with me now for three days and have nothing to eat. If I send them away hungry to their homes, they will faint on the way – and some of them have come from a great distance" (Mk. 8:2; cf. Mt. 14:15–21, Mk. 6:35–44, Lk. 9:10–17, Jn. 6:1–13, and Ja. 2:15).

In summary, the New Testament evidence is, indeed, massively one-sided. To some extent, however, emphasis may fall where it does because family ties, being psychologically so strong, posed a special challenge to the claims of the gospel, not because such ties lacked validity. Perhaps the New Testament takes their legitimacy for granted even as it stresses their limits.[57] 1 Timothy lends credence to this explanation. So does Mark 7:9–12:

Then he said to them, "You have a fine way of rejecting the commandment of God in order to keep your tradition! For Moses said, 'Honor your father and your mother'; and, 'Whoever speaks evil of father or mother must surely die.' But you say that if anyone tells father or mother, 'Whatever support you might have had from me is Corban' (that is, an offering to God) – then you no longer permit doing anything for a father or mother, thus making void the word of God through your tradition that you have handed on."

Nonetheless, this explanation of the imbalance is at best only partial; the New Testament's one-sided insistence does not cease to be suggestive.

By now, a pattern has emerged. Matthew 25:31–46 is suggestive, but it permits no inference regarding EC. The Father's surrender of the Son is suggestive (as are Jesus' analogous choices and Lk. 14:12–14), but it, too, permits no inference. The New Testament's overall stress on aid to the needy rather than the near is suggestive, but it likewise permits no inference. Yet this, at least, can be noted in conclusion, that whereas the New Testament's multiple intimations, even when combined, *do not certainly* favor the neediest over the nearest, for instance in EC, they *certainly do not* support Ewing's contrary verdict. They certainly do not favor the nearest over the neediest.

CHAPTER 4

Patristic positions

Patristic writings address our problem more fully and explicitly than does the New Testament. I shall start with suggestive indications on one side and the other, then consider explicit confrontations between nearest and neediest. I shall then examine, at length, a type of patristic claim which, if valid, may tilt the scales decisively in favor of the neediest.

NEAREST

What Mark 7:9–12 obliquely suggests, the Fathers directly state: honoring one's father and mother consists of more than sentiments and words; it means helping them in their need.[1] However, all should be helped in their need, whereas the Fathers assign a certain priority to parents and other near relatives.[2]

In his commentary on the Song of Songs, Origen states an order of charity preferring relatives to nonrelatives and some relatives to others. Ambrose takes up the theme. "Good-will starts first with those at home, that is, with children, parents, brothers, and goes on from one step to another throughout the world."[3] Augustine agrees: "It is necessary that love, like a fire, should cover the nearest terrain before it spreads farther afield."[4] Caesarius elaborates:

The just and proper order of almsgiving is that first you should provide for yourself and your family sufficient, moderate food and clothing, but nothing rich or luxurious; secondly, as I said, you should generously give whatever you can to those of your relatives who are poor; and, thirdly, you should not allow your servants and maids to be hungry or cold. Whatever God has given you beyond this, except your food and clothing, you should not store up in earthly treasure 'where thieves break in and steal,' but in heaven . . .[5]

And so the doctrine has continued through the centuries (see Wesley in chapter 2, Aquinas in chapter 5). This long-standing tradition accounts for my opening statement, in chapter 1, that Christians have generally agreed that preference should go to one's nearest and dearest, at least to some extent.

The question is: to what extent? An answer may perhaps appear from the reasons given for the preference. Augustine, in particular, recognized that from a Christian viewpoint preference for nearest and dearest required explanation. O'Donovan articulates the problem:

How could such claims be justified in terms of universal neighbor-love? And how could such a love tolerate the special requirements of "love for the brethren"? It was not open to Augustine to find that these restricted claims had their source in some other moral principle than neighbor-love, for it was an avowed part of his ethical program that all obligations of every kind should be traced back to the twin commands of love for God and neighbor. He replied instead that these special responsibilities were imposed by the limitations of time and opportunity. "In the first place, a man bears responsibility for his own: for it is to their care that he has simpler and easier access, whether in the order of nature or in the order of human society."[6]

"All other people are to be loved equally," Augustine explains; "but since you cannot be of assistance to everyone, those especially are to be cared for who are most closely bound to you by place, time, or opportunity, as if by chance."[7] Caesarius's remarks take a similarly utilitarian bent. You should give your own needy parents priority, he explained, since others may then assist those you do not assist, whereas if you do not help your own parents, it is not likely that others will do so.[8]

Recent authors have developed this argument from efficacy, and have applied it specifically to parents' duties toward their children.[9] In this approach, love is basically impartial. The equal good of each person counts equally; hence whatever action maximizes good should be preferred, regardless of who receives the benefit. Generally, good will be maximized by showing special concern for one's own. As Gene Outka notes, "We are capable of helping and harming those with whom we are especially related more deeply and in more ways than those who are less closely related to us."[10] And from intimate acquaintance we are able to judge our obligations toward them with comparatively greater clarity and confidence. Nonetheless, whenever good would be maximized by favoring others, they should be preferred. So if Ewing is right that providing for the starving would save lives, it is clear which way the utility balance tilts: with human lives weighing against a university education, the starving should get the nod.[11]

NEEDIEST

Of the various ways in which early Christian writers stress the duty of aid to the needy, some provide slight or uncertain indication of how aid should be apportioned when the claims of nearest and neediest compete. For example:

Altruism. Then as now, attention typically focused on one's own competing claims and desires rather than on those of one's nearest and dearest. "Whoever cherishes his neighbor as himself," writes Basil, "possesses no more than his neighbor."[12] For Ambrose, "conformity to Christ means not seeking what is another's, not depriving another of anything for one's own benefit."[13] Such sayings offer no clear clue concerning the respective claims of nearest neighbor and neediest neighbor. However, it may be that the needs of children and other dependents are understood as included with one's own. If so, Basil would implicitly be saying that one's family should possess no more than other families – that there should be equality. For example, one's own child should not receive a university education at the expense of other children who are starving.

One family. Ewing's case pits one's nearest and dearest against starving "strangers." The Fathers would contest this character-ization. Those in need, writes Pope Gregory, by the very fact that they are human beings, are not strangers to us.[14] "If we have all sprung from one man whom God made," Lactantius insists, "then, surely, we are relatives . . . Likewise, if we have

all been vivified and inspired by the one God, what else are we
than brothers . . . ?"[15] Tertullian, similarly,

views the world as the "single nation" that gathers all people, the
"single house," the "single flock of God" that has the same God, the
same master, the same shepherd. In all people he notes sameness of
nature, equality of soul, and joint possession of the world. He insists
on this natural unity of humanity and sees there a type of fraternity.
He says to the pagans: "We are your very brothers by virtue of
nature, our common mother."[16]

Basil,[17] Leo,[18] and others[19] sound the same refrain, as does
Gregory Nazianzen.

The Christian, says Gregory, follows not only reason, but Him who is
Supreme Reason, and therefore knows that God is his creator (ch.
xxxiii), and that the image of God is shared by all men, rich and poor,
bond and free, sick and healthy (ch. viii). Because of this tenet of
human solidarity, Gregory asserts that when we minister to the poor in
their bodily needs, we strengthen our common image; in turning our
backs on them, we risk destroying that image in ourselves . . .[20]

The Fathers' insistence on our common humanity sets
Ewing's case, and those it represents, in proper perspective. "At
this level of depth, men encounter each other not as strangers
but as other selves. On the surface lie all the differences – of
race and nation and culture and creed. At heart, men share a
common human substance."[21] However, the son in need of an
education shares the divine image equally with the starving;
hence the latter's humanity, which makes them "other selves,"
cannot tip the scales in their favor. The son has closer kinship
on his side; they have direr need. Which should count more
weightily?

Christ in the poor. Similar uncertainty arises with respect to
Matthew 25:31–46, which the Fathers so frequently cited.
According to Dale Bruner, "most of the Fathers understood
'brother' as a fellow Christian. What we have called the Faith
or Serving Christians Interpretation was almost the exclusive
teaching of the ancient church."[22] This sounds too strong –
indeed clearly mistaken. In most instances, early Christian
writers simply identify Christ the judge with the needy, without
hint of restriction.[23] And sometimes their universalism

becomes explicit: "In every needy and poor person Christ is fed, covered, visited, given to drink."[24] "You will see him in every poor person, touch him in every guest."[25] "He gives alms who does not cease to share his temporal goods with his brothers, that is, with other people"[26] – with "every person who shares the same human nature."[27]

We have seen in St. Jerome where this universalistic reading might lead: with the son on one side and the starving Christ on the other, a Christian would not hesitate. However, we have also noted the exegetical uncertainty of such a reading, and the further uncertainty as to whether the Son of Man identifies himself with the poor and needy alone. If not, Christ near and dear vies with Christ starving, and Matthew 25 cannot decide in favor of the neediest.

Common property.[28] "Share everything with your neighbor," instructs the letter of Barnabas, "and do not say: 'It is private property.'"[29] "*Mine* and *thine*," insists Chrysostom, "are mere words without substance. If you say a house is yours, the word is empty. Air and earth and matter are the Creator's, as are you who built the house, and all other things . . . Since, therefore, they are not ours, we should share them with our fellow servants."[30] And if they are not ours, but the Creator's, perhaps we should share them evenly, without favoritism. Perhaps the needs of the starving should take precedence over such things as a son's need for a university education. The Fathers would probably agree, given their modest estimate of genuine human needs.

Simplicity. "You know," wrote St. Caesarius, "that, if you are unwilling to give, you take away what belongs to another because, as I said, only what reasonably suffices for ourselves and our family is really ours. God has sent everything over and above that for distribution among the poor."[31] In our day, it might be said that what reasonably suffices for our children includes a good education – as good as their capacities permit. However, the Fathers tended to take a less expansive view. "As the foot is the exact measure of the shoe," wrote Clement of Alexandria, characteristically,[32] "so what the body truly needs is the exact measure of what we should own."[33] "With the

exception of moderate, reasonable food and clothing," Caesarius agreed, "whatever God has conferred upon you as the
result of military service or agriculture He did not give to you
in particular, but He transmitted it through you to be spent
upon the poor."[34] These words of Caesarius, together with his
statement previously quoted, suggest a clear verdict: the money
for the son's university education goes beyond what "reasonably suffices" and therefore should go to the poor – and *a fortiori*
to the starving. Whether such rigorous standards of simplicity
still apply will be for the next chapter to consider.

NEAREST VERSUS NEEDIEST

In the writings of the church Fathers, whenever the near and
the poor appear in competition, as they sometimes do, the
Fathers favor the poor.[35] Thus, when urging more generous
alms, they view with mistrust objections of the kind they
repeatedly envisage and doubtless often heard: "We need
money for our children";[36] "What will be left for our children?";[37] "I'm saving it for my children";[38] "What am I to do
about my children?";[39] "Should I disregard my parents?"[40]
These pleas receive short shrift. "Were the gospels not written
for married people?" inquires St. Basil.[41] "Let us not close our
ears to the prayers of the needy so as to save our wealth for our
children or other relations."[42] "Do not increase your money,"
Augustine admonishes, "under the guise of family piety." On
occasion his urgings grow vehement:

> "I'm saving it for my children"; a marvelous excuse! He's saving it for
> his children. Let's see, shall we? Your father saves it for you, you save
> it for your children, your children for their children, and so on
> through all generations, and not one of them is going to carry out the
> commandments of God . . . So you see, brothers, it's a lie when
> people say "I'm saving it for my children." It's a lie, my brothers, it's
> a lie. People are just greedy.[43]

Despite their forcefulness, such replies, consistently favoring
the needy over the near, offer little guidance for a case like EC.
The Fathers' target, and the motive for their rhetoric, may be
avarice ("People are just greedy"), or inordinate family affec-

tion, not a reasonable preference for one's nearest and dearest such as Augustine elsewhere endorses. From their warnings, then, it does not transpire whether, within limits, kith and kin might legitimately be favored.

The tale of the widow of Zarephath, in 1 Kings 17, elicited more definite indications. For Cyprian, a commentator notes, "Not even parents burdened with numerous children are exempt from the obligations imposed by Christian solidarity, which are the performance of 'good and just works'; for they must consider the poor, in whom Christ resides, before their own children, after the example of the widow who gave Elias the hearth-cake she had made for herself and her own son."[44] Here Cyprian's exegesis may be shaky (he takes no account of the prophet's order, the widow's objections, and the prophet's promise in answer to her objections), but his eisegesis is both revealing and typical.

In Chrysostom, as in Basil,[45] the single son becomes plural children, and the widow's generosity thereby acquires still sharper pertinence.

Are you in want of the very necessity of food to eat? Surely, you are not in greater need than the widow of Sidon. She had fallen to the extreme depths of hunger and was expecting soon to die. The throng of her children stood around her, but not even in these circumstances did she hesitate to give what little she had.[46]

If the single stranger, Elijah, should be preferred to the many children, in equal need, surely the many starving in EC should be preferred to the single, far less needy son.

However, would either Cyprian or Chrysostom really recommend favoring needy strangers over one's equally needy children? In the early Fathers, and particularly in the Cappadocians' preaching, allowance must often be made for overstatement.

When, for instance, Gregory [of Nazianzus] praises the magnanimity of his sister Gorgonia by comparing her to Job ("Her door was opened to all comers; the stranger did not lodge in the street; she was eyes to the blind, feet to the lame, a mother to the orphan."), or describes the same virtue in his mother Nonna by declaring that "she would gladly have sold herself and her children into slavery, had there been any chance of doing so, to expend the proceeds on the poor," such excessive language is, given the rules of rhetoric as applied to panegyric literature, less of an exhibition of stylistic prowess than an admission that human words are unequal to the task of describing what is truly good and beautiful.[47]

Granted the exaggeration, the author of such statements would not likely agree with Ewing. If the harm done to one's child were depriving him of a university education, not selling him into slavery, and the poor were not merely indigent but starving, Gregory would hardly condemn assistance to the starving rather than the son. It appears he would admire such generosity.

However, what is admirable may not be of precept. "Sell all that you possess," Jerome advised a widow, "give to the poor, follow the Savior, and, naked and alone, follow virtue naked and alone. You do not wish to be perfect but to maintain a second level of virtue? Then rid yourself of all you possess, give to your children, give to your relatives. No one condemns you if you take a lower place."[48] Chrysostom might distinguish similarly: What the widow did was admirable, but not obligatory.

Even so, there is no mistaking the general drift of patristic thought.[49] The Fathers, who favored sharing even basic necessities, would more likely praise than blame a parent who sacrificed his son's higher education and chose to feed the starving.[50]

PATRISTIC REASONS

Clement, Cyprian, Basil, Chrysostom, Jerome, Augustine, Caesarius – none of these men who speak so strongly on our theme had families to temper their concern for the needy and balance their judgments, realistically, between the claims of the nearest and those of the neediest. So we must ask: What grounds support the Fathers' tilt in favor of the neediest?[51] In chapter 3 we noted how exegetically shaky is their reliance on Matthew 25:31–45. However, in their writings new, sometimes weighty reasons also appear.

Giving what the needy may take

The *Didache* may already make a claim more clearly formulated later:[52] "By the beginning of the thirteenth century it was generally accepted that the starving thief was innocent of any crime."[53] According to this tradition, echoed by St. Thomas, "in a case of extreme necessity everything becomes common property. Hence a person in extreme need may take another's goods in order to sustain himself, if he can find no one who is willing to give him something."[54] If, then, the starving may legitimately take what they need to survive, may not the father in EC legitimately give it to them? May he not even be obliged to provide for their needs? May he not be bound in justice to do so?[55]

Scholastic authors typically deny such parity between the right to take and the duty to give. "For it is commonly taught that a needy person who takes a huge sum must do so on condition of returning it later if he can, at least if he has any prospect of doing so . . . whereas he has no such obligation if he receives the sum as alms."[56] More to our question, the father may have a special duty which the needy do not share – namely, the duty of partiality toward his nearest and dearest. The starving may have their children to consider, but the father's responsibilities are to his own children, not to theirs. The possibility that he, as a father, may have to consider something more than relative need, blocks any ready inference from the right of the starving to take what they need to the father's corresponding duty to provide it.

A second patristic reason carries greater weight and has prompted much contemporary controversy.

Keeping equated with taking or killing

"The more effectively to urge the precept of almsgiving," writes James O'Neill, "the Fathers teach that the wealthy are God's stewards and dispensers, so much so that where they refuse to aid the needy they are guilty of theft."[57] This suggests that not giving may not differ morally from taking. But it would not be judged permissible, by Ewing or by others, to steal – much less to steal from the needy – in order to finance a son's university education. So if the Fathers are right, Ewing may be wrong. The young man's father not only may but should assist the starving strangers rather than his son.

A famous patristic text, echoing earlier sayings[58] and cited through the centuries,[59] makes a still stronger claim: "Feed those who are dying of hunger, for if you have not fed them, you have killed them."[60] Though not developed, explained, or clarified by context, this assertion, too, has evident pertinence for our case. Neither Ewing nor any other ethician would suggest that a father might kill innocent strangers in order to assure his son a university education.[61] So again, if the Fathers are right it seems that Ewing must be wrong. The father is obliged to save the starving with the funds his son would otherwise receive.

Of these strong patristic pronouncements it has been observed: "One must interpret these oratorical formulas and others of the same style that one meets especially in the Greek Fathers, according to the ensemble of traditional teaching . . . One can even say that the guilty rich person is culpable of injustice and theft, but always in the large sense that he keeps something that he should communicate to another."[62] In this reading, *if* the father is culpable in favoring his son, *then* his failure to feed the starving may be comparable to theft or murder; but it remains to be determined, in some unstated manner, whether he is in fact culpable in so choosing. Did not Augustine, who spoke as vigorously as the rest, place negative duties before positive ("primum ut nulli noceat, deinde ut etiam prosit cui potuerit")?[63]

Yet, however one dilutes the Fathers' bold assertions, the crucial point they raise cannot be finessed: if failure to give stands on a par with taking, and taking is clearly wrong, so is the failure to give. If letting die stands on a par with killing, and killing is clearly wrong, so is letting die. It is as wrong to deny the starving assistance as it would be to deprive them of nourishment and thereby cause their deaths. So what of the parity, vigorously debated today, between action and omission?[64] Is it true that, *"ceteris paribus*, omitting to save a life when we could do so is as morally reprehensible as taking a life"?[65] Is it true that "the bare fact that one act is an act of killing, while another act is an act of 'merely' letting die, is not a morally good reason in support of the judgment that the former is worse than the latter"?[66]

On this general question, I agree with Goodin:

Even if it were possible to establish an analytic distinction between acts and omissions, positive and negative duties, what moral importance attached to that distinction per se would remain unclear. What *is* clear is that various other considerations of undeniable moral significance [e.g., effort, intention, costs, legal rights, negative motivation] are commonly, but only contingently, associated with harmful acts (breaches of negative duties) rather than with omissions (breaches of positive duties to provide aid). Once all these other considerations are factored out, there may be little or nothing of moral significance left in the original distinction.[67]

I shall not argue for this general position but shall focus on confrontations such as Ewing's. There the case for parity looks strong. What is the moral difference between taking from people and thereby causing them to starve, on the one hand, and failing to prevent their starving when we can, on the other? In either case they die. In either case, their dying or surviving lies within the power of those acting or not acting (taking or not giving), and follows from their decision. This strong, pragmatic parity overrides any of the reasons I have seen cited for act-omission disparity.[68] For example:

Sacrifice. "I contend," writes David Conway, "that there is a general reason for letting die that is not present in the case of killing: namely, not letting someone die typically requires one to make some personal sacrifice, whereas not killing someone typically does not require one to make any personal sacrifice."[69] Thus stated, this generalization may be true – at least if the cost is understood financially, not psychically. However, Conway's suggestion does nothing to show that, *other things being equal*, killing is worse than letting die. Besides, how significant is expense? Suppose it would be costly to allow one's competitor to live and inexpensive to do away with him (a touch of cyanide, a blow in an out-of-the-way place). Would the financial advantages of the deed significantly alter its wrongness – significantly enough to make it permissible to kill the competitor in order to provide for a son's university education? If not, what makes it permissible to achieve the same end by allowing many to die?

Intention. According to Robert Boyle, "the possibility of a difference of intention in cases of killing and in cases of letting die requires that the moral evaluation of the one be carried out independently of the moral evaluation of the other."[70] This subjective discrimination does not bear on the objective rightness that concerns us.[71] The father in EC might intentionally withhold assistance from the starving, desiring their deaths as a natural solution to overpopulation; or he might give them no thought, desiring only to put his son through college. Intention, like compassion or lack of compassion, is an independent variable, throwing no light on the objective rightness or wrongness of an action.[72]

Motivation. The same holds for an agent's motives, on which Michael Tooley remarks:

The *motivation* likely to be associated with the two types of actions is different. If someone performs an action he knows will kill someone else, this will usually be grounds for concluding that he wanted to kill that person. In contrast, failing to help someone may indicate only apathy, laziness, selfishness, or an amoral outlook: the fact that a person knowingly allows another to die will not normally be grounds for concluding that he desired that person's death. Someone who knowingly kills another is thus likely to be more seriously defective from a moral point of view than someone who fails to save another's life.[73]

These, too, are subjective considerations. They say nothing about the objective rightness or wrongness of Ewing's verdict.

Rights. To James Rachels's defense of act-omission parity, Edward Regis objects:

Overlooked by Rachels entirely is any consideration pertaining to rights which individuals may possess, such as, for example, the right of freedom from coercive interference into one's life. This type of right would be a powerful instrument for the resolution of this problem, for if such a right could be demonstrated to exist then the wrongness of murder would immediately follow. It would not follow, on the other hand, that if we refrained from feeding those about to die of starvation we would be interfering into their lives, even if partially as a consequence of our refraining they were to die.[74]

Granted, we would not infringe that particular right. But to establish disparity with respect to rights, it would be necessary to exclude any comparable right on the part of the starving. Regis himself overlooks the possibility that the starving also have a right to life, hence a right to assistance – a right that may be as strong as the right not to be killed. A Christian conception of rights, based on charity, will not stress mere differences of causality where lives are equally at stake.

Legality. Whereas laws forbid killing, none forbids letting strangers starve. For this reason, it might be said, the former is worse than the latter. Extra evil attaches to killing, because it is illegal. However, suppose no law forbade killing: would it then be morally permissible to kill others for the sake of a son's university education? The legal difference does not make sufficient moral difference to blunt the patristic objection.[75]

That objection, if correct, is momentous. Theoretically, the assimilation of killing and letting die might point in either direction: instead of heightening the obligation not to let die, it might lessen the obligation not to kill. However, such is not the direction the Fathers' thinking took, nor does it look any more inviting today.[76] Early on, they voiced what still appears the strongest argument against Ewing's verdict. If killing to assist one's son would be wrong, and letting die stands on a par with killing, then letting die, for the same purpose, would be equally wrong.

For possible rebuttal, we shall have to turn to later times and other sources. The next two chapters will attend principally to arguments and objections that might negate, or at least weaken, this preliminary tilt in favor of the starving. Is the patristic verdict final?

CHAPTER 5

The Thomistic tradition

While patristic writings address the issue of nearest versus neediest more fully and directly than does Scripture, later Christian literature treats the question much more fully still. In this literature, Aquinas figures as the chief seminal figure and his *Summa Theologica* as the most influential single work, with its most pertinent sections being those that discuss almsgiving and the order of charity. Subsequent authors, developing these sections, produced the most thorough treatments of our theme in Christian or nonchristian literature. I shall start with Aquinas, then pass to his successors, and finally dwell on three problematic aspects of the Thomistic tradition. If that tradition is right about self-preference, about the relation of self-preference to nearest-preference, and about the importance of social standing, there is reason to reconsider the Fathers' implicit assessment of a case such as EC.

THE ORDER OF CHARITY

By the time of Peter Lombard and Philip the Chancellor, the "order of charity" had taken the following general form: "First, God is to be loved, second ourselves, third our parents, fourth our children, fifth members of our household, sixth strangers."[1] Aquinas inherited this doctrine, and his authority established it for centuries to come.[2] With respect to parents and children he also refined it: "A father naturally loves his son more [than his father] because the son is more closely joined to him, but a son naturally loves his father more as representing a higher good."[3]

In practice, "children's chief duty to parents is honor, whereas parents' chief duty to children is providing for them."[4]

Evidently, this ordering would give preference to one's child over a stranger in equal need, but it does not directly indicate where preference should go when need is unequal, as in EC. Neither do Aquinas's reasons offer any clearer clue. On the side of greater love for children than for parents he argues:

> The degrees of love may also be measured from the standpoint of the lover, and here closer union makes for greater love. On this score, a son is to be loved more than a father, as Aristotle observes in the *Ethics*. First, because parents love their children as being part of themselves, whereas a father is not a part of his son; hence his love for his son is more like a person's love for himself. Secondly, because parents know more surely who their children are than the other way around. Thirdly, because a son, as a part of his father, is therefore closer to him than is the father to the son, where the relationship is one of principle or source. Fourthly, because parents have loved longer: for a father immediately begins to love his son the moment he is born, while it is only in the course of time that the son begins to love his father. But the longer love lasts, the stronger it is, in keeping with *Ecclesiasticus*: *Forsake not an old friend, for a new one will not be like to him.*[5]

If any of these varied reasons validly grounded a preference for one's children, they might suggest the strength of the preference. So doing, they might indicate how strongly one should prefer one's children to strangers and how needy the strangers might have to be in comparison with one's children before one might or should put their needs first. However, these possibilities need not detain us, for the reasons Thomas cites all look weak.

For example, in response to his final point one might suggest that children's love for their parents outlives the parents, hence lasts as long as the parents' love for them. More pertinent, anyone familiar with divorce rates knows that love need not grow stronger with time. Even if it did, as a rule, increase over time, this fact of nature would not automatically be normative, either for our affections or for our benefactions. Our wonder at the world declines with time, our senses grow duller, our ways become more set: should they? As for the citation from

Ecclesiasticus, clearly Thomas applied different exegetical standards than are accepted today, when eisegesis is frowned on.

Even if valid, Aquinas's reasons would shed murky light on his views about the strength of filial preference. One can only surmise, quasi-mathematically, that if children take precedence over other relatives or members of one's household and these others take precedence over strangers, the preference for one's children is more than minimal: it amounts to more than preference in equal need. For more specific indications, one must turn to Aquinas's discussion of almsgiving.

ALMS

St. Thomas took the term "alms" (*eleemosynae*) very broadly, as had Augustine:

The Lord's words: *Give alms; and behold, all things are clean unto you,* hold good of all that is done through practical works of mercy. Hence, not only the man who gives food to the hungry, drink to the thirsty, raiment to the naked, hospitality to the stranger, shelter to the fugitive; who visits the sick and the shut-ins, ransoms the captives, carries the lame, leads the blind, comforts the sorrowful, heals the sick, points out the way to the lost, counsels the perplexed, and gives the necessaries of life to the poor – not such a man only, but also he who pardons the sinner truly gives alms.[6]

Accordingly, spiritual works of mercy as well as corporal figure prominently in Aquinas's treatment of alms.

With respect to the corporal works, he distinguishes between sharing that is wrong and sharing that is obligatory, given the respective needs of ourselves and our dependents on the one hand and of nondependents on the other. It is wrong to deprive ourselves and our dependents of what is necessary for life, whatever another's need;[7] it is obligatory to deprive ourselves of what we need neither for life nor for our social station, when another's need is extreme.[8] Indeed, "There is a time when we sin mortally if we fail to give alms. Such a situation exists when there is evident and urgent need on the part of the recipient, yet no one else appears at hand to help him, and when the giver possesses superfluous goods, which he does not need for the time being, so far as he can judge with probability."[9]

From this much, it is not evident whether in EC the father would be obliged to help the starving. Perhaps Thomas's references to state or condition should be interpreted narrowly rather than broadly – that is, as alluding to a rank within a class (e.g., duke or earl) rather than to the whole class (e.g., nobleman).[10] Even so, Aquinas viewed the requirements of one's state elastically. "The *necessary* considered thus is not an invariable quantity: add much, and it still might not exceed what a person needs in this way; subtract much, and he still might have enough to live decently in keeping with his position."[11] Where does a child's university education belong, for what class of parent, then or now?

When Aquinas pinpoints cases between the two extremes just mentioned (equal need and dire need versus none), uncertainty persists. "It would be inordinate," he writes, "for a person so to impoverish himself by almsgiving that he could no longer live decently on the residue according to his position and business commitments; for nobody should live unbecomingly."[12] However, there are exceptions to this rule, and one of them arises when there is "extreme need on the part of a private individual or some grave necessity of State. For in such cases it would be praiseworthy to forego what seems necessary for the decent maintenance of one's station, so as to provide for the greater need."[13]

Had Thomas spoken, not of what seems needful for the *decent* maintenance of one's station (*ad decentiam sui status*), but simply of what seems necessary for one's station (*ad statum*),[14] the verdict would be clear: Ewing would be wrong. Whether or not the father was obliged to help the starving, he would do well if he did so. For the need of the starving is extreme, and a university education, whether needed or not to maintain one's social standing, is not a life-or-death necessity. Even had Thomas drawn this line more clearly, the question would remain whether the assistance he calls praiseworthy is not only admirable but also obligatory. Commenting on Lombard's *Sentences*, he had stated unconditionally: "The precept of law demands that the absolute need of strangers be met before the conditional need of oneself or one's kin."[15] Does the *Summa* weaken this strong claim, or is Michel Riquet's reading (with emphasis added) the right one: "When the neighbor's need is urgent, extreme and evident, one *should* assist him, not only with one's superfluity but also with *all* that is not presently needed for the life of oneself and one's dependents"?[16]

Aquinas may have felt less need than his commentators to clarify this question.[17] "People do not sin mortally," he remarked, "every time they do not give their superfluity to the poor, but when the need is urgent. However, just how great the need must be to oblige under pain of mortal sin cannot be determined by reason but must be left to the prudence and faith of the prospective donor."[18] The like might be said with regard to sin and no sin. As it is difficult to determine precisely when a given deed falls on this side or that of the line between mortal and venial, so it is difficult to determine precisely when a deed falls on this side or that of the line between precept and counsel. (Indeed, I would say, it is impossible; in neither case can we draw the line itself.)

Nonetheless, the evidence cited suggests that Aquinas might disagree with Ewing. It might be permissible, indeed preferable, for the father to assist the starving rather than his son. If so, why?

Léon Bouvier replies:

Though the obligation to give what is necessary for one's condition in this instance [of extreme necessity] has not been expressly indicated in the course of the preceding article, it could easily be inferred from the principles enunciated earlier concerning the order of charity. That order is of obligation (III Sent., d. 29, q. 1, a. 1, ad 5um, repeated later in 2a, 2ae, 44, 8). But, in charity our love should prefer the neighbor's soul over our own body (2a, 2ae, 26, 5); so logically it should prefer the neighbor's bodily life (in case of extreme necessity) to our exterior goods. Since living decently according to one's condition is precisely such a good, we are bound to take from what is necessary for our condition in order to save the corporal life of a person in extreme necessity.[19]

If bodily death entailed death of the soul, there might be some "logic" in this argument; but doubtless Bouvier himself would not defend such an entailment. Certainly Aquinas would not.

Cajetan, reading between the lines, spots a different argument in *Summa* 2–2, q. 32, a. 5: if those who have what they need for their condition do not help those in extreme need, the needy may legitimately take what they need. "Therefore it is against the natural law not to succor extreme need from what is necessary for one's state."[20] The last chapter noted and critiqued this general argument. Of greater interest, therefore, than Cajetan's reasoning is the way he states his conclusion.

In extreme need, he says, one is obliged to give "from" what is necessary for one's state (*de necessario personae*). This wording suggests that one must give some but not all, and leaves unclear how much the some should be. In EC, would the father be obliged to bypass his son and give to the starving? Cajetan's phrase does not say, but is as indefinite as the *Summa*'s "ad decentiam sui status." The indefiniteness is not resolved in a variant formulation: "A person who has more than enough to live on but not more than enough for his condition, is obliged to help a person in extreme need."[21] How much of his goods he should share, this directive too does not indicate.

For Cajetan's indefiniteness I sense one likely explanation which relates to the whole Thomistic tradition. Suppose that five factors are needful for a person's station: the station is then lost whether the person sacrifices all five factors or only one; thus the part–whole distinction has little relevance. Suppose, instead, that a variable ensemble of factors together establish a person's station but are not singly required for it: the station is then lost by sacrificing all or many of these factors but not by sacrificing any single one of them (e.g., a university education). In this second perspective, the part–whole distinction does have relevance. Cajetan and his successors, not having distinguished between these two perspectives, may not have recognized the need to be more definite. A phrase that has clear implications in one perspective may not in the other.

Given the indefiniteness of the borders between one social condition and another (noted by Aquinas) and given the very different results of losing one condition rather than another (about which he was silent), such niceties may appear irrelevant. Once class considerations are introduced, all precision may seem impossible. However, had Thomas stated clearly in the *Summa* that subsistence needs of one's neighbor override all considerations of station, for oneself and one's own, the verdict for EC would have been evident.

SUBSEQUENT TRADITION

Aquinas's heirs staked out a middle position, not clearly identical with his. On one hand, we are obliged to take something from the needs of our condition ("de necessariis, non ad vitam, sed ad statum"[22]) in order to assist those in extreme need. "This is the common view of theologians."[23] On the other hand, we are not obliged to surrender our condition entirely for the sake of those in even the direst necessity. This, too, is the common view. Concerning what might be the better, more Christian course of action, there has been much less discussion.[24]

Even within the limits of concern for obligation, a verdict on EC might have emerged had there been greater agreement, and greater clarity, on the extent to which people might be obliged to encroach on their condition. "Among theologians," wrote Domingo de Soto, "there is no one who doubts, as we have said, that a person is obliged to give to those in extreme need from what is necessary for his state, and is obliged to diminish his state, indeed to diminish it greatly, if necessary."[25] Only some canonists, he added, have disagreed. Yet the encyclical *Rerum novarum* spoke for many others in the Thomistic tradition when it advised: "No one is commanded to distribute to others that which is required for his own needs and those of his household; nor even to give away what is reasonably required to keep up becomingly his condition in life, 'for no one ought to live other than becomingly.' "[26] Surely, for example, it is only reasonable and becoming for a child to receive a good education, up to the standards of his or her class.

This broad middle ground of the tradition, with demands

ranging from exigent to accommodating, represents an uneasy balance between conflicting arguments:

Ordinarily, help should be given *in extreme temporal need* even at great cost, but not at very great cost. The reason, on the one hand, is that the neighbor's life is a more excellent good than any good of ours; on the other hand, since self-love takes precedence, no one is obliged to suffer so great a loss for others' sake.[27]

According to the first argument, "the order of charity demands, per se and other things equal, that we make more of our neighbor's life than of the dignity of our station in life";[28] for "a neighbor's life is a more important good than one's own position in life."[29] More fully:

The order of charity requires us to prefer the weightiest good of our neighbor to our own far inferior good; but the good required simply for the decency of our state is far inferior to the good of a neighbor in extreme need, since a person is only said to be in extreme need when his life, or faculties, or, as some would have it, his entire reputation or all his goods are at stake.[30]

By itself, this argument from disparate value would warrant a stronger conclusion than that generally drawn from it. The neighbor's life outweighs not only the amenities of one's condition, for oneself and one's dependents, but also that condition itself. However, a second standard argument counteracts the first and keeps the conclusion within bounds. "No one, however wealthy, is obliged to take extraordinary measures to assist a neighbour even in direful straits . . . Nor is a wealthy individual obliged to imperil his social standing to aid a neighbor in extreme need."[31] For well-ordered charity puts love of self before love of others. Accordingly, "as we are not obliged to save our own lives by extraordinary means or at great inconvenience, *a fortiori* no strict obligation exists of giving a large sum of money to save a neighbor's life."[32] "Hence the saying: charity does not oblige with serious inconvenience."[33] And what holds for oneself holds for one's own as well, since, in the Thomistic tradition, they fall within the ambit of one's interests and the responsibilities of one's state.

CRITIQUE

Three aspects of this reasoning, counterbalancing the argument from disparate value, distinguish the Thomistic tradition from patristic writings: (1) the preference given self over neighbor; (2) the inclusion of one's kin and dependents within this preference; and (3) the stress laid on social condition. All three are highly problematic.

(1) I have already touched on the first point in chapter 1, and having treated it much more fully in a previous work, I can be brief here. In summary, self-preference lacks scriptural backing,[34] and the arguments of Aquinas and others reveal no good reason to reject the New Testament's contrary teaching.[35] To illustrate both failings, consider the only one of Aquinas's arguments that mentions Scripture: "We read in *Leviticus* and in *Matthew, You shall love your neighbour as yourself;* from which we see that a man's love for himself is, so to speak, the paradigm of his love for others. Now the paradigm is more than what takes after it. Therefore a man is bound in charity to love himself more than his neighbour."[36] In reply to this oft-repeated rationale, I have observed:

The claim that the paradigm is "more than what takes after it" either makes a tautological assertion of epistemological primacy or Platonically identifies epistemological primacy with valuational primacy. The former interpretation makes the premise irrelevant; the latter makes it weak. No logical link requires that a model be superior in value to what is modeled on it, nor can such superiority be affirmed as de facto true in all cases, without including the instance here at issue and thereby begging the question. Whatever one may think of its truth, there is no incoherence in Luther's counterclaim . . . : "By this commandment 'as yourself' man is not commanded to love himself but he is shown the wicked love with which in fact he loves himself; in other words, it says to him: You are wholly bent on yourself and versed in self-love, and you will not be straightened out and made upright unless you cease entirely to love yourself and, forgetting yourself, love only your neighbor." A model can serve in this way too.[37]

The injunction to love one's neighbor *as* oneself – not *as much as* oneself – does not support even parity between self and others;

and other New Testament passages move beyond parity in the direction of Luther's position. "Whoever wishes to be great among you must be your servant, and whoever wishes to be first among you must be your slave; just as the Son of Man came not to be served but to serve, and to give his life a ransom for many" (Mt. 20:26–28, cf. Mt. 23:11, Mk. 9:35, 10:42–45, 14:24, Lk. 12:37). "If I then, your Lord and Teacher, have washed your feet ["a service traditionally rendered by the lowest servant on the staff of house servants"[38]] you also ought to wash one another's feet" (Jn. 13:14). "Have this mind among yourselves, which is yours in Christ Jesus, who, though he was in the form of God, did not count equality with God a thing to be grasped, but emptied himself, taking the form of a servant" (Phil. 2:5–7). "Through love, be servants of one another" (Gal. 5:13; cf. 1 Cor. 9:19; 2 Cor. 4:5). From texts like these no strictly logical inference can be drawn to the norm I have labeled Self-Subordination (I shall not here make the complex case for that norm); but they do clearly suggest a more altruistic stance than self-preference.

(2) To the extent, then, that preference for one's nearest and dearest is tied to self-preference – either as equally strong or as weaker – it is falsified. Aquinas and his heirs effect the linkage in both these ways. One way typifies discussion of alms, the other discussion of the order of charity.

In the Thomistic treatment of almsgiving, self and nearest form one moral person.[39] Thus, on one side stands the individual and his or her own – together, as a unit – while on the other side stands the needy stranger.[40] The superfluous, wrote Aquinas,

is not to be taken merely with reference to oneself, as if it meant only what is beyond one's own individual needs, but also with reference to one's dependents. For a man's first duty is to provide for himself and those under his care (it is with respect to them that the expression "necessary to the person" is used, while "person," here, implies social rank), and only when that is done, to use what is left to relieve the needs of others.[41]

Thus, distinguishing two levels of necessity, Thomas envisages the case "where a man has only just enough to keep himself with his children and dependents alive," then the case where a man has just enough for life "in keeping with his own and his dependents' social position."[42] Self and nearest remain similarly joined in subsequent Thomistic teaching. "The doctors say that one thing is superfluous for the person and for nature, another for one's state. By 'person' we mean all those of whom we have the care; under 'state' you should consider also the state of one's children."[43]

Thus united with the self, all those within the family circle acquire the same status as the self vis-à-vis outsiders. Since, however, primacy is wrongly accorded the self, what the tradition thus joins must be disjoined, lest family members be demoted along with the self. Not only are children, spouses, parents, and the like to be recognized as our neighbors, and as such to be preferred to oneself, but they are to be regarded as privileged neighbors.

So says my earlier-defended theory. However, the Thomistic approach may appear realistic, not only in other times, when greater togetherness characterized family living, but even today. Most of the decisions which parents make with respect to style of life, they make not only for themselves, individually, but for the whole family. Parents and children do not live in separate houses in separate neighborhoods; they do not take separate vacations nor sit down at separate tables. Nor should they.

These facts help to explain the linking of self and kin, but they do not completely justify it. As EC illustrates, not all a parent's decisions equally affect all members of the family. And family decisions cannot be guided by the single norm of self-preference if in fact identical norms do not hold for oneself and one's family members – as Thomistic moralists themselves acknowledged. When discussing the order of charity, they distinguished between self and others, including one's nearest and dearest, and assigned others a lower place. For even my nearest and dearest are not as close to me as I am to myself, and all rankings follow these two principles of order: God and self.[44] Once, however, the lesser of these two godheads is challenged and dethroned, the ordering derived from it is also called in question.

Neither of these two connections with self – the one that puts the nearest on a par with self and the one that puts the nearest next in line – necessarily falsifies the relationship that concerns us, between nearest and neediest. The first ordering, which accords the nearest the same strong priority as the self, is wrong for the self but may be right for the nearest. The second demotes the nearest vis-à-vis the self, but still rates them above strangers. No doubt this preference is right, to some extent. But how strong the preference should be cannot be judged reliably from the Thomistic tradition. To prevent serious distortions, nearest-preference must be detached from self-preference.

(3) A third innovation in the Thomistic treatment of alms-giving, which I shall consider at greater length (there being no previous study, in this instance, to which I can refer the reader), is its emphasis on social standing, both of oneself and of one's nearest.[45]

The writings of the Fathers reveal no such emphasis.[46] "If you wish to be perfect," wrote Jerome, "and stand at the highest rank of dignity, do what the apostles did: Sell all you have, give to the poor, and follow the Savior."[47] "No one should be ashamed," declared Ambrose, "if from being rich he becomes poor, by giving to the poor; for Christ, who was rich, became poor that by his poverty he might enrich all."[48] "What does it profit," asked Augustine, "to acquire anything temporal or transitory in this world – whether money or physical pleasure or the honor of human praise? Are not all these things mere smoke and wind?"[49] "Seek what things suffice," he advised, "and you will see how few they are."[50] "So give to the poor, my brothers. *If we have food and clothing, let us be content with that*"[51] (1 Tim. 6:8).

Later Christian moralists adopted a more accommodating perspective. To be sure, one should live in Christian simplicity; but a peasant's simplicity differs from an artisan's, an artisan's from a merchant's, a merchant's from a nobleman's, a nobleman's from a prince's, a prince's from a king's.[52] At each higher level, more banqueting, retinue, finery, hospitality – yes, even more outward pomp – are required to maintain one's standing properly.[53] All this costs money. Hence,

The upshot is that property is considered as the endowment of a station in life. Its function and justification is that it enables the occupant of that station to perform properly the duties attaching to it. He must not hold more than he needs to that end. But in so far as what he holds does serve that end, he may hold it with a clear conscience: he is even warned not to give so much away in alms that he is left with less than enough to keep up the way of life appropriate to his station. That would be as much a misuse of property as to hold on to more than he needed. "It would be excessive," said Aquinas, "to take so much out of one's own means to give away to others that with what was left one could not very well keep up the way of life that accords with one's station, and meet contingencies as they arise; no one should live unbecomingly" (*Summa Theologica*, II-II, 32, a, b, c . . .). The needs of one's station, moreover, are conventionally defined: they include the jewellery of the alderman's wife as much as the labourer's bench or bowl.[54]

The needs of a person's station also extend to his or her children, whose station must likewise be fittingly maintained.[55]

Hence, a peasant satisfies his duty, who sends out his children, properly instructed for their occupation, to husbandry, or to any branch of manufacture. Clergymen, lawyers, physicians, officers in the army or navy, gentlemen possessing moderate fortunes of inheritance, or exercising trade in a large or liberal way, are required by the same rule to provide their sons with learned professions, commissions in the army or navy, places in public offices, or reputable branches of merchandise. Providing a child with a situation, includes a competent supply for the expenses of that situation, until the profits of it enable the child to support himself. Noblemen and gentlemen of high rank and fortune may be bound to transmit an inheritance to the representatives of their family, sufficient for their support, without the aid of a trade or profession, to which there is little hope that a youth, who has been flattered with other expectations, will apply himself with diligence or success.[56]

Scope must also be allowed for legitimate social aspirations.[57] "If someone reasonably hopes he will attain a higher station, what he now sets aside to attain that higher station, and properly maintain it afterwards, should by no means be judged superfluous for him."[58] So advised, few supposed that they had any surplus. For, as St. Alphonsus Liguori acknowledged, "whatever is necessary for one's children, one's household, honest gifts, entertainments, hospitality, . . . in view of common contingencies, provision for heirs, future needs, etc. is not superfluous."[59] Toledo, Vasquez, and others concluded that, all things considered, "superfluity is rarely to be found, especially among the laity."[60]

How foreign all this seems to Scripture, and how strange it would sound to patristic ears![61] Circumstances have altered, and with them mentalities. The world of St. Thomas, and still more notably that of his successors, differs from the world of the Fathers or the evangelists. He sees no need to question the importance of social condition (*conditio*) or station (*status*). He sees no need to spell out the meaning of these terms or establish their moral significance.[62] And once the master has spoken, the tradition is fixed. Thereafter, economic, social, and political realities shift massively century by century, and with them the implicit content of the doctrine;[63] yet Thomas's followers do not reconsider or revise his teaching. They stress social standing still more strongly and amplify its necessities, without seriously questioning the Christian warrant for such emphasis. Not till the present century did Arthur Vermeersch recognize the need to take a closer look at this aspect of the tradition.[64]

The wisps of argumentation, if any, proffered by most spokesmen of the tradition betray a familiar viewpoint,[65] captured by the hymn:

> The rich man in his castle,
> The poor man at his gate,
> God made them high or lowly,
> And ordered their estate.[66]

According to this mentality, for the rich man to leave his castle and join the poor man at the gate would subvert God's order. Alms are admirable up to a point, but no one is obliged to go beyond that point. The high should remain high and the low remain low, each in his or her place.

"The Schoolmen of the Middle Ages," notes Henry Brown, "developed a positive view of inequality in two closely related ways: they saw society as an organism, and as an order of hierarchy."[67] "From the notion of an organism, whose being involves a union of like with unlike, was derived the necessity of differences in rank, profession and estate. So that the individuals, who were the elements in ecclesiastical and political bodies, were conceived, not as arithmetically equal units, but as socially grouped and differentiated from each other."[68]

Such was the outlook of Aquinas and his heirs. As Etienne Gilson remarks, for Thomas "the universe appears essentially a hierarchy and the philosophical problem is to indicate its exact arrangement and to place each class of beings in its proper grade."[69] Society, too, is a hierarchy, and the problem for the social theorist is to place each social class and ultimately each individual member of society in the exact status which is due.[70] The corresponding task of the ethician is to keep each individual in his or her proper place. The good of society requires it.

Yet a curious contradiction can be noted. On the one hand we are told that a person cannot be obliged to aid even the neediest at the cost of his or her station, since such a loss would gravely harm society.[71] "Granted, in itself a person's life is more precious than another's standing and whole income; yet in relation to the public good a large sum of goods or money is worth more than the life of a single private individual."[72] "It is more useful to the state that a nobleman retain his station than that the life of some poor individual, which would otherwise last only a short time, not end so quickly."[73] On the other hand, when, for instance, a Francis Borgia abandons his dukedom and enters the Society of Jesus, he is viewed as a saint, a Christian hero. Such "downwardly mobile" people are canonized.[74] Their new condition is regarded as a "state of perfection."[75]

For the present point, notice that it makes no difference to whom such people hand on their titles or their wealth – whether to their children, gratis, or to others, for a sum. Thus, a double standard seems to be at work. When the prospect arises that a person might be obliged to feed the starving at the cost of personal wealth or social standing, the public good is invoked, and the status quo is insisted on. When an Anthony, a Benedict, a Francis, a Clare, and many a successor freely abandons his or her station and worldly prospects, the public good is not invoked, and the status quo is not insisted on.

An additional dichotomy casts further doubt on the weight accorded social standing. On the one hand, according to the Thomistic tradition a qualified person may always aspire to a higher station. On the other hand, even a person who is not specially qualified cannot be required by even the direst need to slip a single notch below the position he presently occupies. Indeed, there is seldom any suggestion that losing one's station might mean descending just one tier in a many-tiered hierarchy. Upward, a gradated series of steps ascends; downward, there yawns only the abyss. To lose one's social status, it sometimes appears, is to be reduced automatically to beggary![76]

Notice, for example, how Juan de Lugo weights the scales at the start of a long argument purporting to show that the rich are not obliged to spend large sums to save those in extreme need: "Life itself without an honest station, and joined with great misery, is a great evil, and for some it is worse to lose their station and live than to keep their station and die."[77] Downward, nothing but the pit! Yet, if a nobleman is forced to engage in trade or a merchant prince is reduced to keeping shop, is that not an honest occupation? Is such a lowering a fate worse than death? Some of de Lugo's contemporaries may have thought so,[78] but discerning Christians need not share their sentiments.

For de Lugo, the wealthy's loss of social standing is a dreadful thing, but not the needy's loss of life: "For life is necessarily brief, and must be lost after a few years. Hence the preservation of life for a short time does not exceed in value the loss of state and fortune, whose preservation, prolonged in posterity, appears somehow eternal; indeed, some legitimately prefer to be thus remembered by posterity than to lead a longer life."[79] The attitude de Lugo cites is familiar enough but his argument is surprising, coming from a Christian moralist. "Vain is the fear," the manualists of Salamanca expostulated, "that you will fall from your high estate by giving to those in extreme need; on the contrary, it is evident that you will be honored by God and men."[80]

Prolonging his *plaidoyer*, de Lugo argues: "When Christians die well their life is not so much lost through death as exchanged for a better life. So the loss of life should not be made so much of that all other goods must be sacrificed in order to prevent it."[81] Here the dice are still heavily loaded. To spend large sums or slip in social standing to save another's life need not entail the loss of *all* other goods. And who knows whether the starving will die well or badly? And even if all were sure to pass to a better life, that would be no reason to speed their departure. Eternal values do not cancel temporal values.

De Lugo's reasons do not improve as they continue, nor are better ones to be found in the Thomistic tradition he represents. I have dwelt on this sampling because de Lugo's apologia is the fullest I have encountered, and because of the theme's enduring importance. Prominent in tradition yet never closely scrutinized, the appeal to social status has not lost its relevance. Social stratification continues, and still affects people's perception of their duties toward the needy.

In all societies, Bernard and Elinor Barber observe,

> the different social classes are characterized by different styles of life, by the different kinds of things they do and by the different possessions they have. Almost anything can become an indicator of a class-typed style of life, but visible consumption items are likely to be the ones that are frequently remarked on. That is why, when he was talking about social class differences in styles of life, Veblen spoke of "conspicuous consumption." In the general sense, all classes consume conspicuously.[82]

What people consume they crave, and what they crave they claim. Thus when American workers in the 1920s acquired cars, radios, washing machines, and the like, these new goods quickly became part of the conventional standard of living expected by the class as a whole, and were therefore considered as needs by the individual workers.[83] Once so viewed, the coveted goods competed more strongly with the claims of the needy, as do more recent "necessities" (television sets, stereos, personal computers, cordless telephones, etc.).

But what is a luxury and what is a necessity, asks Schwartz, and who is to judge the difference between the two?

The answer is, the poor of the world. Since Christ placed our final judgment in the hands of the poor we should get in the habit now of looking at our use of money with their eyes; and we should submit every decision of the luxury-necessity type to their hard scrutiny. A trip to Europe, a summer cottage by the seashore, a new car, a yacht, an expensive pet, a visit to the beauty parlor – luxury or necessity? The criterion is, how would the Lazaruses of the world, covered with sores and longing to fill their bellies with the crumbs which fall from our tables, look upon it?[84]

At first glance, this "criterion" looks puzzling, for it names the ones who should judge but says nothing about the standard by which they should judge. This may be Schwartz's point: the destitute would not nicely discriminate between life necessities and social necessities; the Scholastic distinction has been abrogated.[85] To be sure, these things that we and our loved ones might lose through assistance to the Lazaruses of the world – the trips abroad, cottages by the seashore, new cars, yachts, expensive pets, visits to beauty parlors, and so forth – are all desirable, but not because they set a person apart as belonging to this or that class. For a Christian, the claims of social rank, as such, should be minimal or nil. Thus in EC a university education is indeed a worthy goal, but not because it situates a person in the "well-educated" sector of society, not because it makes a person superior.

Worldly people, Loyola observed, "love and seek with such great diligence honors, fame, and esteem for a great name on earth, as the world teaches them," but the followers of Christ do not.[86] Class, rank, social standing, and the like do not deserve the weight accorded them in the Thomistic tradition. More specifically, they do not support the consensus which developed as a result of such weighting, according to which a person is not obliged to sacrifice his social status in order to assist another in extreme need. In biblical terms, the well-dressed may not say to the naked: "I am an upper-class, two-tunic person, not a lower-class, one-tunic person; therefore I need not help you" (cf. Luke 3:7).

Sometimes, to be sure, class expectations must be taken into account, since they affect personal relations and worthwhile endeavors.[87] Often, however, they have no such implications.[88] Will the executive's effectiveness really decline if she does not wear a designer suit? Will the doctor's patients suffer if he drives a compact-size car? The possibility that the answer may be "yes" is my reason for granting that class may deserve at least minimal consideration. However, it would be more accurate to say that class expectations and genuine class advantages deserve consideration, not class itself.

Figuratively, if the hen that lays the golden eggs cannot lay such fine eggs in a shack, that is one reason – though perhaps not an overriding reason – for preferring finer lodgings.[89] Another is the fact that the shack is much less attractive, comfortable, and convenient than the apartment, house, or mansion. But the fact that only lower-class folk live in shacks, whereas upper-class people live in mansions, should carry no extra weight with Christians discerning their responsibilities toward the destitute. "Let the same mind be in you that was in Christ Jesus, who, though he was in the form of God, did not regard equality with God as something to be exploited, but emptied himself, taking the form of a slave" (Phil. 2:5–7).

A NEGLECTED CONSIDERATION: NUMBERS

It may be that for Aquinas, early and late, it is praiseworthy, even obligatory, to sacrifice one's state and that of one's dependents when in the presence of "extreme need on the part of a private individual or some grave necessity of State"[90] – provided, that is, that the pressing need requires it. However, some have questioned whether such would ever be the case.

For, as Lorca sagely remarks, . . . the amount required to succor the extreme need of this or that individual cannot greatly reduce a person's state. And if the need was of many and could not be met without loss of one's state, as for instance if a great famine brought distress to a whole province or country, then no single individual would be bound to meet the entire needs of all the indigent, but all would be bound to.[91]

In either alternative, this reasoning goes, there would be no call to surrender one's social standing completely – either because the needs of a single individual would not be that great or because the needs of many individuals would be the responsibility of many potential providers, or of the state.

Our paradigm case suggests the inadequacy of this viewpoint, especially today, when remediable misery so far exceeds any provision likely to be made for it. In EC, the need of the single child vies with the much greater need of several starving persons. If the discrepancy in their respective needs does not prove decisive, this numerical discrepancy may. Despite the weight he accorded social standing, St. Thomas may have thought it right, in the *Summa* as in the commentary on the *Sentences*, to sacrifice one's standing to save another person's life. Subtract the social weighting and multiply the lives saved, and there may no longer be any doubt which way the preference should go. A close call is no longer a close call if the weight on one side is much reduced and the weight on the other side is multiplied by five or six – or more.

Of legislation introduced in 1984, Arthur Simon recounts: "When the legislation was first proposed, James P. Grant, director of UNICEF, told me that for every $100 spent on child-survival efforts with provisions of this type, at least one child's life would be saved."[92] Recent UNICEF estimates put the cost per child somewhat higher: saving the 100 million children likely to perish of readily remediable ailments during the 1990s would cost about $25 billion – or $250 per child.[93] Whichever decade one chooses, and whichever sum, a university education would cost many times as much as saving a child.

In summary, then, chapter 4's challenge to Ewing's verdict not only stands, but is strengthened. The Thomistic tradition's new, distinctive traits – self-preference, the bond between self-preference and nearest-preference, the weight attached to social standing – do not succeed in weakening the challenge; and this final, numerical consideration, neglected by the tradition, reinforces it. This does not mean that no case can be made for Ewing's verdict. It just means that if we are to find arguments that strengthen or confirm his position we shall have to look elsewhere than in the sources so far considered – Scripture, the Fathers, and the Thomistic tradition.

CHAPTER 6

Contemporary considerations

The New Testament favors the neediest rather than the nearest, though not as decisively as Matthew 25:31–46 might suggest. The Church Fathers speak more explicitly on the same side, and their comparison of letting die with killing tells weightily against Ewing's verdict. Innovations in the Thomistic tradition might blunt this objection but do not, since they lack validity. And the fact that in EC many would die, not just one, further strengthens the case for the neediest. However, a final judgment must wait; for contemporary discussions add new arguments on both sides – especially Ewing's. The present chapter builds to a confrontation between the strongest arguments for and against his verdict.

FOR THE NEEDIEST

Aside from stressing the preciousness of every human life, within a Christian perspective,[1] it seems that little more can be said against Ewing's stance and in favor of the starving. If, for example, it is urged that the starving have a right to assistance, it may be countered that the son, too, has rights: a right to paternal support, and a right to a good education. If it is alleged that the father's bank account is traceable, in part, to First-World exploitation of the poor, even so his prosperity cannot be traced to the particular persons who might benefit from his assistance, hence cannot establish a right of those persons to restitution. If divine impartiality is proposed as a model ("He has the same loving concern for each person he has created"[2]), it may be noted that all are equally children of

God but all are not equally children of any human parent, and that this difference may have moral significance. If it is agreed that "the right form of impersonal regard for everyone . . . gives preferential weight to improvements in the lives of those who are worse off as against adding to the advantages of those better off,"[3] this amounts to recognizing a principle of need in competition with whatever principles of nearness there may be; it says nothing about the principles' respective weights. If the equal, God-given dignity of all human persons is stressed, as "the norm by which the adequacy of all forms of human behavior and all the moral principles which are formulated to guide behavior are to be judged,"[4] other norms may be cited, not reducible to this one,[5] and the norm of nearest-preference may be one of them. Similarly, if the principle of equality is interpreted "as the claim that every man should enjoy an equal level of well-being,"[6] Ewing's verdict need not be affected: the principle need not and should not be taken as the sole principle of distribution; so it does not preclude a legitimate, perhaps powerful, preference for one's nearest and dearest.

Possibly more might be made of one or the other of these suggestions. However, till now I have noted more reasons against Ewing's verdict than for it. And the new arguments that favor his judgment look more impressive, on the whole, than the new arguments that oppose it. And only the supporting considerations might reverse the judgment of the preceding chapters. So I shall dwell on them. First, however, I should mention a pair of reflections that may occasion as deep misgivings about Ewing's stance as do any outright arguments against it.

First, consider the following scenario. A father is driving with his son along a country road bordered on both sides by a ditch and a barbed-wire fence. Rounding a curve they come suddenly on a cluster of children walking in the middle of the road. There is no chance of stopping in time, but a turn of the wheel could take the car into the ditch on the right. Continuing on the road would result in death or serious injury to the children, whereas turning into the ditch might cause injury, possibly death, to the father or the son. What would be the better thing to do? The difference in the numbers and in the seriousness of the risk in each alternative suggests that it would be better to take the action of turning the wheel rather than doing nothing and letting the car continue on its course. But if so, how can Ewing's verdict be correct? The risk to the son's life and limb is comparable in importance to a son's university education. The risk to the children in the road is comparable to that of the starving. Furthermore, in this instance the father's welfare is also put at risk as well as the son's, so that, were Ewing right, the verdict here would favor the son more decidedly than in EC. But does it? Would it be wrong to turn the wheel? Wouldn't that be the preferable course of action, rather than plowing through the children?

In constructing this comparison, I have done several things. I have maintained a parallel with EC by making the deaths result from inaction. At the same time, I have whipped aside the shroud of anonymity and revealed flesh and blood children, there in the road. Similarly, I have made their deaths immediate, tangible, dreadful. These changes have a psychological effect. However, in order to have an argument, I do need the concession that, at the very least, it would not be wrong to turn the wheel; and that concession may not be forthcoming. Even here, the son's high priority may be urged. So I cite this comparable case merely as a source of misgivings, similar to those expressed in chapter 1 with regard to Mrs. Rhi and the Eskimos.

Serious misgivings also have a further source. I have suggested that purely utilitarian, cost-benefit considerations would not justify Ewing's position. The parent-child relationship, as such, must carry strong, independent weight if his verdict is to stand. Ewing makes no case for such independent weighting, nor does it seem likely that he could. At this level of abstraction, prescinding from benefits, intuition would have to replace argument. However, ethnic comparisons call such intuition in question. Whereas Ewing and the culture he speaks for put the advantages of one's children over the lives of strangers, other peoples have viewed things differently.

In *The Origin and Development of the Moral Ideas* Edward

Westermarck noted that many peoples have practiced widespread infanticide without qualms – but also, in many instances, without any diminution of their love for the infants they have spared. "In Fiji 'such children as are allowed to live are treated with a foolish fondness.' Among the Narrinyeri, 'only let it be determined that an infant's life shall be saved, and there are no bounds to the fondness and indulgence with which it is treated.' "[7] Others have cherished their young from the start, but only for a time. Either their parental affection terminates with the age of helplessness, or, as for the Fuegians, it "gradually decreases in proportion as the child grows older, and ceases entirely when it reaches the age of seven or eight; thenceforth the parents in no way meddle with the affairs of their son, who may leave them if he likes."[8] How sharp is the contrast with Ewing's attitude and that of the society he speaks for! So the question comes unbidden: who is right? Whose intuition is the more accurate? Have we of the West arrived, without argument, at the sole correct viewpoint? Have we unerringly struck a perfect balance between deficient parental concern and excessive?

Such cultural contrasts need not breed skepticism. Viewpoints differ because societies differ. The facts are not the same. The Fuegian child could make his own way at seven; a contemporary child could not. A university education is possible, but expensive, in our society; for Fuegian youngsters there was no such possibility or corresponding "need." Multiply such contrasts and it becomes evident why both viewpoints – the Fuegians' and Ewing's – might have some validity. However, if Ewing's verdict rests on such comparative advantages and disadvantages, it cannot stand. In terms of sheer utility, the starving win over the would-be student. What such cultural comparisons suggest is that nothing more may underlie contemporary Western "intuitions."

FOR THE NEAREST

John Cottingham highlights a transcultural value obscured by this line of thought:

Special concern towards particular human beings is essential to the functioning of those close relationships which the overwhelming mass of mankind seek as a major source of psychological enrichment. And if such concern has a successful outcome, so that the agent is able to witness the flourishing of the loved one, and if, further, it is reciprocated, so that the parties are bound together in mutual ties of affection, then the resulting situation constitutes what is one of the principal satisfactions of human life. The justification of philophilic partialism is thus extremely simple. If I give no extra weight to the fact that this is *my* lover, *my* friend, *my* spouse, *my* child, if I assess these people's needs purely on their merits (in such a way as an impartial observer might do), then that special concern which constitutes the essence of love and friendship will be eliminated. Partiality to loved ones is justified because it is an essential ingredient in one of the highest of human goods.[9]

This good warrants some partiality.[10] It might warrant more partiality than would, for example, the son's education alone, in competition with the claims of the starving. However, to do so it would have to compete with their claims; and it is not clear that it does. For, as Rachels remarks:

There is a lot about parental love that is consistent with a large measure of impartiality. Loving someone is not only a matter of preferring their interests. Love involves, among other things, intimacy and the sharing of experiences. A parent shows love by listening to the child's jokes, by talking, by being a considerate companion, by praising, and even by scolding when that is needed.[11]

Thus, love need not be expensive. The starving may be fed and mutual affection between parent and child may still flourish. "The companionship, the listening, the talking, and the praising and scolding are what make personal relationships *personal.* That is why the psychic benefits that accompany such relationships are more closely associated with these matters than with such relatively impersonal things as being fed."[12]

Of Origen's childhood the story is told that each night as his father came home, he would enter the room where the child lay sleeping, and there he would kiss the child's naked breast, saying that this "was the temple of the Holy Spirit and he was never nearer that Spirit than when he imprinted those kisses there." Morton Kelsey comments: "You may think that this is a little overdone, but this father was not just a sentimental peasant; he was a courageous Christian martyr. He knew and expressed the truth that children who have not known this kind of tenderness and affection seldom grow up into persons capable of independence and love."[13] His example also illustrates the truth that paternal love may take forms that do not compete with concern for the destitute. A father may both foster a loving relationship with his son and also feed the starving.[14]

But at the expense of something as desired, important, and taken for granted as a university education? This may be doubted, for reasons that appear from a second line of thought favoring Ewing's position.

Roles and expectations

A series of claims centers in on EC. In general, when a person, either by express promise or by conduct, has encouraged another to rely on his acting in a certain way, obligation arises to act in that way.[15] Deviations are likely to generate surprise, disappointment, or disapproval – especially if society inculcates similar expectations.[16] Specifically, family members are expected to attend more to each other's interests and needs than they do to those of strangers. More specifically, parents are expected to devote special care to nurturing their children. Still more specifically, they are expected to promote not only their children's health, well-being, and happiness, but also their education and socialization.[17] Thus, "if a man applies in the training of his children standards not generally accepted in their circle, and fails to bring the children themselves to accept them, the result is likely to be an alienation of the children, both from their father and from his standards."[18]

Does it follow, then, in EC, that the father, in order to honor his commitments, to conform to societal expectations, and to avoid the risk of alienation, should finance his son's university education and let the starving perish? The answer depends in part on the sureness and seriousness of the risk of estrangement, and how weightily it therefore tells against the countervailing benefits. Anecdotal evidence suggests that the risk may be less than it appears – that the son's reaction might even be admiration rather than resentment. Close to our case is one that Anne Colby and William Damon recount in *Some Do Care*.

Suzie Valadez is known in south Texas as the "Queen of the Dump," a title she came by after years spent feeding , clothing, and providing medical care to thousands of poor Mexicans living in the environs of the huge Ciudad Juarez garbage dump. Valadez's children were required to make real sacrifices in the interests of their mother's cause and grew up with little beyond the bare necessities. This their mother felt deeply, and yet, as Colby and Damon explain:

It was her abiding faith that God would provide for her and her family that allowed her to give so much to others, trusting that she and her children would be all right. "When the Lord called me, when he gave me that vision, he told me that if I dedicated my life to serving He would take care of my children. And He has. So I have a beautiful, beautiful family and I thank the Lord for it." Although during their childhood Suzie's children had ambivalent feelings about their mother's overriding dedication to the mission, they were left with no bitterness and as adults have joined their mother in her work. Her son Danny has been most explicit about this, calling his mother's devotion a "great gift" that more than compensated for his materially humble childhood.[19]

This reaction reveals the one-sidedness of the argument from role expectations and potential alienation. It does not mention possible benefits to the children, of the kind that her son cites and that also appear in Schwartz's account of Mrs. Rhi ("the whole family seemed to have inherited the mother's generous heart") or in a *New York Times* review of David Hilfiker's *Not All of Us Are Saints*:

Among the poignant passages are those where the author confronts the contradictions of a white middle-class family living in the inner city of Washington among poor black alcoholics and drug addicts. His own children sometimes reproach him for indulging his commitment to social justice at their expense. His 13-year-old daughter does not understand why he works for less money than he could earn, or "why we live here in the middle of the city with all these poor people." Dr. Hilfiker's answers do not entirely satisfy his children.

But, he says, "living one floor above 34 homeless men teaches our children that every person has worth and value despite external circumstances." More generally, he writes, "our obedience to the demands of justice can bring us the possibility of a far deeper happiness, security and sense of integrity than can any commitment to individual wealth or personal comfort."[20]

It is clear that in Hilfiker's view these important benefits help to tip the scales in favor of his work for the destitute.[21] The son in EC might profit similarly. True, as Rachels remarks,

> Children in such families would be worse off, in an obvious sense, than the children of affluent parents who continued to live according to the dictates of extreme bias or the most common view. However, we might hope that they would not regard themselves as deprived, for they might learn the moral value of giving up their luxuries so that the other children do not starve. They might even come to see their parents as morally admirable people.[22]

Furthermore, the son's likely feelings are not the only ones to consider. The physical distress of the starving, their relentless anxiety, their despair as they watch their children perish, their grief over loved ones lost – these easily counterbalance, in sureness and gravity, the son's possible disappointment or resentment.

All things considered, then, the scales still seem to tip in favor of the neediest: on one side the value of a single person's university education (and all he might do with it), on the other side the value of numerous people's lives (and all they might do with them); on one side the son's likely distress, on the other side the far greater distress of the starving and those who love them. So preference, it seems, should go to the starving. However, familiar objections against "charity" and "alms" press on the other side of the scales and call this verdict in question.

The evils of giving

Targeting both donor and recipient, the objections to philanthropy have been many and varied.

Those who considered altruism as a cloak-masking evil had a "realistic" if not cynical view of human nature. They unmasked altruism by revealing the Machiavellian motives underlying altruistic acts. Their cost accounting demonstrated that in the end the giver benefited at the expense of the recipient. The recipient would learn to depend on charity or would not correct his pernicious ways as a result of receiving charity (Brinton, 1933; Pray, 1933; Stuart, 1933). Or the donor would suffer because the recipient took advantage of his generosity.[23]

If directed solely against aid to the starving, such arguments would back Ewing's stance. However, all the same objections might apply to child support – for instance, to financing a child's university education. The father, too, might have mixed motives for his action; and the son might learn to depend on his father's assistance, or might take advantage of his father's generosity and not apply himself to his studies.

However, the litany of complaints continues:

While the fear-inducing woodcuts of the Last Judgment no longer haunt people's consciousness, the soulful gaze of underfed waifs from the Third World has that power today. Contributors to children's funds and adoption schemes buy satisfaction through their giving. Having relieved their guilt they go their way, giving scant thought to the political and economic structures that permit – perhaps even cause – the miserable conditions under which such children exist.

Such spurious charity drains human energy away from the political task of social and economic change, and helps perpetuate a political economy of which poverty is a necessary component. The meritorious charity of medieval feudalism is replaced by "analgesic" charity. In both cases the poor serve the needs of the rich.[24]

Such charity is also considered demeaning. Whoever wishes to help the needy "cannot adopt the direct method of distributing his money in the shape of alms, which would increase the spending power of poorer recipients, without degrading or pauperising them. He cannot even adopt the indirect method of supplying the needs of the poor by the support of charities or by carefully planned benefactions, without introducing an element of patronage which can never now be desirable."[25]

To place such objections in proper perspective, imagine the man on the road to Jericho waving off the Good Samaritan:

"Don't degrade me with your help, or make me dependent on your assistance! No patronizing! No airs of superiority! Don't use me to salve your bourgeois conscience! Tend to your civic duties!" Such a response would sound no more likely and no more realistic on the lips of the starving.[26] We need not choose exclusively between feeding and empowering, or between meeting immediate needs and working to improve political and economic structures.

One also wonders about the double standard apparently at work in thus stigmatizing aid to strangers while exempting assistance to one's nearest and dearest. If assistance to those in need by those not in need is inherently demeaning to the recipients, it is so for the son in EC as well as for the starving. If assistance automatically creates dependence, it does so for the son as well as for the starving. Indeed, the implications carry farther: we all are demeaned, we all are made dependent; for, as Pope remarks, "we are all, in different ways and at different times, objects of the care of one another"[27] – and of God.

Justice versus charity

Goodin notes an argument which directly targets our issue and our case:

> One explanation of why, traditionally, it is thought that special duties should take priority over general duties of aid builds on the distinction between duties arising out of considerations of *justice* and those arising out of *charity* or *benevolence*. Discharging our special responsibilities, especially insofar as those responsibilities are seen to have been voluntarily self-assumed, is ordinarily regarded as a matter of justice. Duties falling under that heading are duties to specific other individuals, who may legitimately enter claims against us for the particular performances that are their due.[28]

Thus the father, it might be argued, having assumed responsibilities toward his son, owes him an education, as a matter of justice, whereas he has assumed no responsibilities toward the starving and therefore owes them nothing. Accordingly, if, in Sidgwick's phrase, "Benevolence begins where Justice ends,"[29]

Ewing is right: the father should finance his son's university education rather than feed the starving.

Goodin rightly resists such reasoning: "It is all well and good in theory to say that charity should pick up where justice leaves off. The crucial question then, however, becomes exactly where justice *does* leave off; and my objection is precisely that the peculiar notion of 'justice' at work here has been expanded so far that the notion of 'charity,' so called, hardly ever gets a chance to operate."[30] Coming upon a person in desperate need by the roadside, we may still be allowed to offer assistance and thereby break a promise to meet a friend for lunch. Benevolence may prevail over justice this once, but not often.

The same example suggests a stronger, complementary line of response;[31] for it shows that even with an expanded notion of justice, the general thesis of lexical priority is false: justice does not always win over benevolence. So to decide Ewing's case, we must determine when and why justice does or should prevail; and that sends us in search of other considerations, more decisive than the mere labels "justice" and "benevolence."

Fair shares

Suppose that ten million are starving, that fifty dollars per person would save them all, and that fifty million people are as well placed as the EC father to assist them. Then, if each does his or her fair share and chips in ten dollars, there is no problem: the starving can be fed and the son can get his university education. Suppose, though, that there is no prospect that the fifty million people will all contribute their share, that the probable number is more like five thousand, and that the father is aware of these odds. If he really wants to save the starving, shouldn't he give much more? Shouldn't he give ten thousand dollars rather than ten?

According to Jonathan Cohen, he is under no such obligation:

It does not follow that each affluent individual has the duty to do whatever is both possible and necessary, in the actual situation, to relieve the famine. His or her duty is only to play a fair part in the performance of what is collectively obligatory. Burdens, like benefits, ought to be fairly distributed, and *ceteris paribus* no-one is morally required to take on more than his fair share of a burden because someone else defects. . . .[32]

From a utilitarian viewpoint, this appeal to fairness does not work, or legitimize the father's favoring his son over the starving (ten thousand dollars for him, ten for them). As Dan Brock points out:

The failure of others to act is simply one of the background circumstances in which he acts, and in which the utility of different alternatives is to be calculated; it is like the famine itself, in making the need he could alleviate greater than it would otherwise be. Thus, the failure of others to help will often increase what one ought on utilitarian grounds to do in aiding situations; their failure will not limit what a particular individual must as a result provide.[33]

In reply, Cohen concedes that "all who can afford it have a moral duty to take a fair share, and even rather more than a fair share, in the urgent task of working to alleviate, and eventually prevent, the grave shortages of foodstuffs that continue to occur in many parts of the world." However, "this duty falls a long way short of requiring those of us who do contribute to make up in full for the deficiencies of those who do not. If that requirement became an acknowledged principle, it could have disastrous results."[34] "For," he explains, "the presence of such a principle in the community's acknowledged moral code could encourage many to believe that the world would be no worse off if they themselves contributed nothing at all."[35]

This argument may be understood in either of two ways. First, it may rest on a causal surmise: acting on the remedial principle might bring general acceptance of the principle, with the attendant danger of free-loading; so we should not act on the principle. This version would work only on the question-begging supposition that general acceptance of the principle would not be a great benefit, more than compensating for the risk cited. Second, the argument may make no causal assumptions but may presuppose some form of ideal-rule-utilitarianism. But what form? Not: "An act is right if and only if it conforms to a set of rules general *conformity* to which would maximize utility" (for Cohen envisages and regrets likely lapses). Nor: "An act is right if and only if it conforms to a set of rules general *acceptance* of which would maximize utility, where acceptance of a rule is thought of as falling somewhat short of conformity to it"[36] (for Cohen complains of that short-fall). So one suspects a possible conflation of these alternative forms. There seems no way to make the argument succeed.

This is not surprising, for imagine what would happen to any altruistic norm – for example to the Golden Rule – if similar reasoning were applied to it. Any rule that enjoined assistance to the needy and that was generally accepted, could invite the same reaction: "Others will provide, so I need not bother." The fact that the Golden Rule is in fact widely accepted reveals a further flaw in the argument: those who made the dreaded inference from general acceptance ("the community's acknowl- edged moral code") to general practice would have to be unusually ignorant of human nature.

If, therefore, appeal is thus made to consequences, the fair- share argument looks weak. However, the norm of Value- Maximization accords weight to more than consequences – for instance to fairness as a value in itself. So perhaps a non- utilitarian approach would do better: It is simply unfair for the father to have to give so much – so unfair that he is under no such obligation. To this complaint a simple response seems adequate: It would be far more unfair that the starving should die, through no fault of their own. So they should be favored.

Incomparable values

The arguments of preceding chapters have assumed, with Ewing, that "the money spent by a man in order to provide his son with a university education could save the lives of many people who were perishing of hunger in a famine" and that saving the lives of these people would be more beneficial than providing the son with a university education. John Whelan challenges both of these assumptions: "First, I will show that it is impossible, by contributing to any actual charity, to prevent people from starving in the way that those who argue as I described above typically suppose; second, I will show that the actual benefit paid for by giving money to a charity cannot unfavorably be compared with the benefit paid for by any frivolous purchases"[37] – or by financing a son's university education.

Pleas for the starving look strong, Whelan suggests, because we dimly imagine something like this: "My $25 is sent to some charity and starving people get to eat $25 worth of food; my money is not sent and these people continue to starve: I imagine that my money can make this significant difference in the life of these starving people, and I wonder how, in the face of their need, I can use it to bring about small pleasures."[38] Such thoughts, Whelan argues, are a delusion; my money cannot make that imagined difference.

No charitable organization will alter the amount of money budgeted for food because my $25 does or does not arrive. Furthermore, it is senseless to think that my money could be, so to speak, "tracked" and we could thereby determine what effect its arriving on some particular day has or lacks. Finally, charities need to pay for all sorts of things – salaries, vacations, paper, advertising, equipment, and so forth – so my $25 cannot be said to make the difference between no food or $25 worth of food for people who are starving. If I do not send my money to some charity, then that charity will have that much less money to pay for all of the things that it needs to buy; its ability to help people who are starving will be slightly less because I will have failed to pay for a fractional share of all the kinds of things the charity buys.[39]

These considerations need not prove troubling, provided the organization is reasonably efficient; but they lead to Whelan's second, more serious objection – the claim of incomparability. A human life and a university education might be compared (Whelan urges no general thesis of value-incommensurability). But replace the human life with "a fractional share of all the kinds of things the charity buys," and comparison, he claims, is no longer possible. "We have absolutely no idea what the answer is, and no idea how to find out."[40]

Is this because of the contribution's fractionality or because of the variety of things the organization does? Consider each alternative. First, suppose the organization did nothing but feed starving people, and suppose it saved one hundred thousand of them per year with an income of ten million dollars. In that case, despite overhead costs a contribution of one hundred thousandth of that income (that is, of a hundred dollars) would equivalently save the life of one person, and a comparison could be made between that benefit and a competing benefit for oneself or one's kin. Second, suppose instead that the organization diversified its efforts in ways it judged of roughly equal effectiveness – not just feeding the starving, but saving children from dying of diarrhea; not just saving those in distress but remedying the causes of distress. In that case, a similar comparison could be made, but now disjunctively. The hundred dollars would either feed one starving person *or* prevent one person from starving; it would either go half-way toward feeding two people *or* half-way toward preventing two people from starving; it would either make a one-thousandth contribution toward feeding a thousand *or* a one-thousandth contribution toward preventing a thousand from starving; and so forth. Such indefiniteness in what the money did would make no difference, provided these were the sorts of things it did. The photographs of starving children with bowls of food in their hands would aptly symbolize the needs met and the good achieved.

Dubious effectiveness

Problems of tracking need not prove troubling, I have suggested, provided that the aid organization is reasonably efficient. In most instances, this may appear a realistic assumption, given the expertise of the foremost aid providers.[41] Yet Tony Jackson, in a broad study drawing on the published findings of food-aid institutions themselves and on independent evaluations carried out on behalf of the governments for whom the agencies act as custodians, concluded specifically with regard to famine relief: "Food aid is often sent and distributed in a haphazard and ill-planned way. Many calls for help are answered late or inappropriately; often there is no need to hand out the food free of charge and, sometimes, food may not be what is needed at all."[42] To the extent that these and similar charges hold true today, fifteen years later, they lend some support to Ewing's verdict.[43] Objectively, the benefits to the starving may not be as great or as certain as he assumed. Subjectively, even if they are that great, potential donors may not know that they are, and may therefore be justified in according less weight to aiding distant strangers rather than their own next-of-kin. To the extent that genuine uncertainties are present, we must correspondingly discount our acts' anticipated benefits.[44]

Yet how certain, for their part, are the benefits Ewing envisages for the son? How well does that competing value pass the same test? A reply might resemble Jackson's: Educational goals and decisions often reflect parental wishes more than children's desires or abilities; children easily err in their own choices of career, institution, or program of studies; children who do not finance their own university education often squander their parents' resources, attending more to their social lives than their studies; frequently, a delay of a year or two would be beneficial; a later change of direction may negate much of the value of the education so far received; and so forth. From such a catalog of pitfalls parents should not conclude that financing a child's education is a waste of money; but neither should they conclude from Jackson's similar litany of errors that assisting the starving is a misuse of funds. Thus, at this stage of the discussion, personal, parental fallibility may balance out collective, organizational fallibility.

More troubling than potential inefficiency in assisting the starving is the possibility that the starving should not be assisted. Jackson challenges "the commonly-held belief that food aid is a matter of life and death and that the poor are dependent on it."[45] Disagreeing, Garrett Hardin believes that the poor do depend on food aid but should, for the most part, be allowed to die, so as to avert still greater misery later on. Like Hardin, Peter Singer accepts the dependence on aid but rejects Hardin's pessimistic conclusion. Thus,

Hardin, Singer, and Jackson point to *radically* different action and policies. If Hardin is right, Singer advocated not merely a suboptimal but a gravely wrong line of action, and conversely. Similarly if Jackson is right, both Hardin and Singer advocate action and policies that not merely could be improved but are actually wrong because likely to produce much more suffering and less benefit than alternative policies.[46]

If the father must decide all such disputes before adjudicating Ewing's case, he may be excused if he settles for a relatively sure thing and funds his boy's studies. No comparable debates have arisen concerning the value of a university education.

However, Ewing's dilemma centers specifically on famine relief, and on that topic there has been less dispute. Though Jackson contends that, in general, the poor require money rather than food, he agrees with Singer and others on the need to give a much higher priority to food aid for relief after natural and man-made disasters.[47] The aid should just be made more effective. True, the wisdom even of famine relief has been challenged: "In situations where reproduction has outstripped productivity, to give food would only increase the population without raising the rate of production (GNP), thus increasing the number of starving people and so producing a net loss of life and a net increase of human misery."[48] Yet to this draconian argument others rightly reply that starvation is by no means the only effective form of population control,[49] and that "This thought of the disastrous further future is a fallacious rationalization, at odds with the great bulk of available evidence."[50] On one hand, as Amartya Sen has pointed out, "not only over the two centuries since Malthus's time, but also during recent decades, the rise in food output has been significantly and consistently outpacing the expansion of world population"[51] (and the discrepancy would have been still greater had not oversupply depressed world food markets[52]). On the other hand, "conditions of economic security and affluence, wider availability of contraceptive methods, expansion of education (particularly female education) and lower mortality rates have had – and are currently having – quite substantial effects in reducing birth rates in different parts of the world."[53] Most directly pertinent for our purposes, a review of major famines during the last fifty or sixty years reveals some which, at the time, may have seemed possible candidates for Hardin's hard-nosed treatment; fewer which, in retrospect, still seem plausible candidates; and none of which we can now say with any assurance: "It was better in the long run, or would have been better, to let millions die."[54] Besides, even were pessimism more warranted, the patristic challenge persists: Would Hardin consider it acceptable to *kill* millions of people in order to forestall future starvation? And isn't death by starvation a harsher fate than death by bullet or injection?

There remains, however, one final argument which may have cast its shadow over this whole discussion from the start and which, more than any other, lends credence to a judgment favoring the son: the contrary verdict is just too difficult, too demanding. Any assessment which asks so much cannot be right.

Excessive burden

Owen Flanagan states a "Principle of Minimal Psychological Realism" that moral prescriptions must satisfy: "Make sure when constructing a moral theory or projecting a moral ideal that the character, decision processing, and behavior prescribed are possible, or are perceived to be possible, for creatures like us."[55] This sounds reasonable. It also poses a challenge to Christian ethics, for the love commandment is often interpreted in a way that makes it impossible or at least exceedingly difficult to fulfill.[56] The challenge extends, specifically, to EC. According to St. Alphonsus and others whom he cites, "not even in extreme necessity of the poor is a rich person required to furnish a large sum of money, since these means are extremely difficult and almost morally impossible."[57] In EC the sum required for the son's university education would in fact be large, and such a sacrifice on behalf of the starving might indeed be "almost morally impossible" for a typical father. If so, might he legitimately help his son rather than the starving, as Alphonsus suggests?

Examples from the past signal caution. As a possible object lesson, consider the renowned Francisco de Vitoria, a man of intellectual integrity and moral conviction, who was also extremely well informed about events and conditions in the Indies and who took seriously the question whether pagan nations could be forcefully compelled to accept the faith. As Terrance Walsh recounts, "Vitoria's treatment proceeded from genuine pastoral concern, to reflection on Scripture, and finally to the application of theological and legal principle to the concrete case. But something went wrong along the way. For after having argued that there were no theological grounds to justify either Spanish occupation or the imposition of faith, Vitoria concluded that the abandonment of Spanish commerce and interests 'would be intolerable.' "[58] Having reached a similar point in our discussion, should we now play this final card? With persuasive grounds favoring the starving, should we reverse the verdict by citing excessive burden?

Had the natives been few, the Spaniards might have found it tolerable to let them go free. Were the starving only one or two, the father might manage to spare them a hundred dollars and still finance his son's education. Thus, as Massillon remarks, the very multitude of the poor may serve as pretext for not aiding them. "Yes, my brethren, that which ought to excite and to animate charity, extinguishes it; the multitude of the unfortunate hardens you to their wants; the more the duty increases, the more do you think yourselves dispensed from its practice, and you become cruel by having too many occasions of being charitable."[59] If duty relates inversely to difficulty, then the more needy people there are and the worse off they are, the less we are obliged to help them. Finally, if thousands or millions are starving, as in EC, we have no obligation at all, since the burden is then far too great to bear. We can spare a few dollars for a beggar, but who can feed such a multitude? Clearly, however, this pretext will not do. So we are led to ask: Just how weightily does the difficulty of aiding the starving tell against a duty to assist them, and why?

In their better moments, Christian ethicians have rejected the notion, now advanced by some philosophers,[60] that whatever requires heroism must be supererogatory.[61] Countless martyrs, Christian and non-Christian, have done what they were morally required to do – heroically. Besides, as chapter 2 explained, our concern is not solely with the obligatory but more generally with the better. So let us pass on.[62] The argument from difficulty takes a more serious form than the conflation of heroism with supererogation.

Singer summarizes it thus: "Human nature being what it is, we cannot achieve so high a standard, and since it is absurd to say that we ought to do what we cannot do, we must reject the claim that we ought to give so much."[63] The like might be said of the claim that it would be better, more admirable, to give so much. Regardless of what some objective ideal may require, what we cannot do we cannot do. As for the ideal, if it is unattainable by creatures like us, it violates Flanagan's principle of psychological realism. In Nagel's words: "If real people find it psychologically very difficult or even impossible to live as the theory requires, or to adopt the relevant institutions, that should carry some weight against the ideal."[64]

How much weight it should carry depends on the nature and degree of the difficulty. As Flanagan notes, a course of action may be impossible for "creatures like us" in the strong sense that "it requires that we not possess certain characteristics that typically come with our kind of biology and cannot be modified, suppressed, or otherwise inactivated,"[65] or in the weaker sense that it is impossible for us, individually, given our character and/or circumstances. But our characters might change, and so might our circumstances. An ideal that is currently beyond us and our society need not remain so forever.[66] So Flanagan's summation sounds right:

An adequate understanding of human psychology leads to the conclusion that for every token person, there will be things he cannot do, and ways he cannot be, once he is formed in a certain manner. It may follow from this that we should make significant adjustments to our schemes of assessing individual responsibility. But it by no means follows that we need to revise our conception of what is right or good. Nor does it suggest that our ethical conceptions cannot set their ideals at heights which particular persons cannot reach.[67]

Even if people fall short of an ideal, they may come closer by trying to reach it than they would if they did not hold it as an ideal or strive to achieve it.[68] And, as Dorothy Day observed, time may work a change: "What we avert our eyes from today can be borne tomorrow when we have learned a little more about love."[69]

In a case like EC, our natures do not preclude opting for the starving. Yet such an option is rendered difficult in all four ways that Bibb Latané and John Darley cite to explain bystander inactivity: (1) "Others serve as an audience to one's actions, inhibiting him from doing foolish things" (like denying his son a university education for the sake of far-off strangers). (2) "Others serve as guides to behavior, and if they are inactive, they will lead the observer to be inactive also" (e.g., vis-à-vis the starving). (3) "The interactive effect of these two processes will be much greater than either alone; if each bystander sees other bystanders momentarily frozen by audience inhibition, each may be misled into thinking the situation must not be serious" (he can't really be obliged, or be obliged as seriously, as the famine situation suggests). (4) "The presence of other people dilutes the responsibility felt by any single bystander, making him feel that it is less necessary for himself to act" (he is not required "in justice" to do so).[70]

In a case like EC, where the starving are distant, further factors come into play:

First, the strength of the degree of compassion which one is liable to feel at another's plight is, in part, a function of how vividly one can bring that other's condition before one's consciousness; and, secondly, the further away in physical distance a person in need is from one, the less vividly, other things being equal, is one able to bring that other's condition before one's consciousness.[71]

"The sufferings of China," for example, "are known to us only abstractly and in outline, and only in outline can our sympathies be accorded. But a case which comes under our immediate inspection, disclosing all its significant details, is a different matter."[72] Moreover, in EC the starving are not only distant but also foreign, different, alien. And as Gordon Allport documents in *The Nature of Prejudice*, reflex preference for the familiar grips us all. We resemble the seven-year-olds he describes. Asked, "Which are better, the children in this town or in Smithfield (a neighboring town)?" almost all replied, "The children in this town." When asked why, they typically replied, "I don't know the kids in Smithfield." What is alien, Allport notes, is regarded as somehow inferior, less good.[73]

For the Eskimos in chapter 1, none of the factors I have cited was operative; for the father in EC, all are. If, in addition to these and other influences, one assumes strong parental affection – not just for "one's own child" but specifically for Tim or Tom – the father may have no choice. For him there may be no other live option than the one Ewing urges. External and internal forces may hold him fast.

These reflections suggest a final verdict on EC. Given the valid claims of the needy, on the one hand, and the great difficulty of meeting these claims on the other, the gospel saying applies: "Let anyone accept this who can" (Mt. 19:12).[74] Let anyone who can, feed the starving even at the expense of a child's university education. Since, however, not everyone can, and nobody knows who really can, let no one cast aspersions on a parent who favors a child. As for the parent – for instance the father in EC – if he favors his son, let him neither condemn himself (perhaps he can't do otherwise than prefer his own child) nor feel complacent (perhaps he could help the starving instead). If he favors the starving, he will certainly not feel complacent (not in our society), but neither should he condemn himself: strong considerations back his decision.

A solution can therefore be given for what Thomas Mautner terms "a genuine dilemma": "One kind of theory will inevitably make us always feel morally at fault, no matter how hard we try. But if we reject that kind of theory, there will be scope for moral complacency, and again we will be at fault."[75] What has not been furnished, though, is any verdict for a real-life father or any decision procedure by which he might form his conscience. An ideal has been suggested, no more, in reply to chapter 2's focal question. It would be good for him to save the starving, if he can. It would be good for him to become the kind of person who can save them, if he can.[76] But whether he can is left for him to determine, as best he can. And that may be difficult.

To illustrate the difficulty, consider the case of Enrique ("Kiki") Camarena, the Drug Enforcement Administration agent murdered in Mexico. When his captors asked him the names of DEA informers and fellow agents, plus other information crucial for the anti-drug effort, he could have told himself: "Keeping silent will be extremely difficult; therefore I'm not obliged." So reflecting, he might have spoken straight away, and spared himself much agony. But no: though he knew he was already a dead man, he also knew that, if he could, he should withhold the information. As it turned out, he couldn't. But how could he know that in advance, before they mangled his body?

Though less dramatic, the father's case may be comparable. The appeal may be strong on both sides, as it was for Camarena, and he may therefore have great difficulty knowing what he should do. If he thinks of his son, he may conclude: "Too much: I can't deny my own flesh and blood." If he thinks of the starving, he may conclude: "I must do what I can." Objectively, however, in his case as in Camarena's, the reasons tilt toward the many rather than the one and toward life itself rather than the great but lesser good that competes with it. Granted, in both instances there is some uncertainty about outcomes (as Camarena could not be sure that the agents and informers would die, or how many, if he revealed their names, so the father may not be sure that starving people will die, or how many, if he withholds his aid from even the most discerning, efficient agency). Yet the uncertainty does not suffice to alter the verdict.

Objections

"Let anyone accept this who can," I have suggested – that is, let anyone who can, feed the starving even at the expense of a child's university education. Yet would I speak the same way about actively causing people to die? Would I say, "Let anyone who can, refrain from killing other people?" If not, what becomes of the parallel between killing and letting die, on which I have largely rested my case?

In answer, consider Camarena. Naming his fellow agents' names – that action – would seriously endanger their lives. So in ordinary circumstances, his obligation would be clear. However, his circumstances are not ordinary; hence his obligation is not clear. Keeping silent would be enormously difficult, perhaps impossible, and no one is obliged to do the impossible. Accordingly, a modified verdict applies, as for EC: Be silent – if you can. Keep from actively endangering these people's lives, if you can. The likely loss of life poses an obligation, one which the difficulty of keeping silent does not remove. What precludes a clear statement of obligation is the uncertainty whether it really is possible for Camarena to keep silent. The like may hold for the father in EC.

In both these cases, a more fully Christian perspective might seem to bring greater clarity, and with it a more certain obligation. "My grace is sufficient for you," Paul was assured, "for power is made perfect in weakness" (2 Cor. 12:9). "I can do all things," he confidently asserted, "through him who strengthens me" (Phil. 4:13). Christian magnanimity "has at its disposal encouragements, examples, and forces of superhuman elevation."[77] Rather, then, than exhort Camarena and the EC father to do the best they can, perhaps we should admonish them: "Why are you fearful, you of little faith?" Utter no word to your torturers! Feed the starving! "If you, who are evil, know how to give good gifts to your children, how much more will the heavenly Father give the Holy Spirit to those who ask him!" (Lk. 11:13).

Such clarity, alas, is not to be had. Concerning Paul's declaration in Phil. 4:13, Gordon Fee observes:

"Everything" in this case, of course, refers first of all to his living in "want or plenty". . . . Missing this grammatical and contextual point has allowed some to quote this sentence out of context as a kind of eternal "gnomic" promise of Christ's help for any and everything, sometimes in a triumphalistic way that stands in total contradiction to its intent. On the other hand, to limit it merely to "want" or "plenty" . . . is too constricting, since for Paul it does in fact express the reality of his entire life.[78]

This balanced assessment may do justice to the text, but it leaves us as uncertain as before. If faith does not invest us with surrogate omnipotence, where does the happy mean lie between presumption and pusillanimity?

More enlightening in this regard than the abstract definitions and distinctions of moralists is the experience of many, from Moses to John Woolman, anguished by the difficulty of what they felt called to do. Suzie Valadez, who sacrificed her children's interests for those in greater need, recounts:

A lot of times I cried. A lot of times I thought I was in the wrong field. And I used to get away from the house and away from my kids and I used to ask the Lord "Am I in the right place? Is this where you send me?" Because if I didn't have that vision I would have gone back because of what I was going through. But now my faith is stronger. See, at that time when I started it was weak. I was just going by that vision.[79]

Her vision, the preceding discussion suggests, was not a delusion – despite the cost to herself and to her children. And the experience of the father in EC might prove similar. Good angels, notes Aquinas, may frighten people by their coming, but the terror ends and consolation succeeds it.[80]

To recapitulate: no, a mere counsel to favor the starving does not undermine the parallel between killing and letting die, on which the counsel rests; no, the promise of divine assistance does not negate the reason for stopping short of stating a clear obligation. So the previous verdict stands: to the extent that he can, the father should give preference to the starving. This may appear a minimal result for such an extended inquiry, and by itself, it is. The time has come to take a broader view. If, for the reasons cited, it would be better for the father to assist the starving rather than his son, or for parents generally to favor the destitute over their less needy children, what follows for the cloud of varied cases that surround this single paradigm?

CHAPTER 7

Comparable conflicts

Sixty pages on a single case! Did casuistry in its heyday ever go to such an extreme? Perhaps not, but even at its most particular, traditional casuistry aimed at more than the solution of individual moral dilemmas: its inquiries were to raise general issues and its solutions were to exemplify general principles. And so it is here. Although a verdict on EC furnishes no implicit general rule and no automatic decisions for kindred cases, the considerations that have proved relevant in this instance may prove relevant in countless others.

These considerations exhibit little overlap with the ones Grisez listed in chapter 2. In order to resolve quandaries such as EC's, recall, he suggested, "how Jesus identifies with those in need, and the consequences for those who do not succor him in the poor." Yet our examination of Matthew 25:31–46, and of how and with whom Jesus identifies himself, has established nothing more than special concern for the needy, and this we have assumed from the start. "Bear in mind the universal destination of goods," Grisez further advised, then "apply the Golden Rule"; but the universal destination of goods establishes no preference and the Golden Rule concerns self and others, not nearest versus neediest. We therefore need a new list of checkpoints to replace Grisez's.

The considerations which figure most prominently in the preceding chapters' discussion of EC would figure prominently in any of countless comparable cases pitting the near against the needy, with endless variations of nearness and necessity. These considerations include, in the order of their appearance:

- the parity, other things equal, of acts and omissions, which holds not only for failure to feed the starving but also for the failures Matthew 25 cites, plus others;
- the irrelevance of class distinctions, as such;
- the equal worth of persons, so that numbers matter;
- the respective efficacy of the contemplated assistance, to the near and to the needy;
- the relevance – limited and difficult to estimate, but real – of personal possibilities vis-à-vis the Christian ideal.

Of these five points, the first three favor the starving while the last two tend to favor the son.

This new list looks less distinctively Christian than Grisez's, so may give the impression that Christian ethics can make little or no distinctive contribution to the issue of nearest versus neediest, either in terms of final verdicts or in terms of underlying reasons for the verdicts. However, this impression is mistaken. The contribution which Christian ethics makes is strong, both negatively and positively – that is, both in what it excludes and in what it includes and powerfully supports.

Negatively, the Christian gospel vetoes two major considerations often cited on the side of the nearest. First, with the "near" defined in relation to the self, and the self often accorded priority relative to others, weight shifts toward the nearest. We should have a greater love for those more closely united with us, and a much greater love for those most closely united with us – for instance for a son who desires a university education. The New Testament, however, to which many Christian ethicians have stayed true, shifts preference from the self to others. At the same time, and sometimes in the same passages, it speaks against pride of place as a legitimate motive blocking assistance to the needy. In the Matthean words of Jesus: "Whoever wishes to be great among you must be your servant, and whoever wishes to be first among you must be your slave; just as the Son of Man came not to be served but to serve, and to give his life a ransom for many" (Mt. 20: 26–28). In the words of St. Paul: "Let the same mind be in you that was in Christ Jesus, who, though he was in the form of God, did not regard equality with God as something to be exploited, but emptied himself, taking the form of a slave" (Phil. 2:5–7; cf. Ja. 2:1–13).

With similar, distinctive force the New Testament backs the two positive points in the list above – the first and the third – that tell most strongly in favor of the starving. With regard to the third, equal worth, "there is no longer Jew or Greek, there is no longer slave or free, there is no longer male and female" (Gal. 3:28).[1] Those who are far off are brought near (Acts 2:39; Eph. 2:13). The lowly and despised are beloved of God (1 Cor. 1:26–28). The hairs on the head of each and every person are all numbered (Mt. 10:30; Lk. 12:7). Accordingly, the plight of the starving is of utmost concern, whoever and wherever they may be. Contemporary philosophers have debated more fully, pro and con, the parity of killing and letting die, but it is not by chance that Christians first urged such parity, early on. It was their way of according full, universal weight to the claims of the neediest. "Suppose," James had written, "that a brother or a sister is in rags with not enough food for the day, and one of you says, 'Good luck to you, keep yourselves warm, and have plenty to eat,' but does nothing to supply their bodily needs, what is the good of that?" (Ja. 2:15–16). Suppose, instead, that a brother or sister for whom Christ died not only lacks food for the day but is starving to death, and is treated similarly: how can the followers of Christ view such a refusal of help as a "mere omission"?

These Christian considerations – the preciousness of every life, fundamental equality, rank by loving service, other-preference – have wide application. So do the considerations listed from the preceding discussion. So do others more briefly touched on. Collectively, all these might furnish adequate points of reference for many problematic cases, and suffice for many a verdict. Vary the kinship and vary the need, and a judgment might emerge, as it has for EC. However, many other cases require that horizons be widened beyond the bounds of kinship and beyond the bounds of personal morality.

Ewing's case, I suggested at the start, pits the nearest of the near (one's own children) against the neediest of the needy (starving strangers). If, then, preference should ideally go to the starving over a son's university education, as the preceding chapters suggest, preference should go to the starving over lesser yet costly needs of one's children (a car, a trip abroad) and over equal or lesser needs of those less closely related than one's children (a nephew, a friend, a compatriot). With top ranking among the near accorded to one's children and top ranking among the needy accorded to the starving, such inferences might spread far. However, the moment has come to examine the assumption that one's children, or one's next of kin, merit top rating, as "nearest of the near."

In the traditional "order of charity," the closest competitors with offspring for primacy have been parents and spouses. "It is not easy," some have acknowledged, "to determine who among spouse, children and parents has the prior claim to help in instances of equal necessity."[2] More broadly, though, "in external beneficence the following order should be observed: God, ourselves, kin according to their degree, others connected with us according to the kind of connection, strangers, and enemies."[3] Carnal conjunction outranks spiritual or civil, and spiritual outranks civil.[4] So most have agreed – in the Thomistic tradition.

Other writings attest other priorities. Among the people specially related to oneself, next of kin have had three chief rivals for primacy: coreligionists, friends, and compatriots.[5] If any of these succeed in their challenge, the path of inference is cut for that group: no conclusions can be drawn from EC in the manner just suggested. That is, from the verdict on EC it does not follow that, at a similar cost to a coreligionist, friend, or compatriot as to the son, one should favor the starving. True, the same reasons that support the verdict in EC might support a similar verdict in other instances; but I shall leave that question till the end, after a preliminary review. What are the credentials of each of these rivals? What advantages might they enjoy over children or other close kin in confrontations between nearest and neediest?

FELLOW CHRISTIANS

Matthew 5's proclamation of universal neighbor-love contrasts with John 13's proclamation of Christian brother-love.[6] Galatians 6:10 combines both emphases: "Let us work for the good of all, and especially for those of the family of faith." From early on, Christian tradition has maintained the same balance – and the same tension – in practice and in teaching.[7] Often, the Matthean, universalistic strain has sounded strongly, as in St. Paulinus of Aquileia:

Let us work for the good of all: of all, I say – not partially, not of one or two or three, but of all. For Christ did not die for the holy alone, but for the sinful, impious, and reprobate he ascended the cross, and by his passion recalled us all to life. Not to the holy alone did God give the sun and the moon and the rain, and everything sprouting from the earth, and all the fruits of the land, but he gave them in common to all – he who "makes his sun to rise on the good and the bad, and his rain to fall on the just and unjust" (Matt. 5:96). Thus he gave these things to all people in common, so that our goods, and our alms, and our charity, and our patience, and our humility in common might be distributed to all.[8]

So they were. Even the Emperor Julian bore witness that the heathen were included among those who received alms from the Church.[9] Yet Paul's ecclesial preference was not forgotten, in teaching or in practice. "Lucian (described by Inge as 'the Voltaire of antiquity') said scornfully of Christians 'their original lawgiver had taught them that they were all brethren one of another . . . They become incredibly alert when anything happens which affects their common interests; on such occasions, no expense is grudged.' "[10]

As we have seen, early Christians also expressed a preference for kith and kin. Yet that did not prevent their siding strongly with the destitute, nor would Galatians 6:10. To reverse the EC verdict favoring the starving, something stronger than Paul's simple preference for Christian brethren would be needed.

This extra impetus might derive from the conception of the church as a "higher comradeship" than any natural society, including the family.[11] Already, Stephen Barton notes, such a "suprafamilial" thrust characterizes Matthew's gospel, as well as Mark's: "The kingdom of heaven, the fatherhood of God and belonging to the 'spiritual' family over which Jesus is the 'lord' and 'householder' are what is of supreme importance: and every earthly and mundane tie is subordinate to that new, eschatological reality."[12] In like vein Ignatius of Antioch writes: "I sing the praises of the churches and pray that they be united with the flesh and spirit of Jesus Christ, who is our eternal life; a union in faith and love, to which nothing must be preferred."[13] Of this supreme union, a later writer declared: "Such is the chain that unites and binds us – a chain of gold a thousand times stronger than those of flesh and blood, interest or friendship."[14] Carnal kinship cannot compete with spiritual as the prime social link.

Luis de Granada spells out fully the contrast with mere ties of flesh and blood:

Consider . . . what a love relations have for one another, upon no other account but the communication of a little flesh and blood; and blush that grace should not have as much power over you as nature, or the spiritual alliance as the carnal. If you should say, that this is a union and participation from the same root and the same blood, which is common to both parties, consider how much more noble those alliances are, which the apostle has put between the faithful; since they have all one father and one mother, one Lord, one baptism, one faith, one hope, one nourishment, and one spirit that enlivens them; they have all one Father, which is God; one mother, which is the church; one Lord, which is Jesus Christ; one faith, which is a supernatural light, of which we all partake, and which distinguishes us from the rest of mankind; one hope, which is the same inheritance of glory, in which we shall all have but one heart and but one soul; one baptism, by which we have been all adopted for the children of one and the same father, and consequently made brothers to one another; one nourishment, which is the most adorable sacrament of the body of Christ, by which we are all united to and made one and the same thing with him; just as of several grains of corn is made a loaf, and the same wine of a great many bunches of grapes. And besides all this, we partake of the same spirit, which is the Holy Ghost, who resides in all the souls of the faithful, either by faith alone, or by grace and faith joined together, enlivening them and supporting them in this life . . . If, then, the bare union of flesh and blood be enough to make relations love one another so entirely, how much more force ought so many and such straight unions and alliances have over us![15]

It would seem, then, that the Thomistic order of charity should be revised. Our fellow Christians, not our kin, should lead the list. And so they sometimes do: "Seeing, then, we cannot benefit all the world by our Alms . . . it is fit that the little portion, which we are masters of, be placed upon those, whose circumstances are best suited to our own. Objects so particularly fit, are those in our Church, our family, our neighborhood."[16] "If it be necessary to observe an order in our charity, that is, when we cannot supply and suffice for all our opportunities of mercy, then 'let not the Brethren of our Lord go away ashamed'; and in other things observe the order and propriety of your own relations, and where there is otherwise no difference, the degree of the necessity is first to be considered."[17]

If, then, Christian fellowship takes precedence over kinship, and the son in EC is a fellow Christian, the verdict based on kinship may need to be reconsidered. Perhaps preference should go to the son rather than the starving. However, one will seek far in Christian literature for any such suggestion based on the claims of Christian fellowship.

Various reasons may explain this silence. From the start, the universalistic understanding of charity has predominated over the particularistic. (Consider, for example, the usual universalistic understanding of Matthew 25:31–46, despite the contrary evidence cited by contemporary exegetes.[18]) From the start, Christian fellowship has turned outward as well as inward ("Go, therefore, teach all nations"). From the start, it has been recognized that similarities across sectarian boundaries may count for more than similarities within them ("Whoever does the will of my Father in heaven is my brother and sister and mother"). "In God's ineffable foreknowledge," Augustine remarked, "many who appear to be outside are within and many who appear to be within are outside."[19]

Recent Christian thought goes farther, not only recognizing but emphasizing cross-denominational unity, and not only emphasizing such underlying unity but celebrating diversity.

Since Catholicism has been by far the most historically rooted and culturally defined of Europe's faiths, the new approach seems most remarkable when it comes from the Vatican Council in an all but unanimous affirmation of the bishops of the Church that they must seek and love the purity of Buddhist asceticism, the mystical sense of the Hindus, the dedicated monotheism of the Moslems, the vision of God the Father and Creator shared by Jews and Christians in the stupendous images of the Old Testament; more, that they must find and respect the compassion for man and the devotion to his service among many who would call themselves non-believers, humanists, Marxists, even atheists in the strictest sense.[20]

This new perspective negates nothing in Granada's paean to Christian fellowship but it does correct its one-sidedness, thereby blunting the case for strong Christian-preference.[21] Among all the cited traits, shared and not shared, what might make such a decisive difference as to warrant a verdict similar to Ewing's? Given the variations among Christians, what might tilt the scales in favor of a single far less needy fellow Christian over numerous starving non-Christians?

"Baptism," it has been said, "with its act of faith, is the primary element of the visible unity which still remains between Christians and is the basis for their search for a more visible unity."[22] Is it also a basis for preferential treatment, or for strongly preferential treatment? Is the baptism of Joseph Stalin, with his parents' faith, reason for preferring a non-starving Stalin to starving unbaptized infants? Can this single factor – "one baptism" – of all those Granada cites, carry such weight?

At this juncture, an important parallel surfaces: if based on nothing more than sheer kinship, Ewing's verdict might sound equally far-fetched. Consider the following filled-out version of EC. When a few days old, the son was given up for adoption and lost sight of. Eighteen years later, a call comes from the adoptive parents, who have discovered the father's identity: "Your biological son desires a university education, but he can't pay for it and neither can we." Is the father, who may not have set eyes on this son, even as an infant, now as strongly obliged as Ewing alleges? Would Ewing say he was? These queries suggest the possibility that a close personal relationship between father and son, taken for granted, may account more for Ewing's verdict than does their genetic relationship.[23] The decisive factor may be friendship.[24] So let us pass to a second agent-related class – one with stronger current appeal – that competes with next of kin for preeminence.

FRIENDS

Jonathan preferred David, his friend, over Saul, his father. For David was dear to him as his own self, and Saul, we may surmise, was not (1 Sam. 18–19). The example suggests that when loyalties conflict, friendship may count for more than kinship, and that kinship alone may not be what gives special weight to the preferential status of immediate kin. Often, one's parents, children, spouses, siblings are not only nearest but also dearest.

In some societies, friendship has clearly outranked kinship,[25] and contemporary Western culture shows signs of a similar discrimination. As Michael Lawler recounts:

A major study of family in the United States, funded by Massachusetts Mutual Life in 1989, offered respondents three definitions of family and asked them to select the one that best fitted their understanding. The three definitions were: 1) a group of people related by blood, marriage or adoption; 2) a group of people living in one household; 3) a group of people who love and care for one another. The first definition, used by both the Census Bureau and the U.S. Catholic bishops when they speak of family, was selected by a mere 22 percent of respondents; the second by 3 percent, the third by an overwhelming 74 percent. The traditional definition of family, based on blood and law, has been supplanted for three out of four adult Americans by another definition, based on love and nurture.[26]

Though suspect as conceptual evidence, this account does suggest current values – values that transcend familial boundaries.

"Certainly friendship is the greatest bond in the world," declares Jeremy Taylor;[27] indeed, it is *"the nearest love and the nearest society* of which . . . persons are capable."[28] More recently, friendship, not family, has been proclaimed "the normative relationship,"[29] "the foundation of our social fabric,"[30] "the dominant paradigm."[31] It "is becoming a preeminent intimate relationship in this era of widespread decline in both the role of extended families and the cohesion of nuclear families."[32] In support of this preeminence, relative to kinship, both a quantitative and a qualitative case can be sketched.

Quantitatively, the active circle of our friends typically extends more widely than does that of our kin. Particularly far-reaching are the "associative" friendships that form casually in the course of everyday life: "The classmates in a school, the neighbors on a street, the members of a committee, the congregants of a church, the staff of an office, a faculty, fraternity brothers, the list could go on and on."[33]

Sometimes the friends are useful to each other in pursuing a common purpose, for example, members of an athletic team, fellow citizens devoted to the civic common good, business partners. Sometimes they are useful to each other in like ways for each other's private purpose; such is often the case with politicians or with those who do business with each other. Sometimes the friends are useful to each other in correlative ways, for example, lawyers and clients, doctors and patients, leaders and followers.[34]

According to Taylor, friendship's reach should extend still more widely. "Christian Charity is Friendship to all the world," he writes[35] "We must be friends to all: That is, apt to do good, loving them really, and doing to them all the benefits which we can, and which they are capable of. The Friendship is equall [*sic*] to all the World, and of it self hath no difference; but is differenced onely [*sic*] by accidents, and by the capacity or incapacity of them that receive it."[36] And yet, Taylor acknowledges, "as I cannot do benefits to all alike: so neither am I tyed [*sic*] to love all alike: for although there is much reason to love every man; yet there are more reasons to love some more than others."[37] The breadth and depth of friendship tend to be inversely related.[38]

Qualitatively, the most perfect friendship may outrank all

other relationships. The highest kind has been variously described. For example, John Reisman contrasts merely "associative" friendship with "reciprocal":

A friendship of reciprocity exists when both parties feel love and loyalty to one another. It is their affection and loyalty that enable them to be honest, without experiencing their honesty as cruel and threatening. They feel a freedom to be critical, secure that their friendship provides a firm basis for frankness. A reciprocal relationship of this kind, between persons who view each other as equals, has been, and is, regarded by authorities and people in general as the most ideal and desirable form of human association.[39]

Jules Toner detects further depths in the most perfect friendships:

Sharing lives in friendship comprises a number of factors, each after the first depending on and growing out of the preceding one. These are: being together, mutual intimate self-revelation, each experiencing the other as another self, each knowing the other's life from within, each experiencing the other's life as his or hers in the other and his or her life as the other's in him or her.[40]

Surely those of whom all this can be said are nearest of the near and dearest of the dear;[41] but what implications does this special nearness hold for preferential treatment? Suppose we replace the son in EC with an intimate friend (or suppose the son is also an intimate friend): should preference now go to the friend rather than the starving? On what grounds?

I have suggested earlier that the strength of feelings does not translate automatically into strength of obligation. I have also noted that the acts of affection that cement a parent-child relationship need not be expensive. The like holds for acts of friendship. Indeed, with regard to friendship "utility . . . is thought to be a base consideration, and to the extent that it enters into the determination of the relationship, people tend to believe, along with Cicero, that it dilutes the purity of friendship and makes it less precious."[42] Most of the definitions of friendship that Reisman catalogs do not mention beneficence or generosity.[43]

More serious, the suggestion of preferential treatment sharpens the apparent conflict between friendship and agape:

Agape, the distinctive Christian love, is not preferential, but universal. It is a love restricted to no one and open to everyone. When we hold both loves up side-by-side, what do we see? In friendship we see an exclusive, preferential, reciprocal love based on what people find attractive in one another. In agape we see an inclusive, universal love that goes out to anyone regardless of whether that love is returned, regardless of whether we find the person easy to love or not.[44]

Friendship as affection may entail no exclusion (one simply loves some more than others), but friendship as active preference does. The friend, for example, receives the university education while the starving are left to die. How might such preference be justified?

Elizabeth Telfer replies:

> A plausible line of defense seems to be an appeal to a Rule-Utilitarian position. Thus it might be argued that many sets of rights and duties which set up special claims not obviously required by justice, are justified by the conduciveness of their observance to the general good. If for example a parent is asked why he should support his child, he will reply that it is one of the duties of a parent. If he is then asked *why* parents should be held to have special duties to their children, instead of their being the responsibility of the State or of grand-parents, he will say that it is best for all concerned that parents should have special responsibility for children. In the same way, then, we may suggest that the general welfare is best served by our regarding friends as having a special claim on us. We may defend this view on the grounds that more happiness overall is produced if each man makes the welfare of a few others his special concern, for two reasons: he will be able to be more effective if he concentrates his energies, and he will be able to know more precisely what the needs of a small group are.[45]

Lawrence Blum contests this rule-utilitarian justification. "For one could imagine another practice which was the same as friendship except that one helped the other in preference to one's friend in situations in which one did in fact know what another needed, in which one was equally able to meet that need, and in which that need was manifestly greater than one's friend's need."[46] Friendship need not expire if one party has compassion for the starving. Telfer herself acknowledges that her defense establishes, "if not a prior claim, at least a competing claim."[47] And that does not suffice. As we recognized a competing claim for children, so we might for friends without altering the verdict in favor of the starving. So the question remains: what about friendship might establish a claim strong enough to reverse the judgment in EC? What aspect of this very special relationship might outweigh, or override, the claims of the starving?

Personal friendship requires liking; and liking, for Telfer, is "roughly specifiable as 'finding a person to one's taste,' and depends partly on such things as his physical appearance, mannerisms, voice and speech, and style of life; partly on his traits of character, moral and other."[48] Aristotle stresses the last. In his view, the highest friendship has the highest basis: it rests, not on pleasure or utility but on moral excellence. Here is a feature not considered under kinship which might affect the balance in EC. However, whereas the father knows his lack of kinship with the starving, he knows nothing about their virtue. Furthermore, if virtue warrants preference, it warrants it from all alike, whether friends or total strangers; the fact of friendship is irrelevant to the preference. So, given our focus on special, agent-centered relationships, let us continue our search and inquire more pointedly: what agent-related feature of friendship might affect the balance between nearest and neediest?

Aquinas answers: "In as much as the friendship of comrades originates through their own choice, love of this kind takes precedence of the love of kindred in matters where we are free to do as we choose, for instance in matters of action."[49] I question the explicit and implicit premises of this inference, as well as the conclusion drawn from them. Kinship may involve full choice (spouses) or no choice (parents). And the like holds for friendship. A necessary condition of friendship may be "that the existence of the passions of friendship in both parties, and the practice on both sides of acting on them, once established, be *acknowledged* by the parties."[50] But choice need not initiate friendship, still less choice in the form of a commitment to favor one's friend over one's kin – or those in far greater need. Even if made, the commitment would have to be legitimate in order to justify the chosen preference.

There is danger here, I recognize, of picking off leaf after leaf in search of the artichoke, and concluding that the artichoke does not exist. What is special about friendship, or its highest form, may be friendship, or its highest form, rather than any single feature. However, from a holistic, undifferentiated perception of friendship as something wonderful no inference directly follows for a case like EC. A serious challenge to the claims of the destitute would require an extra premise, to the effect that aid to the starving rather than one's friend would threaten the friendship. If it did, one might legitimately question the worth of the friend and of the friendship.[51] Besides, evidence in chapter 6 suggests that, for friends as for dependent children, an equally likely result might be admiration, and heightened sensitivity to the claims of the destitute, rather than resentment.

COMPATRIOTS

Conationality may appear too weak a link to challenge either kinship or friendship for primacy. And yet it has been said: "As a cultural ideal, nationalism is the claim that while men and women have many identities, it is the nation that provides them with their primary form of belonging."[52] Regarding the present strength of this cultural ideal, Ninian Smart goes so far as to assert:

Nations are the most powerful entities, at least emotionally, in today's world. They have their individual myths of identity, purveyed by histories, often colored. They demand great loyalty. E. M. Forster once said that he would rather betray his country than his friends, but this remark was not well received. You are expected to pay huge swathes of your income and often high taxes on everything you buy, and to lay down your life if necessary, all for the nation-state to which you belong.[53]

For the ardent patriot, the claims of country trump all others. Thus Gabriele D'Annunzio declaims: "Italy is not in those who live on her, trafficking with her and slandering her shamelessly, but in those who live for her alone, and suffer for her alone and for her alone are ready to die."[54] More soberly, yet strongly,

Cardinal Mercier affirms: "Family interests, class interests, party interests, and the material good of the individual take their place, in the scale of values, below the ideal of patriotism."[55] Such sentiments are not confined to a D'Annunzio, Mercier, Frederick the Great,[56] or Ernst Arndt.[57] As Barbara Ward notes, "every single one of us feels the tug of separateness, of nationalism, of ultimate loyalties devoted exclusively to our own community and not concerned with that wider, larger, and admittedly vaguer community of mankind. The natural instinct is to feel united and identified with one's own group, and to forget any wider kinship."[58]

Strong preference for one's country begets strong preference for one's "fellow countrymen," in legislature, voting booth, cabinet meeting, philanthropic enterprise, or private conversation.[59] Indeed, the preference may be stronger, more exclusive, than any we would state for family or friends.[60] "Many people seem . . . to believe that any assignment of duties to aid that extends beyond national boundaries is for that very reason unfair, because one cannot have duties to aid toward anyone but members of one's own society, where one's own society is taken to be, roughly, national."[61] Charity, maybe, but duties, no. Even this concession to charity may be challenged: "Those who urge the Government of the United States to serve interests broader than those of the American people put it in a false position. The benevolent intentions of the government of a sovereign state presuming to act for interests broader than its own will not be taken at face value; and such a government is open to charges of hypocrisy brought by other countries."[62] As evidence *for* national egoism, this argument is flimsy; as evidence *of* national egoism, both in the speaker and in those spoken of, it is cogent.

Peter Singer remarks: "I have written and lectured on the subject of overseas aid, arguing that our affluence puts us under an obligation to do much more than we are now doing to help people in real need. At the popular level, the most frequent response is that we should look after our own poor first."[63] Goodin's perception agrees: "Far and away the most standard objection to foreign aid is the notion that charity begins at home. Any moral duties we may have with respect to needy foreigners are allegedly overridden by our stronger special responsibilities with respect to our compatriots."[64] Given the disparity between most poor people in a country like the United States and those in impoverished lands, this reaction parallels Ewing's: for Ewing, lesser needs of children come before greater needs of strangers; for most citizens of affluent nations, lesser needs of compatriots come before more pressing needs of foreigners.[65] On what grounds?

Peter Henriot suggests at least partial vindication, for a country such as the United States:

It is true that the poverty conditions of many parts of Asia, Africa and Latin America are indeed severe. But the poor in this country also suffer greatly – from hunger, homelessness, poor health, powerlessness. And their poverty is compounded by the fact that it is experienced in the midst of an affluent society. The inner city or rural child who cannot go to school because of lack of decent shoes also knows from television that a consumerist ethos drives the majority of people in North America to a conspicuous and wasteful lifestyle. The child may measure her or his self-worth against the lifestyle of the rich and famous. In North America, more than elsewhere, the poor are subject to a loss of dignity, a self-contempt, which can lead to self-destructive behavior.[66]

This assessment may contain some truth, but an equally plausible case might be made on the other side. Poverty in other lands, being more severe, contrasts more sharply not only with the lifestyle of local elites but also, in a world grown small, with the conspicuous consumption of whole populations. And in lands where no remedy or redress for the condition of the poor seems possible or likely, deeper destitution may lead to deeper desperation.

So the question returns: if foreigners are starving and compatriots are not, why should I favor the latter? Why should I not instead allot my aid to those deprived of subsistence? "I know of no one," replies Shue, "who has adequately answered – or even straightforwardly and systematically tackled – these questions in defence of the thesis that compatriots take priority even when the compatriots' own subsistence rights are more than adequately fulfilled and the subsistence rights of non-compatriots are ignored by those around them. Priority for compatriots as a moral theory is at best unproven, however widely assumed."[67]

From a Christian perspective, proof looks badly needed. With her customary vigor, Barbara Ward asks:

Can Christians accept such limits? Are they no more than nationalists or tribalists? Is their faith based on the formula "I will love my neighbor as myself – provided he is a fellow-American, Briton, Frenchman, German"? Must we rewrite every parable in the Bible to point out that the man in the ditch was really a Samaritan too, that Christ explicitly established that all the lepers were Jews before He cleansed them, that His condition for a cure was that the dumb man would only speak Hebrew, that the Centurion himself and his servant, far from being praised as Gentiles, had to accept citizenship in Israel before the healing words could be spoken?[68]

Utilitarian arguments such as we have seen for kin and friends may establish limited preference for compatriots over foreigners,[69] but not preference strong enough to tip the scales in EC-type cases, where benefit to the desperate is relatively sure.[70] If anything, the case for compatriots looks weaker than for next-of-kin or close friends.[71] Smart tellingly observes:

The power of national identity is strange since that identity can be formed in so many different ways: by language and some obscurely defined ethnicity beyond, in the case of Czechs or Poles or Italians; by religion as with the Croats versus the Serbs; by both language and religion, as with the Turkish and Greek Cypriots; by history and prehistory, as with Egyptians over against, say, Saudis; by sub-religion as with the Saudis (namely the Wahhabi connection, as well as a fading Bedouinness); by pure and recent history, as with Singapore; by partial unity of language and long memories, as with the Chinese; by a sense of historical and partly religious identity modernistically reinterpreted, as with India; by memory and a bit by religion, as with the Scots (also a sense of antagonism, mildly felt, towards the English); and so on. The United States depends on history and loyalty to ideas, enshrined in the Constitution. The Swiss lean on history and a sense of decent federalism.[72]

It is psychologically strange, and ethically stranger, that this hodgepodge should be credited with high moral prerogatives.

If, as David Miller acknowledges, "no objective criterion, such as language, race, or religion, will be adequate to mark all national distinctions,"[73] should we focus on the state rather than the nation, and on shared citizenship in the state as the factor that warrants strong preference for our fellow countrymen? In its motivation and result, this move resembles two already noted: defining kin by blood relationship, apart from knowledge, affection, shared experiences, and the like; and defining coreligionists by baptism, apart from faith, virtue, shared community, and the like. Similarly reduced, to the sheer legal fact of cocitizenship, the national relationship no longer appears very special or ethically compelling.[74]

The power of national sentiment has deeper roots, roots which the family lacks. It derives, for instance, from a sense of national greatness, of size and power and world significance. It draws strength from the idealization that vagueness and vastness permit ("O beautiful for spacious skies, for waves of amber grain"). Yet these attractions furnish no basis for national preference at the expense of starving humanity. Planet Earth, with its teeming billions, looms still larger, still greater, still more mystic in its significance than any single nation, however rich and powerful.

PUBLIC IMPLICATIONS

Our one-by-one examination of competing relations has revealed no difference that makes a difference – no peculiarity of coreligionists, friends, or compatriots that might give them a stronger claim than a son to assistance, and warrant their being preferred over the starving. For all three relationships, we can now further note: (1) The chief argument backing the verdict in EC remains unaffected if a coreligionist, friend, or compatriot replaces the son: letting the starving die still looks on a par with killing them (chapter 4). (2) The two chief objections raised against the verdict – the uncertain outcome of the assistance, the difficulty of denying one's own child (chapter 6) – are not strengthened, but if anything are weakened, by such a substitution. The assistance to the starving is equally effective regardless of whether a son, or a coreligionist, friend, or compatriot is the person passed over. And for the decision to prove as difficult in the case of a coreligionist or compatriot as in the case of one's child, we would have to suppose strong personal affection, comparable to that typically felt for one's child, and strong public expectations, comparable to those for child-support. (3) Overall, therefore, in a situation similar to EC's the verdict remains the same as for EC. An individual contemplating reasonably effective aid to the starving versus aid to a much less needy coreligionist, friend, or compatriot, would do better, objectively, to assist the starving.

A final question, further widening the focus of preceding chapters, is whether such verdicts transfer to the public sphere. If, for example, a person acting as a private individual should favor starving foreigners over less needy compatriots, should the same person, acting as voter, legislator, house speaker, cabinet member, president, or prime minister, show the same preference?

The transition from personal to public morality might occur in two ways, one holistic and the other atomistic. In the first, the norms which govern people's private decisions would extend by analogy to collectivities – to cities, counties, states, nations – and thereby to individual members of the collectivities.[75] (If, for example, wealthy people should aid destitute people, wealthy states should aid destitute states, and such should be the policy supported and pursued by the wealthy states' members.) In the second, the norms which govern people's private decisions would extend directly to their public decisions – as citizens, legislators, public officials.[76] (If, for example, people with private means at their disposal should favor starving foreigners over compatriots, people with public means at their disposal should show the same preference.) Let us start with the first alternative and, by way of illustration, focus on nation-states, the currently most powerful, influential form of political collectivity, and the one to which the strongest loyalties attach.

Considerable grounds exist, I suggested in a previous work, for viewing at least some social entities as moral agents, with conflicting interests to which preference-rules apply.[77] Particularly for nation-states, "the analogies with individual persons are multiple and strong. Nations, too, have points of view on the world, perspectives fixed by their unique stream of experience; they, too, have hopes and fears and aspirations; they, too, may be said to take pride in their achievements, make choices, and attempt to better their lot. Like individuals, they 'conclude contracts, take precautions, apologize for actions, and make promises.' "[78] More directly pertinent, some national states are nearest and dearest (think of the "special relationship" between the United States and Great Britain to which Churchill appealed);[79] and some are neediest (think of Bangladesh or Chad). Furthermore, the claims of the nearest and the neediest may conflict. So, with EC as our guide, should we conclude that nations should prefer the neediest of their fellow states over the "nearest"? And is that, therefore, the policy which individual citizens, legislators, and officials should pursue in their political activities?[80]

Of greater practical moment, should the analogical reasoning perhaps take this further form, with respect to a nation's own interests: (1) The norms for individual persons hold also, *mutatis mutandis*, for moral persons such as nation-states; (2) the Christian norm for individual persons is Self-Subordination (see chapter 1); hence, (3) nation-states, too, should subordinate their interests to those of other states? Each state may and should give independent consideration to its own benefit, but only on the condition that maximum benefit to other states is first assured (whether directly, or indirectly through benefit to itself). Even when, for example, one state has as great need as another, if it can meet the other state's needs as effectively as its own, then, other things equal, it should give preference to the other state. Accordingly, on the individual level such is the policy which voters, legislators, and public officials should pursue. They should prefer the citizens of other lands over their own compatriots.

This conclusion, stronger than anything the verdict on EC would suggest, invites closer scrutiny of the analogy that underlies these extensions from personal to national morality. Consider first the prospective recipients of assistance. Nations do not starve – people do. And aid to a nation may do little for its neediest citizens. In such a corporate "person," the mouth may gorge while the members go hungry. Further disanalogy appears for the donor nations and their decision-making. One-person rule may bear some resemblance to the fiat of an individual will, but even there the person-state analogy breaks down; for the single ruler has relatives, friends, compatriots, toward whom he or she may have special responsibilities. In a more democratic system, the many voters, legislators, and executives who set policy all have similar relationships, vying for recognition. What, then, is the individual to do: favor compatriots, as personal morality suggests, or favor other nations, as the argument extending Self-Subordination recommends? Rather than struggle with this dilemma, engendered by a shaky analogy, I think it best to switch to the second perspective, focusing on individual citizens rather than whole nations.[81]

Although entities such as nations may be said to have duties, to make decisions, and to carry them out,[82] the decisions of nations are made by individuals and the actions of nations are performed by individuals.[83] Directly or indirectly, voters, lobbyists, legislators, and public officials support or oppose specific provisions – on immigration,[84] development, trade,[85] foreign aid, world finance[86] – that do or do not favor conationals vis-à-vis the needy of the world. In all such matters, these varied agents might take cognizance of EC and the foregoing discussion. The question is, should they?[87] What the father should or should not do for his child may indicate what he should or should not do for a coreligionist, friend, or compatriot in his private life; but do the same standards apply to his public life – as voter, legislator, elected official, or the like? Can inferences pass, unimpeded, from one sector to the other?

For voters, they can. For legislators and elected officials, there may be obstacles. In a country with strict party discipline, legislators may be freer to influence party policy than to disregard it and vote their consciences.[88] In a country like the United States, with looser party discipline, the freedom of both legislators and elected officials may be limited by their role as representatives. The constraints on their freedom would be greatest in the following suppositions: (1) The electorate as a whole views them as delegates, carrying out the wishes of their constituents, and not as trustees, entitled to follow their personal judgment;[89] (2) the electorate agrees – with regard, for example, to the treatment of compatriots and noncompatriots – and has made its wishes known. Given these restraints, representatives might be as tightly bound as are physicians and lawyers by their clients' preferences. However, neither supposition looks realistic in the majority of instances, in this country or elsewhere.

Consider William Brown's counterclaim with respect to US voters: "When the people of the United States elect a President and Congress, they entrust to them one primary responsibility – to safeguard and promote the welfare, prosperity, and security of the United States. By the nature of their office they must act in the American interest. They are not and could not be entrusted by the American electorate with the responsibility for the welfare of other countries."[90] In an obvious sense, this is true (the US government is not the government of Italy or Iran); but that sense is compatible with the public's readiness, and politicians' duty, to assist needy peoples. In 1945 and again in 1946 the Gallup Poll showed seventy percent of the US populace willing to go back to food rationing in order to send food to people in other countries.[91] Divided though it may be on questions of foreign aid, the US electorate has issued no mandate against assisting the world's needy.

Neither does it betray a uniform conception of the President and Congress as mere conduits of the popular will, responsive to the latest poll. As I write, President Clinton is bucking public opinion on sending troops to Bosnia, yet winning higher ratings for his show of leadership. As for Congress, some legislators view themselves as delegates, but others do not;[92] and I know no reason to believe that the populace as a whole sides with one group or the other. Thus Nancy Schwartz notes: "Recent empirical literature has begun to label the delegate/trustee model as obsolete, unhelpful to describing the complex realities of our times. In its stead, the most powerful alternative conceptualization has been that of 'responsiveness.' The representative is supposed to be responsive to the needs and wants of the constituents."[93]

To see how this conception might play out, consider President Franklin Roosevelt's situation as throngs of Jews tried to flee Nazi Germany. Their need was as dire as that of the starving; most of those who did not escape would soon perish. But US immigration quotas were tight and were tightly enforced, especially for Jews. Loosening the restrictions would have cost US citizens little if anything, and Roosevelt had the power to loosen them. He also had the right. Some citizens opposed increased Jewish immigration; others pleaded for it. He could have been "responsive" either way, without having had to ascertain percentages. Morally, his hands were free: he could have done more than he did – and he should have.[94]

Granted, in politics there are trade-offs, as there are in private life. Voters for candidates must consider more than any single policy or personality trait. Legislators must consider more than the single bill before them. Presidents must view each move within a larger, strategic perspective. (Would the attempt to raise quotas for Jewish refugees, and not merely loosen restrictions on existing quotas, have cost political capital needed for other, more important efforts, as FDR believed?) However, other things being equal, voters, legislators, presidents, and other office-holders should follow the same standards as for private individuals. Within the leeway allowed them, they should, for example, favor the dire needs of foreigners over the much less pressing needs of compatriots. The implications of EC can carry through, largely unhindered, from the private to the public sphere.

It appears, then, that the preceding inquiry's broad relevance is vindicated. Here, too, in Diana Meyers's words, "what is ultimately at stake is not only the nature and justification of our private responsibilities, but also the ethical model and the array of values that can best guide our deliberations about law and public policy – that is, our deliberations about the overall direction of our society as a whole."[95] However, realism requires that the inquiry's limits also be noted. What it provides is a paradigm, a term of comparison, not some universal norm by which all cases might be judged. And the paradigm carries no farther than the second step in John Bennett's scheme of Christian social ethics:

(1) the setting forth of the Christian ethic in its fullness without dilution or compromise; (2) the recognition that within the Christian Church all norms for action in society remain under the judgment of this radical ethic; (3) the responsibility of Christians to find the best course of action in the world in the light of this judgment; (4) the possibility of developing structures and institutions in the world that are more in harmony than others with a Christian ethic, and in which Christians can live according to their vocation as Christians.[96]

To stop at the second point, with the Christian ideal, may appear unsatisfactory;[97] but to proffer quick solutions to complex policy issues or personal quandaries would be still less satisfactory.[98] Thus, though I noted at the start that an EC verdict in favor of the starving might carry alarming implications, I did not say then and will not determine now just what that verdict's implications really are. My queries were not answers; my misgivings were not judgments. It would be far too facile, for example, to infer straightway that if the father should not finance his son's higher education, all institutions of higher education should be abolished.

And yet, some current policies and practices rather clearly do fail the EC test. For example, millions of present-day refugees live in desperate conditions; their claims are therefore comparable to those of the starving. On the other hand, the claims of compatriots are weaker than those of one's children, and for affluent countries to admit more refugees would cost the average citizen far less than a university education. (Indeed, as Peter Singer notes, we should not too readily assume that residents of the receiving nations would be adversely affected.[99]) True, such a comparison does not spell out what precise policy a given country should adopt – does not indicate how many people, of what categories, should be admitted, under what conditions. It just points the way. That, however, is more important than the details. Where no need for change is sensed, none will be undertaken. And no need of change may be sensed so long as the common sentiment "Charity begins at home" goes unexamined. The saying contains some truth, for family, friends, coreligionists, compatriots, and others; but how much truth? When the claims of nearest and neediest conflict, as they repeatedly do, where should preference go? If my wavering flashlight has cast some light on this particular patch of darkness, that is enough.

Notes

1 Ewing, *Ethics*, 37–8.
2 Rachels, "Morality, Parents, and Children," 58–9. For similar assessments, see Cottingham, "Partiality, Favouritism and Morality," 357; Goodin, *Protecting the Vulnerable*, 23–4; Sharp, *Ethics*, 44–5; Singer, *The Expanding Circle*, 32.
3 Sharp, *Ethics*, 44.
4 Ibid.
5 For the son's side, see Finnis, "Consistent Ethic," 156; Unger, *Living High and Letting Die*, 150. Cf. Vacek, *Love, Human and Divine*, 306; Wasserstrom, "Lawyers as Professionals," 4; Clarke, *Almsgiving*, 106–7 ("No one can be expected willingly to accept for his children a lower standard of education than his father provided for him").
6 E.g., Peeters, *Manuale theologiae moralis*, vol. 2, 291–2; Koch, *A Handbook of Moral Theology*, vol. 5, 176; Shue, *Basic Rights*, 112 ("No excuse is adequate for depriving any person of subsistence, except the extraordinary situation in which someone else's subsistence cannot possibly be provided at any price by any other means"); Singer, *Practical Ethics*, 233–4.
7 Hardwig, "Search," 79–80; Donaldson, "Morally Privileged Relationships," 35; Friedman, *What Are Friends For?*, 86n.
8 Virginia Chudgar, in "Feedback" to Mahoney, "Let's Junk the Profit Motive," 16.
9 Haughey, *The Holy Use of Money*, e.g. 143, 173.
10 "When selecting judges who will be most likely to conduct a fair trial and facilitate a just verdict, we are inclined to disqualify someone from trying his or her own child in view of the loyalties, the particular passions, and interests present in such a relationship" (Dyck, "Questions on Ethics," 470).

11 Kagan, *Limits of Morality*, 258. See Glover, *Causing Death and Saving Lives*, 287–8; Singer, *The Expanding Circle*, 157.
12 Hume, *Treatise*, 3.2.2.
13 Singer, "Famine, Affluence, and Morality," 29.
14 Ewing, *Ethics*, 38.
15 Haughey, *The Holy Use of Money*, 163; Narveson, "Morality and Starvation," 61–2; Tambasco, "Option for the Poor," 38: "As understood by liberation theologians, 'option for the poor' includes as a primary ingredient what they describe as the 'hermeneutic privilege of the poor,' i.e., that the poor have a privileged position for interpreting the meaning of their poverty and for judging the work of justice that addresses itself to that situation."
16 Cf. Mill, *Utilitarianism*, 258–9.
17 Sneed, "A Utilitarian Framework," 103.
18 James, "The Duty to Relieve Suffering," 4. Cf. Unger, *Living High and Letting Die*, 14–20; Ward, *The Lopsided World*, 99–101.
19 Aloysius Schwartz, *The Starved and the Silent*, 76.
20 Westermarck, *Origin*, vol. 1, 542–3.
21 In further illustration, see Hallie, *Lest Innocent Blood Be Shed*, 140–5; Tec, *When Light Pierced the Darkness*, 64–7.
22 "Properly understood, . . . the term conveys a very important truth about the Christian attitude toward poverty: that remedial action should be concentrated upon those experiencing greatest distress" (Wogaman, "Toward a Christian Definition," 23).
23 To these might be added our better understanding of the dire results of deprivation: "When famine strikes, relatively few people die 'of hunger.' They die for the most part of illnesses they would easily have survived if hunger had not weakened them. They die of 'flu and of intestinal troubles, and disproportionately many of those who die are very young or old. When there is famine, the survivors too are affected in hidden ways. Children may suffer brain damage as a result of early malnutrition; whole populations may be listless and lethargic, unable to muster the energy needed for economic advance, still living but permanently weakened" (Onora O'Neill, "Moral Perplexities," 300–1).
24 "The idea that the majority could have access to a little modest affluence is wholly new, the break-through of whole communities to national wealth totally unprecedented" (Ward, *Rich Nations*, 38–9).
25 From Bread for the World's report, "Hunger, 1994" (see "Antihunger Groups," 1266). "Today one of every five human beings lives in poverty so extreme that their survival is daily in doubt" ("The Oxford Declaration," 5).

26 Mary Smith, "The Haves," 3.
27 Temple, *Christianity and Social Order*, 21.
28 Winkler, "Utilitarian Idealism and Personal Relations," 279.
29 Rachels, "Morality, Parents, and Children," 54. See Onora O'Neill, "Moral Perplexities," 294–5; Shue, "Mediating Duties," 693.
30 E.g., Concina, *Theologia christiana dogmatico-moralis*, vol. 2, 22 ("Rarissima haec sunt"); Lehmkuhl, *Theologia moralis*, vol. 1, 363 ("qualis utique extrema necessitas non est, quae raro sese offert, rarius evidens fit"); Pelt, *De tribus bonorum operum generibus*, 42 ("non ita frequenter usu venire soleat"); Vasquez, "Tractatus de eleemosyna," 3: "Et sane Sancti Patres adeo reprehendunt auaros, qui pauperibus subuenire negligunt, quod esset superfluum, & nullius fructus, si tantum tenerentur in extrema necessitate, quae nunquam, aut rarissime occurret." Cf. Damen, "De recto uso," 68 ("Quid faciendum sit, si v.g. in longinqua regione millia millium hominum fame pereunt, a moralistis vix consideratur").
31 Recently, Stephen Pope and Stephen Post, in particular, have noted the issue of nearest versus neediest and its importance but have not grappled with it, in depth or in detail. (See chapter 2.)
32 Two authors who may deserve mention but whose works I have not been able to consult are Louis Thomassin (*Traité de l'aumône*, Paris, 1695) and Joseph de l'Isle (*Traité dogmatique et historique touchant l'obligation de faire l'aumône*, Neufchâteau, 1736).
33 See chapter 2 ("Christian intuition").
34 Sherlock, *Nature and Measure*, 17.
35 Hallett, *Christian Moral Reasoning*, chap. 1, and *Christian Neighbor-Love*, chap. 2.
36 Boff and Pixley, *Bible*, 184. "Christian effort 'should henceforth be turned from charitable paternalism to the realization of more equal justice in the distribution of wealth'" (Muelder, "Ethical Aspects," 320–1, quoting John Bennett on the Oxford Conference of 1937). "The preferential option [for the poor] is not a commitment to *working for* the poor in a paternalistic way, but rather involves *working with* and humbly *learning from* the poor" (Pope, "Preferential Option," 165).
37 Metz, Glaube in *Geschichte und Gessellschaft*, 68.
38 Michael R. Becker, in feedback to Brennan, "Charity."
39 Aloysius Schwartz, *Poverty*, 109. See Singer, *Practical Ethics*, 241–2; Narveson, "Aesthetics, Charity, Utility," 530.
40 Dorr, *Option for the Poor*, 11.
41 Pope, "Proper and Improper Partiality," 269.
42 E.g., "Paul VI formulait en 1967 une série d'interrogations qui

frappèrent beaucoup l'attention: 'Tout homme de ce temps est-il prêt à soutenir de ses deniers les oeuvres et les missions organisées en faveur des plus pauvres? A payer davantage d'impôts pour que les pouvoirs publics intensifient leur effort pour le développement? A acheter plus cher les produits importés pour rémunérer plus justement le producteur? A s'expatrier lui-même au besoin, s'il est jeune, pour aider cette croissance des jeunes nations?' (PP 47)" (Calvez, *Une éthique pour nos sociétés*, 86).

43 Goodin, *Protecting the Vulnerable*, 1–2.

44 Singer, "Reconsidering the Famine Relief Argument," 42. "So far from thinking," writes Hume, "that men have no affection for any thing beyond themselves, I am of opinion, that tho' it be rare to meet with one, who loves any single person better than himself; yet 'tis as rare to meet with one, in whom all the kind affections, taken together, do not over-balance all the selfish. Consult common experience: Do you not see, that tho' the whole expense of the family be generally under the direction of the master of it, yet there are few that do not bestow the largest part of their fortunes on the pleasures of their wives, and the education of their children, reserving the smallest portion for their own proper use and entertainment?" (*Treatise*, 3.2.2) Cf. Bishop Latimer, in Munby, *God and the Rich Society*, 89 ("They will not look on the poor; they must help their children"); Fléchier, *Oeuvres complètes*, vol. 1, 986 ("C'est là le prétexte de la plupart des pères"); Niebuhr, *An Interpretation of Christian Ethics*, 125 ("A narrow family loyalty is a more potent source of injustice than pure individual egoism").

45 Grisez, *Living a Christian Life*, 813–14.

46 Sidgwick, *The Methods of Ethics*, 243.

47 Wayland, *Elements of Moral Science*, 190.

48 Ibid., 160.

49 Harkness, *Christian Ethics*, 113. Cf. Shue, "The Burdens of Justice," 603–6; Gutiérrez, "Preferential Option for the Poor," 180: "Without universality, preference could be a sectarian attitude; without preference, universality could be very abstract. To love everyone is to love no one; the relation between the two is central."

50 "This is the chief thing, which among men of any principles, disputes the bounds of charity" (Sherlock, *Nature and Measure*, 12). See Goodin, *Protecting the Vulnerable*, 1–9, for a very full account of this challenge.

51 Williams, *Spirit*, 239.

52 Frankena, "The Ethics of Love," 22. Cf. Hallett, *Christian Neighbor-Love*, 29, and *Greater Good*, 154–5.

53 Cf. Hallett, *Christian Neighbor-Love*, 33. Reactions to this earlier work illustrate the attitude with special aptness for the present inquiry and suggest the responses it, too, may evoke. My abstracting from character and focusing on conduct, as here, was read as exclusion: "Hallett construes Christian morality in terms of rules for external behavior. Whether an action exemplifies agape depends solely on its conformity to self-subordination rather than on its internal animating spirit" (Pope, "Love in Contemporary Christian Ethics," 172). My focusing on one preference-rule, as here I focus on others, was likewise read exclusively: "Hallett regards all neighbors uniformly as 'others' and refuses to calibrate agape to specific features of particular neighbors or to their connections with the self" (ibid.). See also Post, Review of *Christian Neighbor-Love*, 196.

54 According to Stephen Pope, a reliable response to the issue of nearest versus neediest would require an "adequate theory of the ordering of love," and such a theory would, for example, "have to include a more elaborate account of natural science and attend seriously to relevant social scientific material regarding the human affections, for example, empathy and altruism. It would have to develop a philosophical account not only of love but also of justice, and these accounts would have to be coordinated with the traditional distinction between commands and counsels, duty and supererogation." To be theologically adequate, "a systematic theory of the ordering of love would also have to address the critical source of the Christian tradition, the bible, and particularly the New Testament texts dealing with *agape* and *philia*. It requires not only an adequate interpretation of the various meanings and implications of these notions within the texts themselves, but also a plausible account of how these various texts ought to be coordinated into a coherent whole and related to doctrinal and theological examinations of related notions, such as nature and grace, Incarnation, Trinity, and church. It requires, in short, nothing less than a thorough grounding in systematic theology and Biblical studies" (*The Evolution of Altruism*, 158).

55 Meilaender, *Friendship*, 26; Schüller, "Neuere Beiträge," 159; Sidgwick, *The Methods of Ethics*, 246. Subtly but importantly, Hardwig ("Search," 66–8) distinguishes between truly personal and quasi-personal relationships. In the latter, you are for instance my child, and I wish you well for that reason; in the former, you are one of my ends – as a person, and not merely as my child. In the one case, I would take the same attitude toward any child of mine, precisely because it is my child, whereas in the more fully personal

relationship I wish you well, wish to provide for you, make you happy, precisely because you are my son Tom or my daughter Sarah.

56 Goodin, *Protecting the Vulnerable*, 111; Haughey, *The Holy Use of Money*, 152; Walzer, *Spheres of Justice*, 3.

57 Goodin, *Protecting the Vulnerable*, 111; Hallett, *Christian Neighbor-Love*, 41–3; Haughey, *The Holy Use of Money*, 161.

58 Allen, *Love and Conflict*, 164: "The idea of a need has a troublesome tendency to 'float' in contemporary popular usage. It floats with regard to material possessions, for one thing. Many possessions now taken for granted by the middle and upper classes were once seen as luxuries available only to the few: for example, automobiles or enough money to pay for a college education. The more widely such things are available, the more we view them as indispensable. Yet they are not absolutely necessary to our lives in the sense that food, shelter, and medical care are." Cf. Fairlie, *The Seven Deadly Sins Today*, 136.

59 David Miller, *Social Justice*, 126–34.

60 Bowen, "Major Economic Problems," 78.

61 Singer, "Famine, Affluence, and Morality," 25.

62 Flandrin, *Families in Former Times*, 19. Cf. Suarez, *Opera omnia*, vol. 12, 714.

63 Rosenthal, "The Fertility Market," A1–C6.

64 Becker, *Reciprocity*, 221; Rescher, *Unselfishness*, 14.

65 "We oversimplify matters if we suppose that tensions between universal love and particular roles and practices are all of one kind, or if we fail to examine particular roles and practices in their various historical and social settings" (Outka, "Universal Love and Impartiality," 90).

66 Cf. ibid., 89.

67 Hallett, *Greater Good*, 2. My *Christian Moral Reasoning* proposed the same norm but, having a broader focus, did not expound and defend it as thoroughly and systematically as does this later work.

68 Jeremy Taylor, *Measures*, 64.

69 Cuttaz, *Fraternal Charity*, 119 (following Aquinas, *Summa theologica* 2–2, q. 26, a. 6).

70 Ibid., 123.

71 Henry Davis, *Moral and Pastoral Theology*, vol. 1, 320; Lovasik, *Kindness*, 40–1; Norman, "Self and Others," 193 (quoting Richard Kraut); Oldenquist, "Loyalties," 175; Riquet, *La charité du Christ en action*, 10.

72 Aiken, "Right," 95–6; Sherlock, *Nature and Measure*, 12; Est, *In quatuor libris Sententiarum commentaria*, vol. 3, 92–3; Vermeersch,

Quaestiones de virtutibus, 254; Aquinas, *In 3 Sent.* 29.6: "Praeterea, magis homo debet seipsum diligere quam alios. Ergo, quanto aliqui sunt sibi magis propinqui, magis debet eos diligere."

73 Jonathan Bennett, "Morality and Consequences," 78.
74 E.g., Pelt, *De tribus bonorum operum generibus*, 30–1, 34.
75 Hallett, *Christian Neighbor-Love*, 5.

2: FINDING A FOCUS

1 Soto, *Deliberatio*, quoted in Deuringer, *Probleme der Caritas*, 132.
2 From the Roman Breviary's second reading for the feast of St. Louis (*Acta Sanctorum Augusti* 5 [1868], 546).
3 Sherlock, *Nature and Measure*, 15.
4 Ibid., 12–13.
5 Wesley, "The Use of Money," 277. C. D. Broad terms this concentric-circle perspective "the altruism which common-sense accepts" ("Certain Features," 55). Norman Geisler calls it "biblical" (*The Christian Ethic of Love*, 36). See Wesley, "The Danger of Riches," 459; Aquinas, *Summa theol.* 2–2.32.5; Calvin, *Institutes*, 418; Henry Davis, *Moral and Pastoral Theology*, vol. 1, 325; Geisler, *The Christian Ethic of Love*, 36–8; Goodin, *Protecting the Vulnerable*, 6 (citing Maimonides and Cotton Mather).
6 Pope, "Preferential Option," 163.
7 Post, *A Theory of Agape*, 92.
8 Ibid. Cf. Post, "Love," 506 ("the uniquely powerful duties that correlate with these roles").
9 Post, *Spheres of Love*, chapter 7 ("Love for Strangers").
10 Sheedy, *The Christian Virtues*, 132. Cf. Peter of Poitiers, *Sentent. libri quinque* 3.23 (ML 211, 1108): "et debet unusquisque dare quantum potest, sed non quantumcunque potest."
11 Jeremy Taylor, *The Great Exemplar*, 459.
12 Sherlock, *Nature and Measure*, 17–18.
13 Budde, "Christian Charity," 576.
14 Brandt, *How Much Shall I Give?*, 151. Cf. Sheedy, *The Christian Virtues*, 132: "The best practice for a charitable Catholic is to develop a policy of almsgiving which satisfies his conscience, and then to carry it out."
15 Chiavacci, *Teologia morale e vita economica*, 216.
16 Goodin, *Protecting the Vulnerable*, 28–9 (references omitted).
17 Ibid., 11, 35.
18 Ibid., 33–4.
19 Hallett, *Christian Neighbor-Love*, 3–4.

20 Cf. Donaldson, "Morally Privileged Relationships," 30; Hardwig, "Search," 66–9.

21 Compare David Ross's critique of ideal utilitarianism: "The essential defect of the 'ideal utilitarian' theory is that it ignores, or at least does not do full justice to, the highly personal character of duty. If the only duty is to produce the maximum of good, the question who is to have the good – whether it is myself, or my benefactor, or a person to whom I have made a promise to confer that good on him, or a mere fellow man to whom I stand in no special relation – should make no difference to my having a duty to produce that good. But we are all in fact sure that it makes a vast difference" (*The Right and the Good*, 22). Implicitly, Ross is calling for recognition of relational values over and beyond the maximization of benefits – or minimization of harms.

22 Bishop Butler's words suggest a preference stronger than any of these: "The fact, then appears to be, that we are constituted so as to condemn falsehood, unprovoked violence, injustice, and to approve of benevolence to some preferably to others, abstracted from all consideration which conduct is likeliest to produce an overbalance of happiness or misery" ("On the Nature of Virtue," 373). Cf. Sharp, *Ethics*, 44–5 ("It appeared to them directly self-evident that a member of one's family has a greater claim upon him than any number of outsiders; and the consideration of what course of action would prevent the greater harm seemed to them, in this situation, entirely irrelevant").

23 Singer, *The Expanding Circle*, 153. "The love that springeth out of Christ excludeth no man, neither putteth difference between one and another. In Christ we are all of one degree, without respect of persons" (Tyndale, "Parable," 98). "One's neighbor is not the beloved, for whom you have passionate preference, nor your friend, for whom you have passionate preference . . . No, to love one's neighbor means equality" (Kierkegaard, *Works*, 72). Cf. Ede, "Competition between Individuals," 181; Outka, *Agape*, 9–13; Walzer, *Spheres of Justice*, 231 ("A number of writers have argued that the highest form of the ethical life is one where the 'rule of prescriptive altruism' applies universally, and there are no special obligations to kinfolk").

24 Peeters, *Manuale theologiae moralis*, vol. 2, 292. Cf. Augustine, *De doctr. christ.* 1.28.29 (PL 34, 30); Aquinas, *Summa theolog.* 2–2.32.9.ad 2 ("ordo charitatis, secundum quem propinquioribus magis providere debemus, caeteris paribus"); Beugnet, "Aumône," 2570; Cuttaz, *Fraternal Charity*, 122, 171; Geisler, *The*

Christian Ethic of Love, 37–8; Merkelbach, *Summa theologiae moralis*, vol. 1, 700 ("In inaequali necessitate prius succurrendum est illi qui maiorem patitur"); Loyola, Letter to Jaime Cassador, 28 ("other things being equal, I ought to do more for my relatives than for those who are not"); Peschke, *Christian Ethics*, vol. 2, 186; Pope, "The Order of Love," 279.

25 Loyola, Letter to Jaime Cassador, 28.

26 Cf. Jonathan Bennett, "Morality and Consequences," 78 ("I hold myself entitled to give extra weight to a cost or benefit which is to accrue to someone with a special relation to me").

27 Cf. Blum, *Friendship, Altruism and Morality*, 54–5; Cottingham, "Ethics and Impartiality," 89; Goldman, *Moral Foundations*, 4 ("Family members are expected to weigh each other's interests more heavily than those of strangers"); Oldenquist, "Loyalties," 186; Wasserstrom, "Lawyers as Professionals," 4.

28 Parfit, "Prudence," 556 (on "common-sense morality").

29 Rachels, "Morality, Parents, and Children," 58.

30 Ibid., 59. Compare the four positions which Narveson sets out in "Morality and Starvation," 52.

31 Rachels, "Morality, Parents, and Children," 60.

32 Aquinas, *Summa theol.* 2–2.31.3.ad 1. Cf. Welty, *Handbook*, 344–5; Adam Smith, *The Theory of Moral Sentiments*, 226–7; Vio, "De eleemosynae praecepto," 37; Abelard, *Serm.* 30 (PL 178, 567–8): "Cum autem pauperibus sua restituimus, maxima est adhibenda discretio, ne scilicet quod alterius est alteri demus, aut cui magis debemus, minus demus. Est enim discretio mater omnium virtutum."

33 Sherlock, *Nature and Measure*, 15–16. See ibid., 9, 13.

34 Lovasik, *Kindness*, 36.

35 Broglie, *Charité*, 687.

36 Caesarius of Arles, Sermon 29.2 (*Sermons*, 145).

37 William of Auxerre, *Summa aurea*, vol. 3, 273–4: "Nos autem concedimus affectu et effectu magis tenemur diligere domesticos quam extraneos, omnibus circumstantiis paribus . . . mobilia et victus cotidianus plus debentur consanguineis quam bonis extraneis, si sunt in equali necessitate. Sed in necessitate tanta possent esse extranei quod magis tenemur eis dare. Sed in quanta necessitate hoc sit, non determinat ars vel scientia, sed potius 'virtus que est melior et certior omni arte.' *Unctio* enim *docet* nos *de omnibus* huiusmodi."

38 Vermeersch, *Theologiae moralis*, 86.

39 Vermeersch, *Quaestiones de virtutibus*, 258.

40 Vermeersch, *Theologiae moralis*, 86.

41 Grisez, *Living a Christian Life*, 811.
42 Aloysius Schwartz, *Poverty*, 113.
43 Gasque, "Almsgiving," 17.
44 Aquinas, *Summa theol.* 2–2.26.9.c.
45 Vermeersch, *Quaestiones de virtutibus*, 254.
46 Quoted in Jackson, *Against the Grain*, iii.
47 Cf. Hallett, *Christian Neighbor-Love*, 35–7.
48 E.g., Sherlock, *Nature and Measure*, 16; Tenison, *Sermon*, 8–9: "Though a man is not obliged to do always that which, in the abstracted speculation of it, is best; yet true philosophy, as well as theology seemeth to assure us, that *there are no such things as moral counsels which are not also commands*: and that every man is bound to do whatsoever is, in his circumstances, best to be done by him, and easily understood by him to be best."
49 "Justice is a tangible expression of love when there are many neighbors and limited resources. It is *distributive love*" (Niebanck, *Economic Justice*, 106–7).
50 Moralists have argued, essentialistically, that the labeling has practical interest: if aid is owed in justice and is denied, then restitution is required even when the need has passed. The single label, "justice," excludes all variation! Or it is urged, gratuitously, that if an obligation is only of charity, not of justice, then it cannot be legislated (Vykopal, *Interpretazione*, 73). On the contrary, any law that effectively seeks the common good, as laws should, *ipso facto* conforms with charity, whether or not it enforces an obligation of justice.
51 "Sometimes in development circles the point is made by saying that the issue is about 'justice, not charity, for the world's poor.' One of the points made by this important phrase is that justice is something required of us, whereas charity is not. This point is misleading, since appeals to kindness, charity or compassion, can all be seen as ways of stating an important duty, and as such they may require quite as much action – if not more – than appeals to justice" (Dower, "World Poverty," 274).
52 "Concepts of rights have been contested by feminists for relying on an atomistic or asocial conception of human individuals that is inimical to the interconnectedness of close personal relationships and damaging to the intimacy and mutual trust on which those relationships should be based" (Friedman, *What Are Friends For?*, 67, with references).
53 Brian Barry, "Do Countries Have Moral Obligations?," 28. Cf. Reeder, *Killing and Saving*, 16–17.
54 Hume, *Treatise*, 3.2.1.

3: NEW TESTAMENT INTIMATIONS

1 See also Marshall, *The Challenge of New Testament Ethics*, 136–42.
2 Nolan, *Jesus Before Christianity*, 59.
3 Ibid., 59–60.
4 Ibid., 60.
5 Ibid., 61.
6 Ibid..
7 Ibid., 62.
8 Ibid., 63.
9 Ibid., 62. Cf. Melden (*Rights and Persons*, 158) on "the extraordinary concern of a Father Damien for any human being, a concern he recognized to be distinctive in his case, in which the love and affection he felt for any human being was of that special order commonly reserved by parents for their own children, who share their joys and sorrows yet feel keenly their own responsibility for their misdeeds and even their misfortunes. It is one of the marks of the saint that he takes himself to be under an obligation to *any* human being, whoever and wherever he may be, of just that sort that parents have to their children. For him the line between special and human rights has disappeared."
10 Nolan, *Jesus Before Christianity*, 62–3.
11 Fitzmyer, *The Gospel According to Luke*, 1063 (quoting A. Plummer, *A Critical and Exegetical Commentary*, 364).
12 Nolan, *Jesus Before Christianity*, 63. Cf. Lk. 8:20, Mk. 3:31–5.
13 Morris, *Luke*, 169. Stephen Barton notes Mark's special hostility toward Jesus' family, yet comments: "Howard Kee claims that, 'All genetic, familial and sex distinctions are eradicated in this new concept of the true family.' But this is anachronistic and pushes the relatively slender evidence too far. All that the evidence of Mark's Gospel will allow is the claim that, according to the evangelist, obedience to the will of God revealed in Jesus relativizes family (and other) ties and creates the potential for a new, family-like community of God's people. Kee's view loses sight of the metaphorical dimension of 3.35; and makes nonsense of the support of the fifth commandment in 7.10–13 and 10.19, and the teaching on divorce in 10.1–12" (*Discipleship and Family Ties*, 82, citing Kee, *Community*, 109).
14 Meeks, *Moral World*, 129.
15 Many, "Aumône," 1249.
16 Labata, *Thesaurus moralis*, vol. 1, 965.
17 Cano, "Commentarium," 182. Cf. Drexel, *Gazophylacium Christi*,

147. Regarding the school of Salamanca's stress on the identity of Christ with the needy, see Deuringer, *Probleme der Caritas*, 137–8.

18 Jerome, *Epist.* 120.1 (CSEL 55, 474).

19 Sider, *Rich Christians*, 82.

20 Schweizer, *Good News*, 475.

21 E.g., Robinson, "'Parable,'" 226. Cf. Winandy, "La scène du Jugement Dernier," 170–1.

22 Donahue, "'Parable,'" 6. "Matthew probably thought of the *brethren* here as the disciples of Jesus; but in the original parable it may have referred to anyone who was in distress" (Fenton, *The Gospel of Saint Matthew*, 402). See Friedrich, *Gott im Bruder*, 248–9; Lambrecht, "The Parousia Discourse," 338; Schuyler Brown, "Matthew 25:31–46," 178.

23 Bruner, *Matthew*, 913, citing Klostermann, Schlatter, and Schnackenburg.

24 Newman and Stine, *Matthew*, 809.

25 Patte, *The Gospel according to Matthew*, 349. See Beare, *Matthew*, 495; Bruner, *Matthew*, 918; Meier, *Matthew*, 302; Meyer, "Context," 71; Sand, *Das Evangelium nach Matthäus*, 512; Douglas Hare, *Matthew*, 289–90 ("It appears more probable, therefore, that Matthew intends 'brothers' in 25:40 to be taken in a much broader sense than is usual in his Gospel: the poor and the distressed, whoever they may be, should be regarded as Jesus' brothers and sisters").

26 Donahue, "'Parable,'" 25.

27 Ridderbos, *Matthew*, 468. See, e.g., Richard Gardner, *Matthew*, 359; Gray, *The Least of My Brothers*, 357–9; Harrington, *The Gospel of Matthew*, 358; Lohfink, *Option for the Poor*, 76; Morris, *The Gospel According to Matthew*, 639; Niebanck, *Economic Justice*, 77; Oudersluys, "Parable," 155. For finer discrimination of positions, and a listing of proponents up to 1977, see Friedrich, *Gott im Bruder*, part 1, 186–9.

28 Harrington, *The Gospel of Matthew*, 360; Lohfink, *Option for the Poor*, 76; Donahue, "'Parable,'" 30: "Treatment of the least, who I have argued are Christians in mission and witness to the world, becomes the occasion by which the true meaning of justice is revealed. The parable reveals that justice is constituted by acts of loving-kindness and mercy to those in need; the world will be made 'right' or 'just' when the way the least are treated becomes the norm of action. What is done positively *for* them is not to be limited *to* them." This interpretation removes the oddness of judging the nations, or gentiles, not by their acceptance of the Christian message but by their caring for the physical needs of the messengers.

29 Simcox, *First Gospel*, 273.
30 Schweizer, *Good News*, 476.
31 Toussaint, *Behold the King*, 291. Cf. Beare, *The Gospel according to Matthew*, 496: "The King looks upon all who are in need as his brothers, and takes any failure to meet their need as failure to give him honour."
32 Lubich, *When Our Love Is Charity*, 95 (paragraph break omitted). See Oudersluys, "Parable," 155.
33 Preiss, *Life in Christ*, 52. For critique, see Oudersluys, "Parable," 157.
34 Rahner, *Theological Investigations*, vol. 6, 234.
35 Simcox, *The First Gospel*, 273 ("he is personally *in* every human being").
36 "Tout se passe plutôt, si l'on se contente de suivre le déroulé du texte, comme si ce lien qu'établissait Jésus avec ses indigents était seulement temporaire ou momentané, c'est-à-dire seulement partiel, lié à une phase bien précise, s'établissant et se maintenant dans le moment ou ils étaient dans le besoin mais se dissolvant par après" (Farahian, "Relire Matthieu 15, 31–46," 448).
37 "In some passages Jesus identifies himself with the apostles or with those he has sent out; in others, with his followers; and in still others, with every human being" (Lubich, *When Our Love Is Charity*, 94).
38 MacArthur, *Matthew 24–28*, 124.
39 "The Son of Man thus identifies himself with the cause of all men whom, as the Servant of God, Is 53, he purchased with his death" (Jones, *Matthew*, 283). See Lubich, *When Our Love Is Charity*, 97; Oudersluys, "Parable," 156; Simcox, *The First Gospel*, 273.
40 "Jesus considers that what one does to one whom he loves is done to himself, just as I take as done to me what is done to my mother or father or sister or brother" (Kilgallen, *Brief Commentary*, 198).
41 Sider, *Rich Christians*, 78–9.
42 Fitzmyer, *The Gospel According to Luke*, 1045.
43 Ibid.
44 Ibid., 1047.
45 Ibid., 1045.
46 Nolland, *Luke 9:21–18:34*, 751.
47 Ibid.
48 Morris, *The Gospel according to John*, 229.
49 Ibid., 229–30.
50 Fitzmyer, *The Gospel According to Luke*, 465.
51 Ibid., 469.
52 Ibid., 1132.

53 Ibid., 884.
54 Ibid., 1075.
55 Nolan, *Jesus Before Christianity*, 44–5.
56 Ibid., 22.
57 Barton, *Discipleship and Family Ties*, 222; Kelsey, *Caring*, 88: "If there was one point at which Jesus may have underestimated human frailty, it may have been in his failure to see the difficulties his followers might have in their intimate relationships. Jesus simply assumed that we would love our families, our children, our wives, husbands, brothers and sisters, parents and grandparents, our friends and intimates – even as the good heathen do. He was quite clear in what is reported in the Sermon on the Mount: 'If you love only those who love you, what reward can you expect? Surely the tax-gatherers do as much as that. And if you greet only your brothers, what is there extraordinary about that? Even the heathen do as much' (Matthew 5:46–7)."

4: PATRISTIC POSITIONS

1 E.g., Ambrose, *Expos. Evang. sec. Luc.* 8.74–7 (PL 15, 1788–89); Jerome, *In Matth.* 2.15 (PL 26, 105–6); Caesarius of Arles, Sermon 34.1 (*Sermons*, vol. 1, 168; cf. PL 57, 903).
2 Boniface Ramsey, "Almsgiving in the Latin Church," 233.
3 Ambrose, *De offic.* 1.32.169 (PL 16, 72). See Ambrose, *Expos. Evang. sec. Luc.* 8.77,79 (PL 15, 1789–90).
4 Augustine, *In I Ep. Ioh.* 8.4 (PL 35, 2038). Cf. *De civ. Dei* 19.14 (PL 41, 643), and *De doctr. christ.* 1.28.29 (PL 34, 30).
5 Caesarius of Arles, Sermon 34.2 (*Sermons*, vol. 1, 168; cf. PL 57, 903).
6 O'Donovan, *Problem*, 122, quoting from *De civ. Dei* 19.14.
7 Augustine, *De doct. christ.* 1.28.29.
8 Caesarius of Arles, Sermon 34.1 (*Sermons*, vol. 1, 168; cf. PL 57, 903).
9 Broad, "Certain Features," 55–6; Brock, "Utilitarianism and Aiding Others," 227–8; Dewey and Tufts, *Ethics*, 390; R. M. Hare, *Moral Thinking*, 137; Houlgate, "Ethical Theory and the Family," 70–2; Kaufman, *The Context of Decision*, 103–4; Outka, *Agape*, 273–4; Paley, *Moral and Political Philosophy*, 209–10; Paulsen, *A System of Ethics*, 393; Pope, "The Order of Charity," 278–9; Rachels, "Morality, Parents and Children," 53–4; Schüller, *Die Begründung sittlicher Urteile*, 74–5; Singer, *The Expanding Circle*, 36, and *Practical Ethics* (1993), 233, and "Reconsidering the Famine Relief Argument," 44; Sparshott, *An Enquiry into Goodness*, 286.

The utilitarian approach is nicely summarized in Donaldson, "Morally Privileged Relationships," 24–5.

10 Outka, "Love," 746.

11 Becker, *Reciprocity*, 217–18; Singer, *The Expanding Circle*, 153.

12 Basil, *Homil. in divites* (PG 31, 282).

13 Ambrose, *De offic.* 3.3.15 (PL 16, 149).

14 Gregory the Great, *Moralia*, 21.19.31 (PL 76, 208). Cf. ibid., 19.24.41 (PL 76, 124). See Alulfus of Tournai, *Expos. Nov. Test.* 58 (PL 79, 1219): "qui indiget eo ipso quo homo est etiam incognitus non est."

15 Lactantius, *Inst. div.* 6.10 (*The Divine Institutes*, 417). See Spanneut, *Tertullien*, 165–7.

16 Spanneut, *Tertullien*, 28–9.

17 Basil, Sermon 3.3 (PG 32, 1152–3).

18 Leo the Great, *Serm.* 41.3 (PL 54, 274).

19 Maximus of Turin, *Homil.* 64 (PL 57, 382): "Et iterum: *Qui fratrem suum odit homicida est* (I Joann. III). Hoc loco fratrem omnem hominem oportet intelligi; omnes in Christo fratres sumus."

20 Winslow, "Gregory of Nazianzus," 352.

21 Ward, *The Lopsided World*, 23.

22 Bruner, *Matthew*, 923. Cf. Winandy (with equal lack of documentation): "Ce fut, si je ne me trompe, l'opinion, sinon unanime, du moins la plus répandue parmi les anciens" ("La scène du Jugement Dernier," 180).

23 Some examples: Augustine, *Serm.* 25.8.8 (PL 38, 170–1), *Serm.* 36.9.9 (PL 38, 219), *Serm.* 39.6.8 (PL 38, 240), *Serm.* 86.3.3 (PL 38, 524–5), *Serm.* 388.1 (PL 39, 1700), Serm. 390.2 (PL 39, 1706), sermon attributed to Augustine, 51.2 (PL 39, 1842–3); Caesarius of Arles, *De decem virgin.* (PL 67, 1161); Gaudentius, *Serm.* 13 (PL 20, 939–41); Gregory Nazianzen, *De paup. amore* 39–40 (PG 35, 910); Gregory of Nyssa, *De paup. amandis* (PG 46, 472–3); John Chrysostom, *De poenitentia* 7.7 (PG 49, 334), *In Epist. ad Rom.* 15.6 (PG 60, 547); Lawrence of Novara, *Homil.* 2 (PL 66, 107–8); Leo, *Serm.* 18.3 (PL 54, 185), *Serm.* 35.3 (PL 54, 290), *Serm.* 91.3 (PL 54, 452–3), *Serm.* 94.4 (PL 54, 460); Paulinus, *Epist.* 1.1 (PL 61, 154); Maximus of Turin, *Serm.* 18 (PL 57, 570); Peter Chrysologus, *Serm.* 9 (PL 52, 213), *Serm.* 14 (PL 52, 232), *Serm.* 41 (PL 52, 317), *Serm.* 42 (PL 52, 320); *Comment. in LXXV psalm.* 24.4, 36.22, attributed to Rufinus (PL 21, 731, 780); Valerianus, *Homil.* 4.7 (PL 52, 705), *Homil.* 7.3 (PL 52, 714), *Homil.* 8.2 (PL 52, 717), *Homil.* 9.1,2 (PL 52, 719 and 721); Zacchaeus Christianus, *Consult.* (PL 20, 1148–9).

24 Paulinus, *Epist.* 13.22 (PL 61, 220). Cf. Haymo, *Homil.* 29: "Licet in

omnibus pauperibus Christus recipiatur, et in omnibus illi eleemosyna largiatur" (PL 118, 204).

25 Paulinus, *Epist.* 32.20 (PL 61, 340).
26 Rabanus Maurus, *De cleric. instit.* 2.28 (PL 107, 340). See also Maximus of Turin, *Serm.* 18 (PL 57, 570) and 21 (PL 57, 578).
27 Rabanus Maurus, *Homil.* 10 (PL 110, 23).
28 On this theme, see Clement of Alexandria, *Paedag.*, 2. 12 (PG 8, 541–3); Ambrose, *De offic.* 1.28.132–137 (PL 16, 62–3), and *De Nab. Jez.* 1.2 (PL 14, 731); Chrysostom, *In Epist. I ad Tim.* 12.4 (PG 62, 563–4); Basil, Homily 6 (PG 31, 276) and Homily 8.8 (PG 31, 325); Gregory the Great, *Reg. Past.* 3.21 (PL 77, 87); Bouvier, *Précepte de l'aumône*, 179–80; H. Lio, "Determinatio superflui," 108 ("Canonistae . . . explicite et quasi unanimiter docent in statu extremae necessitatis omnia esse communia id est *communicanda*"); Giordani, *Social Message*, 317–19; Healy, "The Fathers," 446; Mollat, *The Poor in the Middle Ages*, 23; *Property: Its Duties and Rights*, 90, 164–5, 175; White, *Christian Ethics*, 56.
29 *Barnabas*, 19.8. See *Didache*, 4.8.
30 Chrysostom, *In Epist. I ad Cor.* 10.3 (PG 61, 85–6). See Zeno of Verona, *Tract.* 1.3.6 (PL 11, 287): "scire cupio, quae sint tua, cum sint timentibus Deum universa communia . . . sicut dies, sol, nox, pluvia, nascendi atque moriendi conditio: quae humano generi, sine personarum aliqua exceptione, aequabiliter justitia est divina largita."
31 Caesarius of Arles, Sermon 34.2 (*Sermons*, vol. 1, 168–9; see PL 57, 903). Cf. Christophe, *Les devoirs moraux des riches*, 211: "Ce qui est constant chez les Pères, c'est que le superflu doit servir à l'usage de tous."
32 "Clement's thought, with its emphasis on detachment and simplicity, is indeed generally representative of Early Christian thought on the subject of wealth except for that of the primitive Palestinian church," which sometimes took a still sterner view of wealth (Countryman, *The Rich Christian*, 89).
33 Clement of Alexandria, *Paedag.* 3.7 (PG 8, 609).
34 Caesarius of Arles, Sermon 34.2 (*Sermons*, vol. 1, 168).
35 In addition to the following examples, see Basil, Homily 7 (PG 31, 297–9); Jerome, *Epist.* 120.1 (CSEL 55, 477), and *Reg. Monach.* 4 (PL 30, 330); Nectarius, *De festo S. Theodori* 18 (PG 39, 1835); Benedict, *Cod. Reg.* (PL 103, 497); *Inter. div. mandat.* 20 (PG 106, 1365); sermons 60 and 64 attributed to Fulgentius (PL 65, 930 and 936). Augustine's letter to Ecdicia contains what might seem an exception to this rule, since he blames her for giving money to some poor monks which might have gone to her children. His

chief complaint, however, is that she gave the money without the knowledge and consent of her husband (PL 33, 1080).

36 Basil, Homily 7 (PG 31, 293).
37 Basil, *In Matt.* 66.4 (PG 58, 630).
38 Augustine, Sermon 9.20 (*Sermons*, vol. 1, 276).
39 Augustine, Sermon 86.11 (*Sermons*, vol. 3, 401).
40 Caesarius, *Epist. ad quosdam Germanos* (PL 67, 1158).
41 Basil, Homily 7 (PG 31, 293).
42 Basil, Homily 21.8 (PG 31, 553).
43 Augustine, Sermon 9.20,21 (*Sermons*, vol. 1, 276, 277). See *Serm.* 86.8.9–12.14 (PL 38, 527–9); *In Psalm.* 38.11–12 (PL 36, 422–4); *In Psalm.* 48 1.14 (PL 36, 552–3).
44 Giordani, *Social Message*, 307, citing Cyprian, *De op. et eleem.* 16,17 (PL 4, 613–15).
45 Basil, Homily 8.6 (PG 31, 321).
46 Chrysostom, *Incomprehensible Nature*, 218 (PG 48, 771). See Chrysostom, *De eleem.* 3 (PG 51, 265), and compare *Homil. in Gen.* 42.6, 7 (PG 54, 393–5). After noting how the widow did not share with her children but gave all to Elijah, Zeno of Verona remarks: "Quapropter si pater bonus, si providus, si utilis esse desideras, sicut ille Abraham, Deum plus debes amare, quam filios, ut habere merearis integros, incolumes, ac beatos" (*Tract.* 1.3.7; PL 11, 288).
47 Winslow, "Gregory of Nazianzus," 350–1.
48 Jerome, *Epist.* 120.1 (CSEL 55, 478). Compare an anonymous early exhortation to monks (PL 18, 76): " 'Thesaurizate autem vobis thesauros in coelo, ubi neque tinea, neque aerugo exterminant, et ubi fures non effodiunt, nec furantur' . . . Hoc enim ei, qui non caret filiis, hortamentum est; qui caret, imperium."
49 Margaret Farley (drawing on Greer, *Broken Lights and Mended Lives*, ch. 4) cites, and questions, a larger patristic framework: "the themes of asceticism, of desire for the vision of God through contemplation, and of the church itself as a substitute family converged to hold in place through centuries a view of marriage and family as subordinate to other forms of Christian living and other spheres of Christian works" ("Family," 373).
50 Accounts of Christians who, despite dependents and relatives, risked their lives for the plague-stricken may be revealing in this regard. See Riquet, *Christian Charity in Action*, 57–8.
51 The Fathers' grounds should be distinguished from the motivation they so often invoked: "Unfortunately, the instincts of pity and unselfish generosity were not sufficiently developed in the average Christian to make it possible to meet the enormous needs of the

time in reliance upon these alone. Some more effective stimulus was needed: and the most effective stimulus of all was to convince a congregation that not only would their alms benefit their brethren, but that they would benefit themselves. Thus the appeal to self-interest which we have noticed making its appearance in the Church writers of the third century became more marked in those of the fourth – in proportion as both the need was greater and the old enthusiasm waxed more faint" (Phillips, *The New Commandment*, 140).

52 *Didache*, 1.5. The question is whether the Greek verb *lambanei* should be translated "take," as by James Kleist (Westminster, MD: Newman, 1948), or "receive," as by Francis Glimm, Joseph Manque, and Gerald Walsh (New York: CIMA, 1947).

53 Mollat, *The Poor in the Middle Ages*, 111.

54 Aquinas, *Summa theol.* 2–2.32.7. ad 3. See also ibid., 2–2.66.7. On later development of this thesis, see, e.g., Deuringer, *Probleme*, 136 (strengthening), and Crofts, *Property and Poverty*, 207–8 (broadening).

55 For a specially full discussion, see de Lugo, *De justitia et de iure*, 318–37 ("Quando necessitas accipientis rem alienam, excuset a furto").

56 Serafino da Lojano, *Institutiones theologiae moralis*, vol. 2, 129.

57 James O'Neill, "Alms and Almsgiving," 329, citing: "Basil, Homil. in illud Lucae, No. 7, P.G. XXXI, 278; St. Gregory of Nyssa, De Pauperibus Amandis, P.G. XLVI, 466; St. Chrysostom, in Ep. I ad Cor., Homil. 10, c. 3, P.G. LXI, 86; St. Ambrose, De Nab. lib. unus, P.L. XIV, 747; St. Augustine, in Ps. cxlvii, P.L. XXXVII, 1922." See also Basil, Homily 6 (PG 31, 276); Chrysostom, *De Lazaro* 1.12 (PG 48, 980), and *In Psalm. 48.2* (PG 55, 515); Jerome, *Reg. monach.* 4 (PL 30, 331); Augustine, *Serm.* 50.2.4 (PL 38, 327) and *Serm.* 206.2 (PL 38, 1041); and those in whom the teaching continued, e.g., Petrus Cantor, *Verbum abbreviatum*, ch. 104 (PL 205, 287); Peter Damian, *De eleemosyna*, ch. 1 (PL 145, 211); Gratian, *Decr.* 47 (PL 187, 248); Vio, "De eleemosynae praecepto," 20–1; Vitoria, *De caritate et prudentia*, 170–1; Tyndale, "Parable," 97; Challoner, *Meditations*, 307.

58 Hermas, *Pastor* 114.3; Zeno of Verona, *Tract.* 1.3.6 (PL 11, 287): "nec intelligis, quia homini inopia morienti, tantis opibus qui cum possit subvenire, non subvenit, ipse eum videtur occidere?"

59 E.g., Abelard, *Serm.* 30 (PL 178, 566–7); Antoninus, *Summa theologica*, vol. 1, 710; Vio, "De eleemosynae praecepto," 34–5; Raymond of Peñafort, *Summa de paenitentia*, 835; Vatican Council II, *Gaudium et spes* 69. Cf. Luther, "The Large Catechism," 391.

60 Early attributed, perhaps correctly, to Leo the Great (PL 54, 490), this dictum acquired great vogue after Gratian, who attributed it to Ambrose (*Decr.* 86.21). In agreement with this saying, Lio ("Finalmente rintracciata," 359–61) cites: Augustine, *Cont. Faustum* 15.7 (PL 42, 310); Pseudo-Caesarius of Arles, *Homil. XVI De decimis* (PL 67, 1079C); Pseudo-Jerome, *Ad Romanos* 13, (PL 30, 734 [rather, 705]); Rabanus Maurus, *In Exod.* 2.12 (PL 108, 99D); Pseudo-Bede, *Quaest. super Exodum* 30 (PL 93, 374–5); *Glossa ordin.*, *In Deuter.* 5.16 (PL 113, 458); *Glossa interlin.*, *Deut.* 5.16–17. See also Basil, Homily 8.7 (PG 31, 321); Lactantius, *Inst. div.*, 6.11 (PL 6, 674); Gregory the Great, *Reg. past.* 3.21 (PL 77, 87).

61 Outka states more generally: "To set boundaries includes the minimal moral prohibitions against our doing anything whatever to those outside the personal relations and social groups with which we identify for the sake of those inside. In the case of friendship, Gilbert Meilaender defends a promising approach by urging us 'to prefer some to others, but to remain open to those others and refuse to harm them for the sake of those we prefer . . .'" ("Universal Love and Impartiality," 90).

62 Beugnet, "Aumône," 2565. See Ch. Antoine, "L'aumône," 321; Albert the Great, *In 4 Sent.* 15.16: "Ad id autem quod obicitur de Ambrosio, dicendum quod ipse loquitur interpretative, non proprie. Et est sensus: 'Si non paveris, occidisti,' id est, per occasionem reputabitur tibi in culpam, licet non tantam, quanta esset si manu occideret; et hoc ideo, quia cum posset dando vitam prolongare, non fecit."

63 Augustine, *De civ. Dei* 19.14 (PL 41, 643).

64 For parity, see, e.g., Nancy Davis, "The Priority of Avoiding Harm," 174 ("moral asymmetry views face serious difficulties"); Glover, *Causing Death and Saving Lives*, ch. 7; Hall, "Acts and Omissions," 407–8 ("I think we must conclude that the act/omission distinction cannot be made except in certain favoured cases, which there is no ground for supposing to have any special moral significance"); Harris, "Bad Samaritans Cause Harm," 69 ("in all cases where we fail to save those we could save we are causally responsible for their fate; they die *because* we do not help them"); Rachels, "Killing and Starving to Death," 159 ("letting die is just as bad as killing"); Peter Singer, *Practical Ethics*, 222 ("If, then, allowing someone to die is not intrinsically different from killing someone, it would seem that we are all murderers"). Against parity, see, e.g., Foot, "The Problem of Abortion," 26–7; Haslett, "Is Allowing Someone to Die"; Kamm, "Killing and Letting Die"; Ross, *The Right and the Good*, 21–2 ("even when we

have come to recognize the duty of beneficence, it appears to me that the duty of non-maleficence is recognized as a distinct one, and as *prima facie* more binding"); Trammell, "Saving Life and Taking Life."

65 Cottingham, "Ethics and Impartiality," 92 (not Cottingham's view).

66 Rachels, "Killing and Starving to Death," 164.

67 Goodin, *Protecting the Vulnerable*, 25. Cohen ("Who Is Starving Whom?", 69–72), Glover (*Causing Death and Saving Lives*, 94–112, 116), and Isaacs ("Moral Theory and Action Theory," 356–63) argue to a similar conclusion.

68 For a similar conclusion but different listing, complementing mine, see Peter Singer, *Practical Ethics*, 228–9.

69 Conway, "Failing to Save Lives," 111. Cf. Singer, *Practical Ethics*, 223.

70 Boyle, "On Killing and Letting Die," 452. Cf. Atkinson, "Ambiguities," 164.

71 Hughes, "Killing and Letting Die," 43–4.

72 Hallett, *Greater Good*, 8–10, 91–9.

73 Tooley, *Abortion and Infanticide*, 188. See Tooley, "An Irrelevant Consideration," 59.

74 Regis, "Rachels," 417. Cf. Foot, "Killing, Letting Die, and Euthanasia."

75 Cf. Glover, *Causing Death and Saving Lives*, 107–8.

76 Psychologically, warns Colin McGinn, "[i]t is a dangerous mistake to elide the distinction between murder and uncharitableness, since this is liable to weaken our condemnation of murder and other abominations" (Review, 57). The danger looks greater on the other side. Whereas no empirical evidence backs McGinn's surmise (have Goodin and like-minded ethicians grown soft on murder?), there is no mistaking the effect which this commonly accepted distinction, between death by commission and death by omission, has had in condoning neglect of the desperately needy.

5: THE THOMISTIC TRADITION

1 Philip the Chancellor, *Summa de bono*, 708. Cf. Lombard, *Sent.* 3.29.3 (PL 192, 817), where enemies replace strangers (the latter being understood). On the early history of this ordering, see Guimet, "Notes," 379–80.

2 Aquinas, *In III Sent.* 29; *Summa theol.* 2–2.26.

3 Aquinas, *Summa theol.* 2–2.26.9. ad 2.

4 Ibid., ad 1. Cf. Aquinas, *De caritate* 9. ad 18: "sed in subventione

necessariorum plus tenetur homo filio quam parenti, quia parentes debent thesaurizare filiis, et non e converso, ut dicitur 1 Corinth. 4."

5 Aquinas, *Summa theol.* 2–2.26.9.c. See Aquinas, *In X lib. Eth.* 8.12.

6 Augustine, *Faith, Hope, and Charity,* 72.

7 Aquinas, *Summa theol.* 2–2.32.6.c.

8 Ibid., a. 5, c.

9 Aquinas, *Summa theol.* 2–2.32.5. ad 3. Cajetan rightly resists a minimalist, conjunctive reading of these two conditions (Vio, "De eleemosynae praecepto," 5–6).

10 Cf. Anderson, *Traditional Europe,* on tenth-century society, in which later distinctions were already present: "The upper class ranged from court nobility to backwoods gentry. Urbanites ranged from common laborers and immigrant peasants to rich merchants and patriarchs hostile to the aristocracy. Peasants ranged from landless serfs to wealthy landholders" (16).

11 Aquinas, *Summa theol.* 2–2.32.6.c. See Aquinas, *In IV Sent.* 15.2.4.3.

12 Aquinas, *Summa theol.* 2–2.32.6.c.

13 Ibid.

14 Compare the contrast between "ad sui status decentem conservationem" (Vio, "De eleemosynae praecepto," 7) and "ad sui status conservationem."

15 Aquinas, *In IV Sent.* 15.2.1.4.sol.4.

16 Riquet, *Le chrétien face à l'argent,* 90 (citing our text, *Summa theol.* 2–2.32.6). *Summa theol.* 2–2.118.4. ad 2 supports the "should," though not the "all." Cf. Bañez, *De fide, spe, et charitate,* 720; Menendez Reigada, "Obligaciones," 351.

17 See Vio, *Commentaria,* vol. 8, 256, and "De eleemosynae praecepto," 5–12; Soto, "Commentarium," 155, n. 55; Bouvier, *Le précepte de l'aumône,* 40–52.

18 Aquinas, *Quod.* 7.12.c. Cf. *Summa theol.* 2–2.185.7. ad 1.

19 Bouvier, *Le précepte de l'aumône,* 51.

20 Vio, "De eleemosynae praecepto," 19.

21 Ibid., 6.

22 Vitoria, *De caritate et prudentia,* 169.

23 Concina, *Theologia christiana dogmatico-moralis,* vol. 2, 22. Cf. Castro Palao, *Operis moralis,* 402 ("sic fere omnes Doctores"); Paul-Gabriel Antoine, *Theologia moralis universa,* pt. 1, 193 (*"Est communis & certa sententia,* inquit Platellius . . . *Ita Suarez, Valentia, Sanchez & alii multi"*). However, concerning the definition of extreme need ("extrema necessitas"), there was not perfect agreement: "Prima dicitur extrema, quae est de rebus necessariis ad vitam conservandam, ita ut si de iis non subveniatur homini, periculum sit

morale quod brevi moriatur. Illud autem, *brevi*, explicat Ledesma II. part. iv. qu. xiii. art. 3. ita ut in una hyeme, vel in uno vere moriatur. Cajetanus vero tom. I. *opusc.* tract. xvi. *de indulgent.* quaest. 3. dicit esse extremam necessitatem, quando non apparet alia via qua illi subveniatur, licet longe sit a morte, Soto lib. V. *de Justitia*, qu. III. art. iv. vers. *Circa tertiam*, dicit esse etiam extremam, quando homo approprinquat periculo morbi incurabilis, aut alterius miseriae, quae homines solet conficere. Angelus, et Bannes apud Sanchez nu. 6 dicunt, esse etiam extremam, quando est in periculo amittendi membrum principale, vel sensus sui corporis" (Lugo, *De iustitia et de iure*, 318–9).

24 Brouillard explains: "C'est au confesseur, aux perplexités de sa conscience, à sa lourde charge de juge que les casuistes ont avant tout songé" ("La doctrine catholique de l'aumône," 24). Only sin concerns the confessor, especially mortal sin (ibid., 27).

25 Soto, "Commentarium," 146. See, e.g., Kol, *Theologia moralis*, vol. 1, 248 ("cum magno incommodo"); Torres, *Disputationes*, 11 ("cum magno aliquo detrimento proprii status"); Zalba, *Theologiae moralis summa*, 745 ("cum magno incommodo"), 746 ("etiam cum notabili sacrificio"). De Vitoria suggests as illustrations: marrying one's daughters less well; going by foot rather than by horse; doing with one manservant rather than four (*De caritate et prudentia*, 170).

26 Leo XIII, *Rerum novarum*, 22. The quotation is from Aquinas, *Summa theol.* 2–2.32.6.

27 Ferreres, *Compendium theologiae moralis*, vol. 1, 191–2 (citing St. Alphonsus, n. 31 and n. 297, q. 3).

28 Sporer, *Theologia moralis*, vol. 1, 465. See Peter La Palu and Durandus, in Vio, "De eleemosynae praecepto," 36; Antonius a S. Joseph, *Compendium Salmanticense*, vol. 1, 191; Bucceroni, *Institutiones theologiae moralis*, vol. 1, 329; Soto, "Commentarium," 146; Bellarmino, *De controversiis christianae fidei*, vol. 4, 721; Prümmer, *Manuale theologiae moralis*, vol. 1, 427; Toledo, *Enarratio*, vol. 2, 202.

29 McHugh and Callan, *Moral Theology*, vol. 1, 494. See, e.g., Bucceroni, *Institutiones theologiae moralis*, vol. 1, 329; Drexel, *Gazophylacium Christi*, 194.

30 Tournely, *De universa theologia morali*, vol. 3, 294. See James O'Neill, "Alms and Almsgiving," 329 (citing Suarez, *De caritate*, Disp. vii, §4, n. 3).

31 James O'Neill, "Alms and Almsgiving," 329. For this standard view, see, e.g., Alsina, *Compendium theologiae moralis*, vol., 355, 357; Beugnet, "Aumône," 2567; Bouquillon, *Institutiones theologiae moralis specialis*, 326; Bucceroni, *Institutiones theologiae moralis*, vol. 1, 329; Häring, *The Law of Christ*, vol. 2, 383; La Croix, *Theologia moralis*,

vol. 1, 106; Lehmkuhl, *Theologia moralis*, vol. 1, 362; Liguori, *Theologia moralis*, vol. 1, 327; Marc and Gestermann, *Institutiones moralis alphonsianae*, vol. 1, 314; Merkelbach, *Summa theologiae moralis*, vol. 1, 709; Vermeersch, *Theologiae moralis*, vol. 2, 82–4.

32 Prümmer, *Manuale theologiae moralis*, vol. 1, 427. For this standard argument, with variations, see, e.g., Billuart, *Summa Summae Sancti Thomae*, vol. 3, 881; Henry Davis, *Moral and Pastoral Theology*, vol. 1, 324; Diana, *Coordinati*, vol. 4, 213; Fanfani, *Manuale theorico-practicum theologiae moralis*, vol. 2, 126, 159; Jone, *Moral Theology*, 87, 144; Lanza and Palazzini, *Theologia moralis*, vol. 2, 204; Menendez Reigada, "Obligaciones," 352; Merkelbach, *Summa theologiae moralis*, vol. 1, 710; Roncaglia, *Universa moralis theologia*, vol. 1, 178; Zalba, *Theologiae moralis summa*, vol. 1, 746.

33 Lanza and Palazzini, *Theologia moralis*, vol. 2, 204.

34 Hallett, *Christian Neighbor-Love*, ch. 4.

35 Ibid., chs. 5 and 6.

36 Aquinas, *Summa theol.* 2–2.26.4 (trans. R. J. Batten). For Aquinas's other arguments, with critique, see Hallett, *Christian Neighbor-Love*, 65–8.

37 Hallett, *Christian Neighbor-Love*, 66–7.

38 Summers, *Commentary on Luke*, 279.

39 Vermeersch, *Theologiae moralis*, vol. 2, 83: "Bona dicuntur *necessaria* aut *superflua*; idque sive respectu vitae cuiuspiam propriae et suorum (quibuscum moraliter pro una persona habetur) sive respectu status seu condicionis."

40 Denis the Carthusian, *Commentaria in Quartum Librum Sententiarum*, 418 ("Exigit ergo praeceptum Dei, ut id quod homini superest ultra decentem sui ipsius ac suorum provisionem, indigentibus communicet et impendat, potissime in necessitate"); Bouvier, *Le précepte de l'aumône*, 22 ("soi, les siens: première catégorie; les étrangers: deuxième catégorie"). Prior to Thomas, cf. Chobham, *Summa confessorum*, 312 ("Potest tamen breviter dici quod omnia illa dicuntur esse necessaria homini que necessaria sunt ad sustentationem suam et ad honestam provisionem familie sue").

41 Aquinas, *Summa theol.* 2–2.32.5.c (Blackfriars translation).

42 Ibid., a. 6, c. Cf. Vasquez, "Tractatus de eleemosyna," 12: "In hac re primo conueniunt omnes cum S. Thom. art. 6. quod dare eleemosynam de necessariis naturae pro se, & sua familia, non obligat . . ."

43 Cano, "Commentarium," 171.

44 Aquinas, *Summa theol.* 2–2.26.6.

45 "Es wäre durchaus verfehlt," insists Otto Schilling, "den Begriff des standesgemässen Lebens aus der Moral zu streichen,

allerdings lässt sich nicht genau bestimmen, was noch zum standesgemässen Auskommen gehört und was nicht mehr, gleichwohl bleibt es ein rationeller, unentbehrlicher Begriff für die christliche Moral, wie er denn ein wesentliches Mittel ist für die christliche Tradition, um die sozialen Forderungen zu bestimmen" (*Handbuch der Moraltheologie*, vol. 3, 105).

46 In the East, see for instance Chrysostom, Homily 28.10 (*Homilies on Genesis*, 189–90), or Basil, Homily 7 (PG 31, 281).

47 Jerome, *Epist.* 120.1 (PL 22, 985).

48 Ambrose, *De offic.* 1.30.151 (PL 16, 67).

49 Augustine, *In Ioann.* 10.2.6 (PL 35, 1469).

50 Augustine, *Enar. in Psalm.* 147.12 (PL 37, 1922).

51 Augustine, Sermon 61.12 (*Sermons*, vol. 3, 147).

52 Savonarola, *De simplicitate christianae vitae*, 99–100.

53 "Hinc *statui* necessaria censentur ea quae requiruntur ad famulos sustentandos, hospites recipiendos, ad honestas donationes, ad convivia de more instauranda, ad moderatam pro conditione pompam, etc. Ita *communiter*" (Ferreres, *Compendium theologiae moralis*, 197). "Immo, ut docet S. Alphonsus (l.3, n.32): 'Necessarium ad decentiam status . . . habet latitudinem eo maiorem quo status est maior'" (Génicot and Salsmans, *Institutiones theologiae moralis*, vol. 1, 174).

54 Henry Brown, *Egalitarianism*, 32. Implicit here is a point which Walter Shewring makes explicit: "In the feudal society of the Middle Ages it was taken for granted that wealth should follow status – that a man of important social functions should have wealth to live comfortably, not that a man who chanced to be wealthy should therefore be given a high social status" (*Rich and Poor*, 21). Cf. Stone, "Class Divisions in England, 1540–1640," 14: "Money was the means of acquiring and retaining status, but it was not the essence of it: the acid test was the mode of life, a concept that involved many factors."

55 "Every man can licitly use his possessions in order to live in accordance with his social status. This would include, for example, the support of his family and the education of his children in order that they might maintain the same social status" (Bender, "Almsgiving," 58).

56 William Paley (no Thomist, but expressing the common view), in *Moral and Political Philosophy*, 215.

57 "Inter ea quae statui necessaria sunt, a multis AA. recensentur ea quae reservantur *ad altiorem statum acquirendum*" (Génicot and Salsmans, *Institutiones theologiae moralis*, vol. 1, 174).

58 Valencia, *Commentariorum theologicorum*, vol. 3, 652–3. See also

Tournely, *De universa theologia morali*, vol. 3, 290–1 (citing Cajetan and Silvius). Bañez adds a rare proviso: "quando in republica sunt graves & urgentes necessitates, non est licitum ascendere ad statum altiorem, si per hoc eleemosynae impediantur" (*De fide, spe, et charitate*, 723). In a still more contrary vein, compare Denis the Carthusian, *Summa de vitiis et virtutibus*, 74: "Si vero possideat tanta sicut progenitores praedecessoresque sui, et nihilo minus enitatur magis ditari, ad majora aspirans, ut ad meliora connubia pro se aut sobole sua, vel ad equitaturam ac familiam copiosiorem, seu ad majores expensas, ut majoribus se aequetur, vel ad abundantiorem thesaurum, sive ad majorem honorem aut famam; vitiosum est et avaritiae vitium."

59 Liguori, *Theologia moralis*, vol. 1, 326.

60 Toledo, *Enarratio*, vol. 2, 198. Cf. Vasquez, "Tractatus de eleemosyna," 20; Brouillard, "La doctrine catholique de l'aumône," 27–8; Lugo, *De iustitia et de iure*, vol. 6, 319: "Secundum genus est eorum quae sunt necessaria ad statum, scilicet ad decentem suum suorumque statum conservandum, habita ratione, non omnium possibilium, sed eorum quae prudenter timeri, et expectari possunt. Ita omnes doctores, quos congerit Sanchez nu. 10. Unde multi sub hoc genere includunt convivia et munera honesta, ac liberalitates moderatas juxta statum. Includit etiam hoc genus, quae reservantur ad dotes filiarum, et ad necessitates communiter occurrentes morborum, bellorum, et famis. Alii extendunt ad id quod reservatur pro alumnis vel consanguineis indigentibus. Imo alii dicunt non censeri superflua statui, quae aliquis ex fine honesto congerit ad dotandas capellanias, vel erigendam ecclesiam, vel etiam ut comparet altiorem statum, ad quem idoneus est. Quod multis adductis, probabile putat Sanchez nu. 19. et Vasquez dub. III. nu. 26. Unde Corduba dicto lib. I. q. 18. infert, paucos esse, qui superflua statui habeant."

61 Where I have highlighted contrast, Henry Brown sees more continuity: "We have seen how the Christian Fathers accepted the existing differences of rank and status, from the highest constituted authority down to and even including slavery. These differences had become necessary to control the vicious propensities of human nature after the Fall. But they could not be maintained unless they were supported by corresponding differences of wealth and income. The Christian Fathers therefore held those differences to be just. What the Church came to teach about both property and wages was that their amount should be appropriate to a man's station in life" (*Egalitarianism*, 31).

62 On the prior history of these and other such terms, see Mollat,

The Poor in the Middle Ages, 105, and Duby, *The Three Orders*, 351. For Aquinas's perception of his own ambiance, see Archibald, "The Concept of Social Hierarchy in the Writings of St. Thomas Aquinas."

63 "During the last six centuries of European history there has been a basic change in the structure of differential evaluation of occupational roles. In the earlier part of this period, the military, landowning-and-managing, governmental, and religious official roles were more highly evaluated than commercial, industrial, scientific, teaching, and various other professional roles . . . Gradually, and everywhere, the functional importance, the number and the relative prestige of 'modern' occupational roles increased in all countries, but the gradual processes involved have not been precisely charted in the way in which, say, the gradual processes of governmental transformations have been studied" (Barber and Barber, *European Social Class*, 2–3).

64 Vermeersch, *Quaestiones de virtutibus*, 258–64.

65 Marshall, *Challenge*, 162; Plant et al., *Political Philosophy and Social Welfare*, 224–5.

66 Even as he exhorted his hearers to greater generosity, Esprit Fléchier, bishop of Nimes, conceded: "Je sais que comme il se trouve diverses demeures dans la maison du Père céleste, il se trouve de même plusieurs états dans le royaume visible de Jésus-Christ; qu'il y a une décence et une splendeur de condition, selon la naissance ou les emplois de chacun, que l'Écriture même approuve, quand on les règle par la loi de Dieu et par la prudence chrétienne, et qui fait parmi les hommes une distinction et une magnificence nécessaire pour autoriser la vertu et pour attirer le respect des peuples" (*Oeuvres complètes*, vol. 1, 980).

67 Henry Brown, *Egalitarianism*, 26.

68 Ibid., 27, quoting F. W. Maitland. "Until quite recently," write Bernard and Elinor Barber, "the predominant type of norm concerning attitudes toward social mobility has been what has been called the 'caste' norm – that is, a norm that disapproves of social mobility" (*European Social Classes*, 8).

69 Gilson, *Christian Philosophy*, 361.

70 Archibald, "The Concept of Social Hierarchy," 53–4.

71 Bouquillon, *Institutiones theologiae moralis specialis*, 326: "amissio totalis vel partialis status reputatur malum gravissimum et societati valde nocivum; cfr. Aeg. De Coninck, I.c.n.134–139; Herinckx, I.c.n.46; Castropalao, l.c.n.6, etc., quorum sententiam maxime fundatam et solide probabilem existimamus." See also, e.g., Concina, *Theologia christiana dogmatico-moralis*, vol. 2, 22.

72 Billuart, *Summa Summae Sancti Thomae*, vol. 8, 81. See Diana, *Coordinati*, vol. 4, 213; Lugo, *De iustitia et de iure*, 324; Fanfani, *Manuale theorico-practicum theologiae moralis*, vol. 2, 159; Piscetta and Gennaro, *Elementa theologiae moralis*, vol. 2, 147.

73 Reiffenstuel, *Theologia moralis*, 102. Cf. Berardi, *Theologia moralis theorico-practica*, vol. 2, 67: "Quod autem divites *non totum* superfluum teneantur dare pauperibus, patet tum communi sensu theologorum; tum quia, sublata facultate adaugendi propria capitalia, ipsi animo deiicerentur, et (cum damno communi) fundorum melioramenta bonaeque agriculturae regulas negligerent, et otio vitiisque magis magisque indulgerent."

74 Shewring, *Rich and Poor*, 8–9.

75 "The doctrine austerely taught by St. Thomas is lovingly dwelt upon by Angela of Foligno, Simone Fidati, Catherine of Siena and Thomas à Kempis. To put it most simply: poverty, not wealth, is the status of Christ on earth; a life of poverty, not a life of wealth, must be for Christians the pattern of perfection" (Shewring, *Rich and Poor*, 23; paragraph break omitted).

76 "Nemo obligatur ad subveniendum cum gravissimo detrimento sui status; nec tenetur ex nobili plebejum, nec ex divite mendicum fieri" (Antonius a S. Joseph, *Compendium Salmanticense*, vol. 1, 191). "Si proximus versetur in necessitate extrema, tunc . . . adest obligatio (etiam in non divite) eidem succurrendi, non equidem ex bonis necessariis vitae . . . sed ex bonis necessariis statui; ita tamen ut quis non iam a statu suo prorsus decidere (v.g. artifex ad mendicitatem se reducere . . .) teneatur" (Berardi, *Theologia moralis theorico-practica*, vol. 2, 66).

77 Lugo, *De iustitia et de iure*, 323. See Pelt, *De tribus bonorum operum generibus*, 34.

78 "By law in many places, trade was placed beneath the dignity of a nobleman and forbidden. By general agreement, agricultural labor was not honorable for an aristocrat. According to a Provençal ordinance, 'To plough, to dig, to carry a load of wood or manure' were activities that automatically deprived a person of knightly privileges" (Anderson, *Traditional Europe*, 32).

79 Lugo, *De iustitia et de iure*, 323. Cf. Pons, *L'amour chrétien*, 11: "L'idée force, dans ces sociétés restées en grande partie féodales (et *feod* veut dire champ et troupeau), c'était de faire durer l'occupation d'un domaine par des hommes d'un même sang. On regardait plus loin que les couples ou les générations; on considérait les lignages, et ceux-ci ont pu faire l'object d'attachements sincères et mêmes passionnés."

80 College of Salamanca, *Cursus theologiae moralis*, vol. 5, 147–8 (citing Bañez and Tapia in agreement).
81 Lugo, *De iustitia et de iure*, 323–4.
82 Barber and Barber, *European Social Class*, 9.
83 David Miller, *Social Justice*, 137.
84 Aloysius Schwartz, *Poverty*, 117.
85 Cf. Singer, *Practical Ethics*, 221 ("Those who are absolutely affluent are not necessarily affluent by comparison with their neighbors, but they are affluent by any reasonable definition of human needs").
86 Loyola, *Constitutions*, 107–8.
87 Cf. Gasper, "Distribution and Development Ethics," 185.
88 Of the bourgeois anxiety to possess and thereby keep up with the Joneses, Henry Fairlie remarks: "Possessing for the sake of possessing is stifling, in us and in our societies, impulses that are more generous, more strenuous, and even more adventurous; it distracts those who might do more serious work, such as many of our artists and writers, into the avaricious pursuit of possessions that neither their work nor their lives in fact require, and in the end pervert and destroy" (*The Seven Deadly Sins Today*, 138).
89 Cf. Brock, "Utilitarianism and Aiding Others," 230; McHugh and Callan, *Moral Theology*, vol. 1, 494: "A well-to-do person is not obliged to sell his office, conveyance, books, and other things needed for his business or profession, in order to rescue a captive held for ransom by bandits." More might be achieved in the long run by staying in business.
90 Aquinas, *Summa theol.* 2–2.32.6.c.
91 College of Salamanca, *Cursus theologiae moralis*, vol. 5, 148.
92 "It Wouldn't Take a Miracle," 22–4.
93 Hernbäck, "A Chance for Children," 74. For a recent, detailed cost analysis, in general agreement, see Unger, *Living High and Letting Die*, 146–8.

6: CONTEMPORARY CONSIDERATIONS

1 Robert Barry, *Breaking the Thread of Life*, 124–9; Chesterton, introduction to Dudley, *Will Men Be Like Gods?*, viii-x; Korff, *Theologische Ethik*, 38–9; Wogaman, *A Christian Method*, 80–2. Cf. Glover, *Causing Death and Saving Lives*, ch. 3. What Christian faith gives it also takes away: belief in an afterlife, both bodily and spiritual, tends to blunt the force of this argument against letting people die. A non-believer might see human life as less precious but also as more threatened by death through starvation.

2 Sider, *Rich Christians*, 84.
3 Nagel, *Equality and Partiality*, 12.
4 Hollenbach, *Claims in Conflict*, 90.
5 Cf. discussion of Alan Donagan's comparable principle, in Hallett, "Christian Moral Norms" and *Greater Good*, chapter 6.
6 David Miller, *Social Justice*, 143–4.
7 Westermarck, *Origin*, vol. 1, 405.
8 Ibid., vol. 2, 193.
9 Cottingham, "Partiality, Favouritism and Morality," 369. In a similar vein, see Blum, *Friendship, Altruism, and Morality*, ch. 3; Dower, *World Poverty*, 32; Gewirth, "Ethical Universalism and Particularism," 294; Goldman, *Moral Foundations*, 4; Norman, "Self and Others," 193–4. Rachels probes this "Argument from Personal Goods" in "Morality, Parents and Children," 54–5.
10 Cottingham claims nothing more. Since the present study assumes at least minimal partiality, I here bypass some similarly limited arguments.
11 Rachels, "Morality, Parents, and Children," 55 (emphasis omitted). Cf. James ("Hooty") McCown's moving account in *With Crooked Lines*, 59–60 ("What an unmeasurable blessing to have had a father who can be most tenderly remembered for his whippings").
12 Rachels, "Morality, Parents, and Children," 55.
13 Kelsey, *Caring*, 98.
14 In further illustration, see Snarey, *How Fathers Care*, 353–4. In confirmation, consider John Hardwig's complementary remarks: "'I don't want you to take me out,' my wife exploded. 'I just want you to want to go out with me. If you don't want to go out, let's just forget it.' Motives, intentions, and reasons for acting play a *much* larger role in the ethics of personal relationships than they do in the ethics of impersonal relationships. In fact, the motivation of those who are close to us is often more important than the things which result from it. And even when actions are important in personal relationships, it is often because they are seen as symbols or symptoms of underlying feelings, desires, or commitments" ("Search," 74).
15 Mill, *On Liberty*, ch. 5.
16 Andre, "Role Morality," 73. In "Roles and Morality," Richard Wasserstrom critiques such arguments from roles, in ways that complement the present discussion.
17 Donaldson, "Morally Privileged Relationships," 24.
18 Temple, *Christianity and Social Order*, 76. Ronald Preston comments: "The problem is clear, but since one cannot know in advance

whether one will bring one's children to challenge currently accepted standards, Temple's proviso seems to lead to a perpetual support of the *status quo*" (ibid., Introduction, 17).

19 Colby and Damon, *Some Do Care*, 46–7. See ibid., 56, 222–3, and compare Chang, *Wild Swans*, 363.

20 Pear, Review, 8. Cf. Colby and Damon, *Some Do Care*, 56 ("Although Danny believes that his children's lives are invaluably enriched through their association with the mission, he acknowledges that they have felt the sting of material want"), 223 ("Mother Waddles has come to see the mission as primarily a force for good in the children's lives, no matter if it did take their mother away from them").

21 On the importance of such benefits, see Blustein, *Parents and Children*, 128, and Daniel Williams, *Spirit*, 239 ("unless the tensions between self-protection and obligation to the community are acknowledged, family love can become a self-centred existence, protected from learning the larger demands of love by its internal satisfactions").

22 Rachels, "Morality, Parents, and Children," 60. Cf. Hallie, *Lest Innocent Blood Be Shed*, 141–2, on the costs and risks imposed on children for the sake of Jewish fugitives ("Nelly remembers that for her and her brothers their father was a hero and their mother a heroine").

23 Leeds, "Altruism," 238.

24 Niebanck, *Economic Justice*, 83–4.

25 Urwick, *Luxury and Waste of Life*, 205. See Klein, *From Philanthropy to Social Welfare*, 272.

26 Cf. Bremner, *American Philanthropy*, 2: "Many Americans have been concerned lest their countrymen's generosity be abused. But on a deeper level there is something about philanthropy that seems to go against the democratic grain. We may be willing to help others, but we are not humble enough to appreciate the efforts of those who would bend down to help us. 'Don't try to uplift me,' we say. 'I can lift myself.' We expect rich men to be generous with their wealth, and criticize them when they are not; but when they make benefactions, we question their motives, deplore the methods by which they obtained their abundance, and wonder whether their gifts will not do more harm than good."

27 Pope, "Proper and Improper Partiality," 258. Cf. Leo XIII, *Graves de communi*, 64.

28 Goodin, *Protecting the Vulnerable*, 16.

29 Sidgwick, *The Methods of Ethics*, 242.

30 Goodin, *Protecting the Vulnerable*, 17.

31 Cf. ibid., 27 (note).

32 Cohen, "Who Is Starving Whom?", 76. See Henry Brown, *Egalitarianism*, 525–6; Parfit, *Reasons and Persons*, 31. Cf. Aiken's critique of a related "last resort" argument, in "The Right to Be Saved," 93.

33 Brock, "Utilitarianism and Aiding Others," 230. Cf. Singer, "Famine, Affluence, and Morality," 25–7, e.g.: "Should I consider that I am less obliged to pull the drowning child out of the pond if on looking around I see other people, no further away than I am, who have also noticed the child but are doing nothing? One has only to ask this question to see the absurdity of the view that numbers lessen obligation" (25–6).

34 Cohen, "Who Is Starving Whom?", 80.

35 Ibid., 79.

36 Frankena, *Ethics*, 40.

37 Whelan, "Famine and Charity," 158.

38 Ibid.

39 Ibid.

40 Ibid., 160.

41 Ibid., 156 ("there are reputable charities, and with respect to them, these risks are slight"); Michael Taylor, *Good for the Poor*, xi ("there are several organizations, CAFOD, Christian Aid, One World Week, Oxfam, World Development Movement among them, who can supply all the help that is needed by those who, recognizing the moral claims of the poor, or better still hearing the promise of the Gospel of the poor, want to get on and do something").

42 Jackson, *Against the Grain*, 3.

43 More recently, see Brian Smith, *More Than Altruism*, 112–14.

44 See Goodin, *Political Theory and Public Policy*, ch. 9 ("Uncertainty as an Excuse for Myopia").

45 Jackson, *Against the Grain*, 4.

46 Onora O'Neill, "Moral Perplexities," 314.

47 Jackson, *Against the Grain*, 5.

48 Fletcher, "Give If It Helps," 106. See Fletcher, "Feeding the Hungry."

49 Dower, "World Poverty," 276–7; Onora O'Neill, "Moral Perplexities," 304–7; Shue, *Basic Rights*, chapter 4.

50 Unger, *Living High and Letting Die*, 37. See ibid., 36–9.

51 Cf. Kutzner, *World Hunger*, 59–112.

52 Sen, "Population: Delusion and Reality," 66.

53 Ibid., 67.

54 Ibid., 64–5.
55 Flanagan, *Varieties of Moral Personality*, 32. Cf. Singer, *The Expanding Circle*, 157–8.
56 Wallwork, "Thou Shalt Love," 297. See Irving Singer, *The Nature of Love*, 312; Hallett, *Christian Neighbor-Love*, 95–8.
57 Liguori, *Theologia moralis*, vol. 1, 327. Cf. Dower, *World Poverty*, 21–2; Temple, *Christianity and Social Order*, 75–6; Clarke, *Almsgiving*, 91: "The average Christian is not called upon to live greatly within his income. Allowance must be made for habit; for most of us it is a hardship to reduce the standard of living to which we have been accustomed since childhood – not so much as regards quality of food and the service we exact from our fellow-men as in the refinements of life such as a bedroom to ourselves, baths, frequent changes of linen, etc."
58 Walsh, Review, 369.
59 Massillon, "On Charity," 419. See Shue, "The Burdens of Justice," 600–2.
60 E.g., Fishkin, *The Limits of Obligation*, 5; Shue, "Mediating Duties," 697.
61 Marshall, *Challenge*, 139–40. Compare Urmson, "Saints and Heroes," 200–1.
62 For a fuller response, see Hallett, *Christian Neighbor-Love*, 92–3.
63 Singer, *Practical Ethics*, 242. See Goodin, *Protecting the Vulnerable*, 166–7.
64 Nagel, *Equality and Partiality*, 21. Cf. Cooper, *The Diversity of Moral Thinking*, 183. Nagel adds: "On the other hand, this accommodation has its own problems: One has to be careful not to turn it into an excuse for giving up too easily; there is a danger that one will get into the habit of thinking that any radical departure from accustomed patterns is psychologically unrealistic."
65 Flanagan, *Varieties of Moral Personality*, 46. See ibid., 41–2.
66 "Some of the proponents of the view that modern moral theory is too demanding make use of premises which presuppose relatively narrow, socially specific construals of what constitutes extreme demandingness and unrealizability. Because such arguments are in danger of merely reflecting culturally parochial biases and of conflating issues of realizability in the strict sense with issues of degree of difficulty, they will have to be scrutinized especially carefully" (ibid., 46).
67 Ibid., 93–4.
68 Hallett, *Christian Neighbor-Love*, 94–5.
69 Quigley and Garvy, *The Dorothy Day Book*, 11.

70 Latané and Darley, *The Unresponsive Bystander*, 125.
71 Conway, "Is Failing to Save," 110–11. Cf. Cullity, "International Aid," 121; Rachels, "Killing and Starving to Death," 160–1.
72 Palmer, *Altruism*, 51–2.
73 Allport, *The Nature of Prejudice*, 42. See ibid., 43–4, 264. "The remarkable thing," writes Michael Gazzaniga, "is that the more you are near someone, the more positively you come to feel about that person. Propinquity is a powerful draw. Robert Zajonc showed a series of faces to students. The test group viewed certain faces once or twice, while they saw others many more times. The more frequently a face was seen, the more the students liked it" (*Mind Matters*, 169).
74 Cf. Jerome, *Epist.* 120.1 (CSEL 55, 477): "Respondebis: 'difficile, durum est, contra naturam.' Sed dominum tibi audies respondentem: qui potest capere, capiat. Et si vis esse perfecta, non tibi jugum necessitatis imponit, sed potestati tuae liberum concedit arbitrium."
75 Mautner, Review, 117. Singer suggests a different solution: "Ranking our own interests and those of our kin higher than we would if we adopted an impartial point of view is a normal trait in an evolved creature . . . So an ethic for normal human beings will do well to limit the demands it makes – not to the extent that it demands no more than people are inclined to do anyway, but so that the standards it sets can be recommended to people with a realistic hope that many will meet them. An ethic of rules can do this, because rules can be formulated so that obedience is not too difficult" (*The Expanding Circle*, 160). "'Do not kill innocent human beings' is compatible with a normal, relaxed way of life, 'Preserve innocent human lives' could – in a time of famine, for instance – require us to give up everything and work full-time to save the lives of others" (ibid.).
76 "The only defensible form of the requirement that moral demands fit the human frame is the relatively weak one that it must make sense for us to work at them, to see them as relevant ideals" (Griffin, *Well-Being*, 306).
77 Thouvenin, "Magnanimité," 1551.
78 Fee, *Philippians*, 434.
79 Colby and Damon, *Some Do Care*, 44–5.
80 Aquinas, *In Matt.* 1.4.

7: COMPARABLE CONFLICTS

1 James Dunn points out that these were the most profound and obvious differences in Paul's world, and comments: "As distinctions, marking racial, social and gender differentiation, which were thought to indicate or imply relative worth or value or privileged status before God, they no longer have that significance. In particular, in the context it is the Jewish assumption that being 'under the law' showed Jews to be more highly regarded by God than Greeks which governs the force of the sequence. So, by implication, what Paul attacks in this version of a common theological affirmation in Hellenistic Christianity, is the assumption that the slave or the woman is disadvantaged before God or, still more, is an inferior species in the eyes of God" (*The Epistle to the Galatians*, 207).

2 Peschke, *Christian Ethics*, vol. 2, 186–7, citing Bernard Häring.

3 Roey, *De virtute charitatis*, 356.

4 Peinador, *De fide, spe, caritate*, 246–7.

5 Preference has often been accorded to better, holier people; but holiness is not a special relation to any particular person, as is being one's child, one's coreligionist, one's friend, or one's compatriot.

6 Ratschow, "Agape, Nächstenliebe und Bruderliebe," 160–1; Nygren, *Agape and Eros*, 153–4; Wadell, *Friendship and the Moral Life*, 94–5.

7 Fulgentius, *Serm.* 5.4 (PL 65, 738–9); Odo of Cambrai, *Liber de villico iniquitatis* (PL 160, 1150); Hildebert of Turin, *Serm.* 25 (PL 171, 459); White, *The Insights of History*, 20–1 and 42.

8 Paulinus of Aquileia, *Exhortatio* (PL 99, 249–50).

9 Dimont, "Charity, Almsgiving (Christian)," 383, citing *Ep. xxx*, 49. Cf. Herrmann, *La charité*, 49; White, *The Insights of History*, 20.

10 White, *The Insights of History*, 20, quoting Lucian, *The Death of Peregrinus*, 13.

11 Raven, *The Heart of Christ's Religion*, 132.

12 Barton, *Discipleship and Family Ties in Mark and Matthew*, 218. Barton adds the pertinent comment: "there is in Matthew a more explicit communal – in doctrinal terms, ecclesiological – dimension to the material on family ties. The idea of Jesus' followers as his true family is augmented by the idea that the followers are related to Jesus and to one another as 'brothers' . . ." (ibid., 218–19). According to Meeks, as we have seen, "More than a metaphor is involved here, for the Christians are evidently

expected not only to cherish fellow members of the sect with the same care as they would natural siblings, but even to replace natural family ties by those of this new family of God, created by conversion and ritual initiation" (*Moral World*, 129).

13 Translation from *The Liturgy of the Hours* (New York, 1975), vol. 3, 516.

14 Valuy, *Fraternal Charity*, 3. "Verdaderamente," writes Menendez Reigada ("Obligaciones," 353), "que esta unión es muy superior a cualquiera otra unión de orden humano."

15 Granada, *The Sinner's Guide*, 352.

16 Tenison, *Sermon*, 26–7.

17 Jeremy Taylor, *The Great Exemplar*, 461–2.

18 See chapter 4, note 23.

19 Augustine, *De baptismo*, 5.27.38.

20 Ward, *Nationalism and Ideology*, 121–2.

21 Cf. the concluding words of Ratschow's pertinent study: "Die christliche Bruderliebe ist nur gesund, so dürfen wir wohl sagen, wo sie die ganze Weite der Nächstenliebe in sich trägt. Ein Gemeindebewusstsein bleibt nur da echt, wo es die Welt meint, und nicht in curvata est in se" ("Agape, Nächstenliebe und Bruderliebe," 182).

22 Guillon, "Church," 323.

23 Aquinas, *Summa theol.* 2–2.26.8.c ("illi qui sunt nobis magis conjuncti, sunt ex caritate magis diligendi; tum quia intensius diliguntur, tum etiam quia pluribus rationibus diliguntur"); Cottingham, "Partiality, Favouritism and Morality," 372: "What gives such desires and actions moral backing is the close emotional bonding which people develop towards their offspring and the role which such bonding plays in the fulfilment and happiness of those involved. It is this, not the mere fact of consanguinity as such, that provides the moral foundation for any partiality we may show to our close kin."

24 Some deny friendship between parents and children (cf. Reisman, *Anatomy of Friendship*, 42–3) or between family members (cf. ibid., 91; Brain, *Friends and Lovers*, 15); others do not (e.g., Aquinas, *Summa theol.* 2–2.26.8.c; Brain, *Friends and Lovers*, 12–16; Reisman, *Anatomy of Friendship*, 35, 131, 136, 139; Jeremy Taylor, *Measures*, 65). Eschewing veiled redefinitions proposed as theories, I side with the latter.

25 For example, of the Bangwa of Cameroon, Brain writes (*Friends and Lovers*, 35): "Friendship is valued far above kinship; between kin there are niggling debts and witchcraft fears. Friendship lasts

till death; kinship is brittle and involves inequalities of age and wealth and status." Similarly, "In Alcala, friendship between two persons is a sacred relationship, emotionally more meaningful than relations between members of the kin group, except perhaps that of parent and child" (ibid., 44).

26 Lawler, "Family: American and Christian," 20.

27 Jeremy Taylor, *Measures*, 61–2. For Aristotle, no one would choose a friendless existence on condition of having all other good things in the world (*Nicomachean Ethics*, 8.1).

28 Jeremy Taylor, *Measures*, 24 (his italics).

29 Hunt, "Friends and Family Values," 170.

30 Ibid., 172.

31 Ibid., 170.

32 Friedman, *What Are Friends For?*, 2.

33 Reisman, *Anatomy of Friendship*, 23. "If neither party feels loyalty or deep fondness for the other, the friendship is associative" (ibid., 26).

34 Toner, Typescript.

35 Jeremy Taylor, *Measures*, 10. Cf. Wadell, *Friendship and the Moral Life*, 74 ("agape is a kind of friendship extended to the world, to those whom Jesus called our neighbors").

36 Jeremy Taylor, *Measures*, 14.

37 Ibid., 21.

38 Leyton, *The Compact*, ix.

39 Reisman, *Anatomy of Friendship*, 19.

40 Toner, Typescript.

41 Aelred of Rievaulx's rhapsodic account, in *De amicitia* 5 (PL 40, 835), exalts perfect friendship still higher above mere kinship. Notice that the characterizations I have cited, of the highest kinds of friendship, are more germane to my purposes than the "deep analysis of the nature of friendship" urged by one reader. Friendship has no single nature or essence; its most paradigmatic forms are the ones that most plausibly contend for preferential primacy.

42 Reisman, *Anatomy of Friendship*, 39–40.

43 Ibid., 96–7. One may therefore question Reisman's concluding summation: "Scholars have suggested a number of definitions, and though they have their shortcomings and differences, they agree that *a friend is someone who likes and wishes to do well by someone else and who believes those feelings and good intentions are reciprocated*" (ibid., 108).

44 Wadell, *Friendship and the Moral Life*, 70 (on views such as Kierkegaard's and Nygren's). See Meilaender, *Friendship*, 3.

45 Telfer, "Friendship," 235–6.

46 Blum, *Friendship, Altruism and Morality*, 259.
47 Telfer, "Friendship," 235.
48 Ibid., 226.
49 Aquinas, *Summa theol.* 2–2.26.8. ad 1.
50 Telfer, "Friendship," 230.
51 Jecker, "Impartiality and Special Relations," 85–6.
52 Ignatieff, *Blood and Belonging*, 5.
53 Smart, "Friendship and Enmity among Nations," 155. Cf. Hayes, *Nationalism*, 180; David Miller, "The Ethical Significance of Nationality," 653 ("Forster's remark . . . seems now to represent the conventional wisdom"). In the past, compare Brutus's conflict between loyalty to his friend Caesar and loyalty to his country.
54 Snyder, *Varieties of Nationalism*, 50.
55 Ibid., 40.
56 "I love my country ardently . . . Had I a thousand lives, I should with pleasure sacrifice them all, if I could thereby render her any service and show her my gratitude" (ibid., 51).
57 "The most beautiful thing about all this holy zeal and happy confusion was that all differences of position, class, and age were forgotten . . . that the one great feeling for the Fatherland, its freedom and honor, swallowed all other feelings, caused all other considerations and relationships to be forgotten" (ibid., 47).
58 Ward, *Five Ideas*, 151–2.
59 Amdur, "Rawls' Theory of Justice," 457; Beitz, *Political Theory and International Relations*, 163; Walzer, *Spheres of Justice*, 64: "Membership is important because of what the members of a political community owe to one another and to no one else, or to no one else in the same degree. And the first thing they owe is the communal provision of security and welfare."
60 Prior to the recent US intervention in Haiti, a politician declared that the whole of Haiti was not worth a single drop of American blood – a claim more extreme than one would likely hear for a friend or family member.
61 Shue, *Basic Rights*, 131.
62 William Brown, "America's International Economic Responsibilities," 109–10.
63 Singer, *The Expanding Circle*, 32.
64 Goodin, *Protecting the Vulnerable*, 154. See Goodin, "What Is So Special," 667.
65 Nielsen, "Global Justice," 609.
66 Henriot, *Opting for the Poor*, 31.
67 Shue, *Basic Rights*, 139. Cf. Lesser, "Human Needs," 44–5.

68 Ward, *The Lopsided World*, 97–8.
69 Gorovitz, "Bigotry, Loyalty, and Malnutrition," 135–6; Shue, *Basic Rights*, 142; Walzer, *Spheres of Justice*, 64–5; Oldenquist, "Loyalties," 191 ("As a matter of historical and sociological fact, moral motives for good citizenship are marginally effective and harder to produce in the first place; it is primarily group loyalties – group egoism and tribal morality – that have produced the caring and commitment that keep our social worlds going").
70 Cf. the universalist twist which Mazzini, the 19th-century Italian hero, gave utilitarian reasoning: "'You are citizens,' he told his compatriots; 'you have a country in order that in a given and limited sphere of action, the concourse and assistance of a certain number of men, already related to you by language, tendencies, and customs, may enable you to labor more effectively for the good of *all men*, present and to come; a task in which your solitary effort would be lost, falling powerless and needless among the immense multitudes of your fellow beings" (Snyder, *Varieties of Nationalism*, 51).
71 Donaldson, "Morally Privileged Relationships," 36–7.
72 Smart, "Friendship and Enmity among Nations," 155–6. Of the US Tamar Jacoby writes ("The Politics of Identity," 32): "From the beginning, uncertainty about our national identity has been part of what it means to be American. Is the nation by definition a heterogeneous bundling of many? Or can something common be shaped of the whole – and if so, what exactly?"
73 David Miller, "The Ethical Significance of Nationality," 648.
74 Goodin writes: "Special responsibilities are, on my account, assigned merely as an administrative device for discharging our general duties more efficiently" ("What Is So Special," 685). Given current realities, he therefore concludes: "In the present world system, it is often – perhaps ordinarily – wrong to give priority to the claims of our compatriots" (ibid., 686).
75 "In the writings of the classical international jurists, the rules of international relations are derived from domestic morality by analogy; international society is understood as domestic society writ large, with states playing the roles occupied by persons in domestic society. States, not persons, are the subjects of international morality, and the rules that regulate their behavior are supposed to preserve a peaceful order of sovereign states" (Beitz, "Bounded Morality," 408; cf. Kol, *Theologia moralis*, vol. 1, 252).
76 Cf. Beitz, "Cosmopolitan Ideals and National Sentiment," 597.
77 Hallett, *Christian Neighbor-Love*, 124–5.
78 Ibid., 123. Cf. Held, "Can a Random Collection," 471–2.

79 Janssen, "Duties to Underdeveloped Countries," 202–3.
80 Take a historical case. Its sponsors' Anglo-Saxon names suggest why the Johnson-Reed Act of 1924, which introduced the national-origins plan into US immigration policy, assigned the largest quota of all to Great Britain. The British were kith and kin; they were nearest and dearest – personally, nationally. So they received preferential treatment. Later generations branded the Act's quotas unfair, biased, discriminatory, undemocratic. "This system," declared Lyndon Johnson as he signed it out of existence, "violated the basic principle of American democracy – the principle that values and rewards each man on the basis of his merit as a man" (Mann, *Immigrants in American Life*, 169).
81 Cf. Beitz, *Political Theory and International Relations*, 153, and "Bounded Morality," 409; Hoffmann, *Duties Beyond Borders*, 148; Lesser, "Human Needs, Objectivity and Morality," 45; Shue, *Basic Rights*, 141, 151.
82 Hallett, *Christian Moral Reasoning*, 121, 123–5.
83 Goodin, *Protecting the Vulnerable*, 138–9; Smart, "Friendship and Enmity among Nations," 157.
84 "The collective pursuit of prosperity and justice for themselves by the citizens of a nation remains under a shadow while it goes on in a world like ours, where a minority of nations are islands of relative decency in a sea of tyranny and crushing poverty, and the preservation of a high standard of life depends absolutely on strict controls on immigration" (Nagel, *Equality and Partiality*, 179).
85 Hoffmann, *Duties Beyond Borders*, 177; Johnson, *Economic Policies*, 163–206. "Ajoutons ce point, pour les hommes et les femmes des pays développés: beaucoup des mesures évoquées peuvent paraître hors de portée, à première vue, pour la plupart des citoyens ordinaires; inversement, pourtant, tout ou presque dépend réellement d'eux. Les responsables ne peuvent, en effet, agir pour la modification de l'ordre international en faveur des plus pauvres – afin de rétablir au moins une certaine égalité dans les discussions et les négociations et, progressivement, une égalité des chances – que si l'opinion y est favorable ou si beaucoup de citoyens sont disposés à accepter de sacrifier des avantages dont ils bénéficiaient jusque-là. Disposés, par example, à acheter plus cher des produits importés pour rémunérer plus justement le producteur. Ou disposés aux reconversions, requises pour permettre l'entrée sur leurs marchés de produits manufacturés du tiers monde" (Calvez, *Une éthique pour nos sociétés*, 95).

86 Nossiter, *The Global Struggle for More*, 61–3.
87 My question, notice, is not one of strategy. It may be, as some believe, "that people-to-people programs that bridge national borders and link civil societies directly (bypassing governments caught in a morass of bureaucracy and self-serving considerations based on narrow definitions of national interest) can deal more effectively with pieces of such issues [like those cited]" and "that private nonprofit organizations can overcome the limits of ideology and patriotism, and thus help construct an international constituency for global humanistic concerns and offer a nonpartisan pragmatic strategy to fulfill them" (Brian Smith, *More than Altruism*, 19). Regardless of the means, what should be the goal? How narrowly should national interest be defined?
88 On issues of party representation, often lost sight of, see Birch, *Representation*, 97–100.
89 Birch, *Representation*, 112–13; Pennock, "Political Representation," 5, 9–10, 14–21; Nancy Schwartz, *The Blue Guitar*, 24.
90 William Brown, "America's International Economic Responsibilities," 110.
91 John Bennett, *Christian Ethics and Social Policy*, 65.
92 Pennock, "Political Representation," 14.
93 Nancy Schwartz, *The Blue Guitar*, 25.
94 Chernow, *The Warburgs*, 446, 448; Dinnersteen, "Refugees"; Nathan Miller, *FDR*, 429; Morgan, *FDR*, 499, 508.
95 Meyers, Introduction, 17.
96 John Bennett, "Christian Ethics," 202–3.
97 "The contemporary movement in applied ethics is one acknowledgement that ethical writing needs to be brought closer to deliberations of those involved in public affairs if it is not to seem remote, unrealistic or even sentimental" (Onora O'Neill, *Faces of Hunger*, 4).
98 Cf. Beitz, "Bounded Morality," 423: "A possible response to this last point is that the application of moral principles to political practice is more properly the province of the policy scientist than of the moral philosopher. This thought is suggested by Singer's remark that 'there is no real dilemma' about how to distribute aid funds 'so long as we bear in mind that our goal is to prevent as many people as possible from starving.' In fact, there are many real dilemmas, not only about distributing aid funds but, more generally, about preventing as many people as possible from starving. Massive cash transfers *may* succeed only in removing incentives for increasing indigenous food production, and even

institutional reforms like those of the New International Economic Order *may* only reinforce the structural inequalities found in many poor societies."

99 Singer, *Practical Ethics*, 257. Cf. Francis Fukuyama's critique ("No Vacancy") of Roy Beck, *The Case Against Immigration*, and Chilton Williamson, Jr., *The Immigration Mystique*.

Works cited

ABBREVIATIONS

CSEL   Corpus scriptorum ecclesiasticorum latinorum
(Vienna: Apud C. Geroldi filium, 1866 –)
PG   Patrologiae cursus completus, series graeca
(Paris: Migne: 1857–1866)
PL   Patrologiae cursus completus, series latina
(Paris: Migne: 1844–1890)

Aiken, William. "The Right to Be Saved from Starvation." In Aiken and LaFollette, *World Hunger and Moral Obligation*, 85–102.
Aiken, William and Hugh LaFollette, eds. *World Hunger and Moral Obligation*. Englewood Cliffs, NJ: Prentice-Hall, 1977.
Allen, Joseph L. *Love and Conflict: A Covenantal Model of Christian Ethics.* Nashville, Tenn.: Abingdon, 1984.
Allport, Gordon W. *The Nature of Prejudice.* Cambridge, Mass.: Addison-Wesley, 1954.
Alsina, Raymundus. *Compendium theologiae moralis.* 2nd edn. Vol. 1. Barcelona: J. Grabulosa, 1879.
Amdur, Robert. "'Rawls' Theory of Justice: Domestic and International Perspectives." *World Politics* 29 (1976–7): 438–61.
Anderson, Robert. *Traditional Europe: A Study in Anthropology and History.* Belmont, CA.: Wadsworth, 1971.
Andre, Judith. "Role Morality as a Complex Instance of Ordinary Morality." *American Philosophical Quarterly* 28 (1991): 73–80.
"Anithunger Groups Call for US Policy Changes." *Christian Century* 110 (1993): 1265–6.
Antoine, Ch. "L'aumône." *Dictionnaire apologétique de la foi catholique.* Ed. A. D'Alès. Vol. 1. Paris: Beauchesne, 1925. Col. 319–28.
Antoine, Paul-Gabriel. *Theologia moralis universa.* Rome/Venice: Apud Haeredes Balleonios, 1762.

Antonius a S. Joseph. *Compendium Salmanticense.* Vol. 1. Pamplona: B. Cosculluela, 1791.

Archibald, Katherine. "The Concept of Social Hierarchy in the Writings of St. Thomas Aquinas." *The Historian* 12 (1949–50): 28–54.

Atkinson, Gary M. "Ambiguities in 'Killing' and 'Letting Die.'" *Journal of Medicine and Philosophy* 8 (1983): 159–68.

Augustine, St. *Faith, Hope, and Charity.* Trans. Louis A. Arand. Westminster, Md.: Newman, 1947.

——. *Sermons.* 10 vols. *The Works of Saint Augustine,* Part III. Trans. Edmund Hill. Ed. John E. Rotelle. Brooklyn: New City Press, 1990–1995.

Bañez, Domingo. *De fide, spe, et charitate.* Rome: T. and P. de Dianis, 1586.

Barber, Bernard and Elinor G. Barber, eds. *European Social Class: Stability and Change.* New York: Macmillan, 1965.

Barry, Brian. "Do Countries Have Moral Obligations? The Case of World Poverty." In McMurrin, *The Tanner Lectures on Human Values,* 25–44.

Barry, Robert L. *Breaking the Thread of Life: On Rational Suicide.* New Brunswick, NJ: Transaction, 1994.

Barton, Stephen C. *Discipleship and Family Ties in Mark and Matthew.* Cambridge: Cambridge University Press, 1994.

Beare, Francis Wright. *The Gospel according to Matthew.* San Francisco: Harper and Row, 1981.

Becker, Lawrence C. *Reciprocity.* London: Routledge and Kegan Paul, 1986.

Beitz, Charles R. *"Bounded Morality: Justice and the State in World Politics." International Organization* 33 (1979): 405–24.

——. "Cosmopolitan Ideals and National Sentiment." *Journal of Philosophy* 80 (1983): 591–600.

——. *Political Theory and International Relations.* Princeton: Princeton University Press, 1979.

Bellarmino, Roberto. *De controversiis christianae fidei adversus hujus temporis haereticos.* Vol. 4. Naples: Giuliano, 1858.

Bender, Ludovico. "Almsgiving." *Dictionary of Moral Theology.* Ed. Francesco Roberti and Pietro Palazzini. Westminster, Md: Newman, 1962. 57–9.

Bennett, John C. *Christian Ethics and Social Policy.* New York: Scribner's, 1956.

——. "Christian Ethics in Economic Life." In Bennett et al., *Christian Values and Economic Life,* 201–34.

Bennett, John C. et al. *Christian Values and Economic Life.* New York: Harper, 1954.

Bennett, Jonathan. "Morality and Consequences." In McMurrin, *The Tanner Lectures on Human Values*, 45–116.

Berardi, Aemilius. *Theologia moralis theorico-practica*. Vol. 2. Rome: Proganda Fidei; Ratisbon: Pustet, 1904.

Beugnet, A. "Aumône." *Dictionnaire de théologie catholique*. Vol. 1, part 2. Paris: Letouzey, 1931. Col. 2561–71.

Billuart, Charles René. *Summa Summae S. Thomae*. Vol. 3. Rome: Puccinelli, 1834.

Birch, A. H. *Representation*. New York: Praeger, 1971.

Blum, Lawrence A. *Friendship, Altruism and Morality*. London: Routledge and Kegan Paul, 1980.

Blustein, Jeffrey. *Parents and Children: The Ethics of the Family*. New York: Oxford University Press, 1982.

Boff, Clodovis, and George V. Pixley. *The Bible, the Church, and the Poor*. Trans. Paul Burns. Maryknoll, NY: Orbis, 1989.

Bouquillon, Thomas. *Institutiones theologiae moralis specialis: Tractatus de virtutibus theologicis*. Bruges: Beyaert-Storie, 1878.

Bouvier, Léon. *Le précepte de l'aumône chez saint Thomas d'Aquin*. Montreal: College of the Immaculate Conception, 1935.

Bowen, Howard R. "Major Economic Problems." In *Christian Values and Economic Life*, by John C. Bennett et al. New York: Harper, 1954. 68–94.

Boyle, Joseph M., Jr. "On Killing and Letting Die." *New Scholasticism* 51 (1977): 433–52.

Brain, Robert. *Friends and Lovers*. New York: Basic Books, 1976.

Brandt, Lilian. *How Much Shall I Give?* New York: Frontier, 1921.

Bremner, Robert H. *American Philanthropy*. 2nd edn. Chicago: University of Chicago Press, 1988.

Brennan, Todd. "Charity: We Need a New Concept of Giving." *US Catholic and Jubilee* 36, March 1971, 14–18 (with feedback).

Broad, C. D. "Certain Features in Moore's Ethical Doctrines." In *The Philosophy of G. E. Moore*, ed. Paul Arthur Schilpp. 3d edn. La Salle, Ill.: Open Court; London: Cambridge University Press, 1968. 43–67.

Brock, Dan W. "Utilitarianism and Aiding Others." In *The Limits of Utilitarianism*, ed. Harlan B. Miller and William H. Williams. Minneapolis: University of Minnesota Press, 1982. 225–41.

Broglie, Guy de. "Charité: Essai d'une synthèse doctrinale." *Dictionnaire de spiritualité*. Vol. 2, part 1. Paris: Beauchesne, 1953. Col. 661–91.

Brouillard, René. "La doctrine catholique de l'aumône." *Nouvelle Revue Théologique* 54 (1927): 5–36.

Brown, Henry Phelps. *Egalitarianism and the Generation of Inequality*. Oxford: Clarendon, 1988.

Brown, Peter G. and Henry Shue, eds. *Food Policy: The Responsibility of the United States in the Life and Death Choices.* New York: Free Press, 1977.

Brown, Schuyler. "Faith, the Poor and the Gentiles: A Tradition-Historical Reflection on Matthew 25:31–46." *Toronto Journal of Theology* 6 (1990): 171–81.

Brown, William Adams, Jr. "America's International Economic Responsibilities." In Bennett et al., *Christian Values and Economic Life*, 103–16.

Bruner, Dale. *Matthew.* Vol. 2: *The Churchbook Matthew 13–28.* Dallas: Word, 1990.

Bucceroni, Gennaro. *Institutiones theologiae moralis.* 6th edn. Vol. 1. Rome: Pius IX Institute, 1914.

Budde, Gerard J. "Christian Charity: Now and Always. The Fathers of the Church and Almsgiving." *American Ecclesiastical Review* 85 (1931): 561–79.

Butler, Joseph. "On the Nature of Virtue." Appended to *The Analogy of Religion Natural and Revealed.* Ed. Joseph Cummings. New York: Phillips and Hunt; Cincinnati: Cranston and Stowe, 1884.

Caesarius of Arles, St. *Sermons.* Vol. 1. Trans. Sister Mary Magdeleine Mueller. New York: Fathers of the Church, 1956.

Calvez, Jean-Yves. *Une éthique pour nos sociétés.* Paris: Nouvelle Cité, 1988.

Calvin, John. *Institutes of the Christian Religion.* Ed. John T. McNeill. Trans. Ford Lewis Battles. Vol. 1. Library of Christian Classics, 20. Philadelphia: Westminster, 1960.

Cano, Melchior. "Commentarium in II.II.q.32 De eleemosyna (anno 1544)." In Deuringer, *Probleme der Caritas in der Schule von Salamanca,* 158–201.

Castro Palão, Fernando de. *Operis moralis, de virtutibus, et vitiis contrariis. Pars Prima.* Venice: Pezzana, 1702.

Challoner, Richard. *Meditations.* Vol. 1. London: Keating, Brown, 1807.

Chang, Jung. *Wild Swans: Three Daughters of China.* New York: Doubleday, 1992.

Chernow, Ron. *The Warburgs: The Twentieth-Century Odyssey of a Remarkable Jewish Family.* New York: Random House, 1993.

Chiavacci, Enrico. *Teologia morale e vita economica.* Vol. 3/1, *Teologia morale.* Assisi: Cittadella, 1985.

Chobham, Thomas of. *Summa confessorum.* Ed. F. Broomfield. Louvain: Nauwelaerts; Paris: Béatrice-Nauwelaerts, 1968.

Christophe, Paul. *Les devoirs moraux des riches: L'usage chretien du droit de propriété dans l'écriture et la tradition patristique.* Paris: Lethielleux, 1964.

Chrysostom, St. John. *Homilies on Genesis, 18–45.* Trans. Robert C. Hill. Washington: Catholic University of America Press, 1990.
On the Incomprehensible Nature of God. Trans. Paul W. Harkins. The Fathers of the Church, 72. Washington: Catholic University of America Press, 1984.
Clarke, W. K. Lowther. *Almsgiving: A Handbook.* London: Society for Promoting Christian Knowledge, 1936.
Cohen, L. Jonathan. "Who Is Starving Whom?" *Theoria* 47 (1981): 65–81.
Colby, Anne, and William Damon. *Some Do Care: Contemporary Lives of Moral Commitment.* New York: Free Press, 1992.
College of Salamanca. *Cursus theologiae moralis.* 6 vols. in 3. Venice: Pezzana, 1750.
Concina, Daniele. *Theologia christiana dogmatico-moralis.* Vol. 2. Rome; Venice: Occhi, 1749.
Conway, David. "Is Failing to Save Lives as Bad as Killing?" *Journal of Applied Philosophy* 5 (1988): 109–12.
Cooper, Neil. *The Diversity of Moral Thinking.* New York: Oxford University Press, 1981.
Coste, René. *L'amour qui change le monde: Théologie de la charité.* Paris: Éditions S.O.S., 1981.
Cottingham, John "Ethics and Impartiality." *Philosophical Studies* 43 (1983): 83–99.
"Partiality, Favouritism and Morality." *Philosophical Quarterly* 36 (1986): 357–73.
Countryman, L. William. *The Rich Christian in the Church of the Early Empire: Contradictions and Accommodations.* Toronto: Edwin Mellen, 1980.
Crofts, A. M. *Property and Poverty.* Dublin: Irish Rosary Office, 1948.
Cullity, Garrett. "International Aid and the Scope of Kindness." *Ethics* 105 (1994–5): 99–127.
Cuttaz, François. *Fraternal Charity: Its Theology and Its Application.* Trans. Malachy Gerard Carroll. New York: Alba House, 1962.
Damen, Cornelius. "De recto usu bonorum superfluorum." In *Miscellanea Vermeersch,* vol. 1: *Studi di teologia morale e diritto canonico.* Rome: Pontificia Università Gregoriana, 1935. 63–79.
Davis, Henry. *Moral and Pastoral Theology.* Vol. 1: *Human Acts, Law, Sin, Virtue.* 4th edn. London: Sheed and Ward, 1945.
Davis, Nancy. "The Priority of Avoiding Harm." In Steinbock, *Killing and Letting Die,* 173–214.
Denis the Carthusian. *Commentaria in Quartum Librum Sententiarum. Opera omnia.* Vol. 24. Tournai: Typis Cartusiae S. M. de Pratis, 1904.

Summa de vitiis et virtutibus. Opera omnia. Vol. 39. Tournai: Typis Cartusiae S. M. de Pratis, 1910. 7–242.

Deuringer, Karl. *Probleme der Caritas in der Schule von Salamanca.* Freiburg: Herder, 1959.

Dewey, John and James H. Tufts. *Ethics.* New York: Holt, 1908.

Diana, Antonino. *Coordinati, seu omnium resolutionum moralium.* Vol. 4. Venice: Pezzana, 1728.

Dimont, C. T. "Charity, Almsgiving (Christian)." *Encyclopaedia of Religion and Ethics.* Ed. James Hastings. Vol. 3. Edinburgh: T. & T. Clark, 1910. 382–6.

Dinnersteen, Leonard. "Refugees." In *Franklin D. Roosevelt: His Life and Times.* Ed. Otis L. Graham, Jr. and Meghan Robinson Wander. Boston: G. K. Hall, 1985. 348–9.

Donahue, John R. "The 'Parable' of the Sheep and the Goats: A Challenge to Christian Ethics." *Theological Studies* 47 (1986): 3–31.

Donaldson, Thomas. "Morally Privileged Relationships." In Meyers et al., *Kindred Matters,* 21–40.

Dorr, Donal. *Option for the Poor: A Hundred Years of Vatican Social Teaching.* 2nd edn. Maryknoll, NY: Orbis, 1992.

Dower, Nigel. *World Poverty: Challenge and Response.* York, England: Ebor Press, 1983.

"World Poverty." In *A Companion to Ethics,* ed. Peter Singer. Oxford: Blackwell, 1993. 273–83.

Drexel, Jeremias. *Gazophylacium Christi.* In *Opera.* Vol. 3. Lyons: Sumptibus Ioannis-Antonii Huguetan & Marci-Antonii Ravaud, 1658. 141–211.

Duby, Georges. *The Three Orders: Feudal Society Imagined.* Trans. Arthur Goldhammer. Chicago: University of Chicago Press, 1980.

Dudley, Owen Francis. *Will Men Be Like Gods? Humanitarianism or Human Happiness?* London: Longmans, Green, 1937.

Dunn, James D. G. *The Epistle to the Galatians.* Peabody, Mass.: Hendrickson, 1993.

Dyck, Arthur J. "Questions on Ethics." *Harvard Theological Review* 65 (1972): 453–81.

Ede, W. Moore. "Competition between Individuals and Classes, Considered from the Christian Point of View." In *The Elements of Pain and Conflict in Human Life, Considered from a Christian Point of View.* Cambridge: Cambridge University Press, 1916. 173–88.

Est, Willem H. van. *In quatuor libros Sententiarum commentaria.* Vol. 3. Paris: Josse et al., 1680.

Ewing, A. C. *Ethics.* London: English Universities Press, 1953.

Fairlie, Henry. *The Seven Deadly Sins Today.* Washington: New Republic Books, 1978.

Fanfani, Lodovico. *Manuale theorico-practicum theologiae moralis*. Vol. 2. Rome: Libraria "Ferrari," 1950.

Farahian, Edmond. "Relire Matthieu 25, 31–46." *Gregorianum* 72 (1991): 437–57.

Farley, Margaret A. "Family." *The New Dictionary of Catholic Social Thought*. Ed. Judith A. Dwyer. Collegeville, Minneapolis: Liturgical Press, 1994. 371–81.

Fee, Gordon D. *Paul's Letter to the Philippians*. Grand Rapids, Mich.: Eerdmans, 1995.

Fenton, J. C. *The Gospel of St Matthew*. The Pelican New Testament Commentaries. Harmondsworth: Penguin, 1963.

Ferreres, Juan Bautista. *Compendium theologiae moralis*. Revised by A. Mondria. Vol. 1. Barcelona: Subirana, 1949.

Finnis, John. "The Consistent Ethic: A Philosophical Critique." In *Consistent Ethic of Life*, ed. Thomas G. Fuechtmann. Kansas City, MO.: Sheed and Ward, 1988. 140–81.

Fishkin, James S. *The Limits of Obligation*. New Haven: Yale University Press, 1982.

Fitzmyer, Joseph A. *The Gospel According to Luke*. 2 vols. The Anchor Bible. Garden City, NY: Doubleday, 1981, 1985.

Flanagan, Owen. *Varieties of Moral Personality: Ethics and Psychological Realism*. Cambridge: Harvard University Press, 1991.

Flandrin, Jean-Louis. *Families in Former Times: Kinship, Household and Sexuality*. Trans. Richard Southern. Cambridge: Cambridge University Press, 1979.

Fléchier, Esprit. *Oeuvres complètes*. Vol. 1. Paris: Migne, 1856.

Fletcher, Joseph. "Feeding the Hungry: An Ethical Appraisal." In *Lifeboat Ethics: The Moral Dilemmas of World Hunger*. Ed. George R. Lucas, Jr. and Thomas W. Ogletree. New York: Harper and Row, 1976. 52–69.

"Give If It Helps But Not If It Hurts." In Aiken and LaFollette, *World Hunger and Moral Obligation*, 104–14.

Foot, Philippa. "Killing, Letting Die, and Euthanasia: A Reply to Holly Smith Goldman." *Analysis* 41 (1981): 159–60.

"The Problem of Abortion and the Doctrine of Double Effect." *Oxford Review* 5 (1967): 5–15. Rept. in *Virtues and Vices and Other Essays in Moral Philosophy*. Berkeley: University of California Press, 1978. 19–32.

Frankena, William K. *Ethics*. 2nd edn. Englewood Cliffs, NJ: Prentice-Hall, 1973.

"The Ethics of Love Conceived as an Ethics of Virtue." *Journal of Religious Ethics* 1 (1973): 21–36.

Friedman, Marilyn. *What Are Friends For?: Feminist Perspectives on*

Personal Relationships and Moral Theory. Ithaca, NY: Cornell University Press, 1993.

Friedrich, Johannes. *Gott im Bruder: Eine methodenkritische Untersuchung von Redaktion, Überlieferung und Traditionen in Mt. 25, 31–46.* Stuttgart: Calwer Verlag, 1977.

Fukuyama, Francis. "No Vacancy." *New York Times Book Review,* 1 September 1996, 18.

Gardner, Richard B. *Matthew.* Believers Church Bible Commentary. Scottdale, Pa.: Herald, 1991.

Gasper, Desmond. "Distribution and Development Ethics: A Tour." In *Development Studies: Critique and Renewal.* Ed. Raymond Apthorpe and András Kráhl. Leiden: E. J. Brill, 1986. 136–203.

Gasque, W. Ward. "Almsgiving." *Baker's Dictionary of Christian Ethics.* Ed. Carl F. H. Henry. Grand Rapids, Mich.: Baker, 1973. 17.

Gazzaniga, Michael S. *Mind Matters: How Mind and Brain Interact to Create Our Conscious Lives.* Boston: Houghton Mifflin, 1988.

Geisler, Norman L. *The Christian Ethic of Love.* Grand Rapids, Mich.: Zondervan, 1973.

Génicot, Édouard and Joseph Salsmans. *Institutiones theologiae moralis.* 17th edn. Ed. A. Gortebecke. 2 vols. Bruges: Desclée de Brouwer, 1952.

Gewirth, Alan. "Ethical Universalism and Particularism." *Journal of Philosophy* 85 (1988): 283–302.

Gilson, Etienne. *The Christian Philosophy of St. Thomas Aquinas.* Trans. L. K. Shook. New York: Random House, 1956.

Giordani, Igino. *The Social Message of the Early Church Fathers.* Trans. Alba I. Zizzamia. Paterson, NJ: St. Anthony Guild, 1944.

Glover, Jonathan. *Causing Death and Saving Lives.* Harmondsworth: Penguin, 1977.

Goldman, Alan H. *The Moral Foundations of Professional Ethics.* Totowa, NJ: Rowman and Littlefield, 1980.

Goodin, Robert E. *Political Theory and Public Policy.* Chicago: University of Chicago Press, 1982.

Protecting the Vulnerable: A Reanalysis of Our Social Responsibilities. Chicago: University of Chicago Press, 1985.

"What Is So Special about Our Fellow Countrymen?" *Ethics* 98 (1987–8): 663–86.

Gorovitz, Samuel. "Bigotry, Loyalty, and Malnutrition." In Brown and Shue, *Food Policy,* 129–42.

Graham, George and Hugh LaFollette, eds. *Person to Person.* Philadelphia: Temple University Press, 1989.

Granada, Luis de. *The Sinner's Guide.* Translator not named. Philadelphia: Eugene Cummiskey, 1833.

Gray, Sherman W. *The Least of My Brothers: Matthew: 31–46 – A History of Interpretation.* Society of Biblical Literature Dissertation Series, 114. Atlanta: Scholars Press, 1989.

Greer, Rowan A. *Broken Lights and Mended Lives: Theology and Common Life in the Early Church.* University Park, Pa.: Pennsylvania State University Press, 1986.

Griffin, James. *Well-Being: Its Meaning, Measurement, and Moral Importance.* Oxford: Clarendon, 1986.

Grisez, Germain. *Living a Christian Life.* Vol. 2, *The Way of the Lord Jesus.* Quincy, Ill.: Franciscan Press, 1993.

Guillon, Marie-Joseph le. "Church: II. Ecclesiology." *Sacramentum Mundi.* Ed. Karl Rahner et al. Vol. 1. New York: Herder and Herder, 1968. 317–27.

Guimet, Fernand. "Notes en marge d'un texte de Richard de Saint-Victor." *Archives d'histoire doctrinale et littéraire du moyen âge* 14 (1943–5): 371–94.

Gutiérrez, Gustavo. "Preferential Option for the Poor." *SEDOS Bulletin* 24 (1992): 176–81.

Hall, John C. "Acts and Omissions." *Philosophical Quarterly* 39 (1989): 399–408.

Hallett, Garth L. *Christian Moral Reasoning: An Analytic Guide.* Notre Dame: University of Notre Dame Press, 1983.

Christian Neighbor-Love: An Assessment of Six Rival Versions. Washington: Georgetown University Press, 1989.

"Christian Norms of Morality." *The Philosophical Assessment of Theology: Essays in Honour of Frederick C. Copleston.* Ed. Gerard J. Hughes. Washington: Georgetown University Press; Tunbridge Wells: Search Press, 1987. 187–209.

Greater Good: The Case for Proportionalism. Washington: Georgetown University Press, 1995.

Hallie, Philip P. *Lest Innocent Blood Be Shed: The Story of the Village of Le Chambon and How Goodness Happened There.* New York: Harper and Row, 1979.

Hardwig, John. "In Search of an Ethics of Personal Relationships." In Graham and LaFollette, *Person to Person,* 63–81.

Hare, Douglas R. A. *Matthew.* Louisville, Ky.: John Knox, 1993.

Hare, R. M. *Moral Thinking: Its Levels, Method, and Point.* Oxford: Clarendon, 1981.

Häring, Bernard. *The Law of Christ.* Vol. 2: *Special Moral Theology: Life in Fellowship with God and Fellow Man.* Trans. Edwin G. Kaiser. Westminster, Md.: Newman, 1964.

Harkness, Georgia. *Christian Ethics.* New York: Abingdon, 1957.

Harrington, Daniel J. *The Gospel of Matthew.* Sacra Pagina Series, 1. Collegeville, Minneapolis: Liturgical Press, 1991.
Harris, John. "Bad Samaritans Cause Harm." *Philosophical Quarterly* 32 (1982): 60–9.
Haslett, D. W. "Is Allowing Someone to Die the Same as Murder?" *Social Theory and Practice* 10 (1984): 81–95.
Haughey, John. *The Holy Use of Money: Personal Finances in Light of Christian Faith.* Garden City, NY: Doubleday, 1986.
Hayes, Carlton J. *Nationalism: A Religion.* New York: Macmillan, 1960.
Healy, Patrick J. "The Fathers on Wealth and Property." *Catholic University Bulletin* 17 (1911): 434–58.
Held, Virginia. "Can A Random Collection of Individuals Be Morally Responsible?" *Journal of Philosophy* 67 (1970): 471–81.
Henriot, Peter. *Opting for the Poor: A Challenge for North Americans.* Washington: Center of Concern, 1990.
Hernbäck, Eva. "A Chance for Children." *World Press Review,* April 1990, 74.
Herrmann, Robert. *La charité de l'église de ses origines à nos jours.* Mulhouse: Éditions Salvator, 1961.
Hoffmann, Stanley. *Duties Beyond Borders: On the Limits and Possibilities of Ethical International Politics.* Syracuse, NY: Syracuse University Press, 1981.
Hollenbach, David. *Claims in Conflict: Retrieving and Renewing the Catholic Human Rights Tradition.* New York: Paulist, 1979.
Houlgate, Laurence D. "Ethical Theory and the Family." In Meyers et al., *Kindred Matters,* 59–73.
Hughes, Gerard. "Killing and Letting Die." *Month,* n.s. 8 (1975): 42–5.
Hunt, Mary E. "Friends and Family Values: A New Old Song." In Rouner, *The Changing Face of Friendship,* 169–82.
Ignatieff, Michael. *Blood and Belonging: Journeys into the New Nationalism.* New York: Farrar, Straus and Giroux, 1994.
Isaacs, Tracy L. "Moral Theory and Action Theory, Killing and Letting Die." *American Philosophical Quarterly* 32 (1995): 355–68.
"It Wouldn't Take a Miracle to Save the World" (interview with Arthur Simon). *U. S. Catholic,* April 1988, 21–8.
Jackson, Tony with Deborah Eade. *Against the Grain: The Dilemma of Project Food Aid.* Oxford: Oxfam, 1982.
Jacoby, Tamar. "The Politics of Identity." *New York Times Book Review,* 19 November 1995, 32.
James, Susan. "The Duty to Relieve Suffering." *Ethics* 93 (1982–3): 4–21.
Janssen, Leon H. "Duties to Underdeveloped Countries." *Social Order* 8 (1958): 197–205.

Jecker, Nancy S. "Impartiality and Special Relations." In Meyers et al., *Kindred Matters*, 74–89.

Johnson, Harry G. *Economic Policies Toward Less Developed Countries.* Washington: Brookings Institution, 1967.

Jone, Heribert. *Moral Theology.* Trans. and adapted by Urban Adelman. Westminster, Md.: Newman, 1945.

Jones, Alexander. *The Gospel According to St. Matthew: A Text and Commentary for Students.* New York: Sheed and Ward, 1965.

Kagan, Shelly. *Limits of Morality.* Oxford: Clarendon, 1989.

Kamm, Frances Myrna. "Killing and Letting Die: Methodological and Substantive Issues." *Pacific Philosophical Quarterly* 64 (1983): 297–312.

Kaufman, Gordon. *The Context of Decision: A Theological Analysis.* New York: Abingdon, 1961.

Kee, Howard Clark. *Community of the New Age: Studies in Mark's Gospel.* London: SCM, 1977.

Kelsey, Morton T. *Caring: How Can We Love One Another?* New York: Paulist, 1981.

Kierkegaard, Sören. *Works of Love.* 1847. Trans. Howard and Edna Hong. San Francisco: Harper and Row, 1962.

Kilgallen, John J. *A Brief Commentary on the Gospel of Matthew.* Lewiston, NY: Edwin Mellen, 1992.

Klein, Philip. *From Philanthropy to Social Welfare: An American Cultural Perspective.* San Francisco: Jossey-Bass, 1968.

Koch, Antony. *A Handbook of Moral Theology.* Ed. Arthur Preuss. Vol. 5: *Man's Duties to His Fellowmen.* St. Louis and London: B. Herder, 1924.

Kol, Alph van. *Theologia moralis.* Vol. 1. Barcelona: Herder, 1968.

Korff, Wilhelm. *Theologische Ethik: Eine Einführung.* Freiburg: Herder, 1975.

Kutzner, Patricia L. *World Hunger: A Reference Handbook.* Santa Barbara, Ca.: ABC-CLIO, 1991.

Labata, Juan Francisco. *Thesaurus moralis.* 2 vols. Cologne: Impensis Joannis Godofredi Schonwetteri & Gervini Gymnici, 1652.

La Croix, Claude. *Theologia moralis.* 2 vols. Venice: Pezzana, 1738.

Lactantius. *The Divine Institutes.* Books I-VII. Trans. Mary Francis McDonald. Washington: Catholic University of America Press, 1964.

Lambrecht, J. "The Parousia Discourse: Composition and Content in *Mt.*, XXIV-XXV." In *L'Évangile selon Matthieu: Rédaction et théologie.* Ed. M. Didier. Gembloux, Belgium: J. Duculot, 1972. 309–42.

Lanza, Antonio, and Pietro Palazzini. *Theologia moralis.* Vol. 2: *De virtutibus in specie.* Turin: Marietti, 1955.

Latané, Bibb and John M. Darley. *The Unresponsive Bystander: Why Doesn't He Help?* New York: Appleton-Century-Crofts, 1970.

Lawler, Michael G. "Family: American and Christian." *America*, 12 August 1995: 20–2.

Leeds, Ruth. "Altruism and the Norm of Giving." *Merrill-Palmer Quarterly* 9 (1963): 229–40.

Lehmkuhl, August. *Theologia moralis.* 5th edn. Vol. 1. Freiburg: Herder, 1888.

Lesser, Harry. "Human Needs, Objectivity and Morality." In Raymond Plant et al., *Political Philosophy and Social Welfare: Essays on the Normative Basis of Welfare Provision.* London: Routledge and Kegan Paul, 1980. 37–51.

Leyton, Elliott, ed. *The Compact: Selected Dimensions of Friendship.* Toronto: Institute of Social and Economic Research, Memorial University of Newfoundland, 1974.

Liguori, St. Alphonsus. *Theologia moralis.* 9th edn. Ed. Leonard Gaudé. Vol. 1. Rome: Typographia Vaticana, 1905.

Lio, Hermengildus. "Determinatio superflui in doctrina Alexandri Halensis eiusque Scholae." *Antonianum* 27 (1952): 75–168.

"Finalmente rintracciata la fonte del famoso testo patristico: 'Pasce fame morientem . . .' " *Antonianum* 27 (1952): 349–66.

Lohfink, Norbert F. *Option for the Poor: The Basic Principle of Liberation Theology in the Light of the Bible.* Trans. Linda M. Maloney. Ed. Duane L. Christensen. Berkeley, Calif.: BIBAL, 1987.

Lovasik, Lawrence G. *Kindness.* New York: Macmillan, 1962.

Loyola, Saint Ignatius of. *The Constitutions of the Society of Jesus.* Trans. George E. Ganss. St. Louis: The Institute of Jesuit Sources, 1970.

Letter to Jaime Cassador. Trans. Martin E. Palmer. *Studies in the Spirituality of Jesuits,* May 1995: 27–30.

Lubich, Chiara. *When Our Love Is Charity.* Spiritual Writings, 2. Trans. New City Press staff. New York: New City, 1991.

Lugo, Juan de. *De iustitia et de iure.* Vol. 6, *Disputationes scholasticae et morales.* 9th edn. Paris: Vivés, 1868.

Luther, Martin. "The Large Catechism." In *The Book of Concord.* Ed. and trans. Theodore G. Tappert. Philadelphia: Fortress, 1959.

MacArthur, John, Jr. *Matthew 24–28.* The MacArthur New Testament Commentary. Chicago: Moody, 1989.

McCown, James Hart. *With Crooked Lines: Early Years of an Alabama Jesuit.* Mobile, Ala.: Spring Hill College Press, 1990.

McGinn, Colin. Review of Peter Unger, *Living High and Letting Die: Our Illusion of Innocence. The New Republic,* 14 Oct. 1996, 54–7.

McHugh, John A., and Charles J. Callan. *Moral Theology: A Complete Course.* 2 vols. New York: Joseph F. Wagner, 1929.

McMurrin, Sterling M., ed. *The Tanner Lectures on Human Values*. Vol. 2. Salt Lake City: University of Utah Press; Cambridge: Cambridge University Press, 1981.

Mahoney, John. "Let's Junk the Profit Motive." *US Catholic*, June 1972, 14–18 (with feedback).

Mann, Arthur. *Immigrants in American Life: Selected Readings*. Boston: Houghton Mifflin, 1968.

Many, Seraphin. "Aumône." *Dictionnaire de la Bible*. Ed. F. Vigouroux. Vol. 1. Paris: Letouzey, n.d., Col. 1244–53.

Marc, C., and F. X. Gestermann. *Institutiones morales alphonsianae*. 20th edn. Vol. 1. Lyons: Vitte, 1940.

Marshall, L. H. *The Challenge of New Testament Ethics*. New York: Macmillan, 1947.

Massillon, Jean Baptiste. "On Charity." In *20 Centuries of Great Preaching*, vol. 2: *Luther to Massillon*. Ed. Clyde E. Fant, Jr., and William M. Pinson, Jr. Waco, Texas: Word Books, 1971. 410–30.

Mautner, Thomas. Review of Robert E. Goodin, *Protecting the Vulnerable: A Reanalysis of Our Social Responsibilities*. *Journal of Applied Philosophy* 5 (1988): 114–18.

Meeks, Wayne A. *The Moral World of the First Christians*. Philadelphia: Westminster, 1986.

Meier, John P. *Matthew*. Wilmington, Del.: Glazier, 1980.

Meilaender, Gilbert. *Friendship: A Study in Theological Ethics*. Notre Dame: University of Notre Dame Press, 1981.

Melden, A. I. *Rights and Persons*. Berkeley: University of California Press, 1977.

Menendez Reigada, Ignacio G. "Obligaciones de justicia y de caridad de los proprietarios en los teólogos escolásticos." *La Ciencia Tomista* 77 (1950): 333–61.

Merkelbach, Benoît Henri. *Summa theologiae moralis*. 3d edn. Vol. 1: *De principiis*. Paris: Desclée de Brouwer, 1938.

Metz, Johann Baptist. Glaube in *Geschichte und Gessellschaft*: Studien zu einer praktischen Fundamentaltheologie. Mainz: Matthias Grünewald, 1977.

Meyer, Paul W. "Context as a Bearer of Meaning in Matthew." *Union Seminary Quarterly Review* 42, nos. 1–2 (1988): 69–72.

Meyers, Diana Tietjens. Introduction to Part I. In Meyers et al., *Kindred Matters*, 13–20.

Meyers, Diana Tietjens, Kenneth Kipnis, and Cornelius F. Murphy, Jr., eds. *Kindred Matters: Rethinking the Philosophy of the Family*. Ithaca, NY: Cornell University Press, 1993.

Mill, John Stuart. *Utilitarianism*. Vol. 10, *Collected Works of John Stuart*

Mill. Ed. J. M. Robson. Toronto: University of Toronto Press; London: Routledge and Kegan Paul, 1969. 203–59.

Miller, David. "The Ethical Significance of Nationality." *Ethics* 98 (1987–8): 647–62.

Social Justice. Oxford: Clarendon, 1976.

Miller, Nathan. *FDR: An Intimate History*. Garden City, NY: Doubleday, 1983.

Mollat, Michel. *The Poor in the Middle Ages: An Essay in Social History*. Trans. Arthur Goldhammer. New Haven: Yale University Press, 1986.

Morgan, Ted. *FDR: A Biography*. New York: Simon and Schuster, 1985.

Morris, Leon. *The Gospel according to John*. Grand Rapids, Mich.: Eerdmans, 1971.

The Gospel According to Matthew. Grand Rapids, Mich.: Eerdmans; Leicester, England: Inter-Varsity, 1992.

Luke: An Introduction and Commentary. Tyndale New Testament Commentaries. Grand Rapids, Mich.: Eerdmans; Leicester: Inter-Varsity, 1988.

Muelder, Walter G. "Ethical Aspects of Income Distribution and Consumption." In Elizabeth E. Hoyt et al., *American Income and Its Use*. New York: Harper, 1954. 307–41.

Munby, D. L. *God and the Rich Society: A Study of Christians in a World of Abundance*. London: Oxford University Press, 1961.

Nagel, Thomas. *Equality and Partiality*. New York: Oxford University Press, 1991.

Narveson, Jan. "Aesthetics, Charity, Utility, and Distributive Justice." *Monist* 56 (1972): 527–51.

"Morality and Starvation." In Aiken and LaFollette, *World Hunger and Moral Obligation*, 49–65.

Newman, Barclay M., and Philip C. Stine. *A Translator's Handbook on the Gospel of Matthew*. London: United Bible Societies, 1988.

Niebanck, Richard J. *Economic Justice: An Evangelical Perspective*. Christian Social Responsibility Series. NP: Division for Mission in North America, Lutheran Church in America, 1980.

Niebuhr, Reinhold. *An Interpretation of Christian Ethics*. London: SCM, 1936.

Nielsen, Kai. "Global Justice and the Imperatives of Capitalism." *Journal of Philosophy* 80 (1983): 608–10.

Nolan, Albert. *Jesus Before Christianity*. Maryknoll, NY: Orbis, 1978.

Nolland, John. *Luke 9:21–18:34*. Word Biblical Commentary 35B. Dallas: Word Books, 1993.

Norman, Richard. "Self and Others: The Inadequacy of Utilitarianism." In *New Essays on John Stuart Mill and Utilitarianism*, ed.

Wesley E. Cooper, Kai Nielsen, and Steven C. Patten. Guelph, Ont.: Canadian Association for Publishing in Philosophy, 1979. 181–201.

Nossiter, Bernard D. *The Global Struggle for More: Third World Conflicts with Rich Nations.* New York: Harper and Row, 1987.

Nygren, Anders. *Agape and Eros.* Trans. Philip S. Watson. New York: Harper and Row, 1969.

O'Donovan, Oliver. *The Problem of Self-Love in St. Augustine.* New Haven: Yale University Press, 1980.

Oldenquist, Andrew. "Loyalties." *Journal of Philosophy* 79 (1982): 173–93.

O'Neill, James David. "Alms and Almsgiving." *Catholic Encyclopedia.* Vol. 1. New York: Appleton, 1907. 328–31.

O'Neill, Onora. *Faces of Hunger: An Essay on Poverty, Justice and Development.* London: Allen and Unwin, 1986.

"The Moral Perplexities of Famine and World Hunger." In *Matters of Life and Death: New Introductory Essays in Moral Philosophy,* ed. Tom Regan. 2d edn. New York: Random House, 1986. 294–337.

Oudersluys, Richard C. "The Parable of the Sheep and Goats (Matthew 25:31–46): Eschatology and Mission, Then and Now." *Reformed Review* 26 (1972–3): 151–61.

Outka, Gene. *Agape: An Ethical Analysis.* New Haven: Yale University Press, 1972.

"Love." In *Encyclopedia of Ethics.* Ed. Lawrence C. Becker and Charlotte B. Becker. 2 vols. New York: Garland, 1992. 742–51.

"Universal Love and Impartiality." In *The Love Commandments: Essays in Christian Ethics and Moral Philosophy.* Ed. Edmund N. Santurri and William Werpehowski. Washington: Georgetown University Press, 1992. 1–103.

Paley, William. *Moral and Political Philosophy.* Vol. 1, *The Works of William Paley, DD.* London: George Cowie, 1837.

Palmer, George Herbert. *Altruism: Its Nature and Varieties.* New York: Scribner's, 1919.

Parfit, Derek. "Prudence, Morality, and the Prisoner's Dilemma." *Proceedings of the British Academy* 65 (1979): 539–64.

Reasons and Persons. Oxford: Clarendon, 1984.

Patte, Daniel. *The Gospel according to Matthew: A Structural Commentary on Matthew's Faith.* Philadelphia: Fortress, 1987.

Paulsen, Friedrich. *A System of Ethics.* Ed. and trans. F. Tilly. New York: Scribner's, 1911.

Pear, Robert. Review of David Hilfiker, *Not All of Us Are Saints. New York Times Book Review,* 13 Aug. 1994, 8.

Peeters, Hermes. *Manuale theologiae moralis.* Vol. 2. Turin: Marietti, 1962.

Peinador, Antonio. *Cursus brevior theologiae moralis. Pars prior speculativa, tomus II: Theologia moralis specialis.* Vol. 1: *De fide, spe, caritate. De prudentia.* Madrid: Coculsa, 1950.

Pelt, Theodor van. *De tribus bonorum operum generibus.* Ingolstadt: Apud Davidem Sartorium, 1680.

Peñafort, St. Raymond of. *Summa de paenitentia.* Universa Bibliotheca Iuris. Ed. X. Ochoa and A. Diez. Rome: Commentarium pro religiosis, 1976.

Pennock, J. Roland. "Political Representation: An Overview." In *Nomos X: Representation.* Ed. J. Roland Pennock and John W. Chapman. New York: Atherton, 1968. 3–27.

Peschke, Karl H. *Christian Ethics: Moral Theology in the Light of Vatican II.* Vol. 2: *Special Moral Theology.* Alcester, Warwickshire: C. Goodliffe Neale, 1985.

Philip the Chancellor. *Summa de bono.* Ed. Nikolaus Wicki. Corpus Philosophorum Medii Aevi. Opera philosophica mediae aetatis selecta, 2. Berne: Francke, 1985.

Phillips, C. S. *The New Commandment: An Inquiry into the Social Precept and Practice of the Ancient Church.* London: Society for Promoting Christian Knowledge, 1930.

Piscetta, Aloysius, and Andrea Gennaro. *Elementa theologiae moralis.* 3rd edn. Vol. 2. Turin: Società Editrice Internazionale, 1935.

Plant, Raymond, Harry Lesser and Peter Taylor-Gooby. *Political Philosophy and Social Welfare: Essays on the Normative Basis of Welfare Provision.* London: Routledge and Kegan Paul, 1980.

Plummer, Alfred. *A Critical and Exegetical Commentary on the Gospel According to S. Luke.* 5th edn. New York: Scribner, 1922.

Pons, Blaise, ed. *L'amour chrétien.* Paris: Éditions François Beauval, 1969.

Pope, Stephen J. *The Evolution of Altruism and the Ordering of Love.* Washington: Georgetown University Press, 1994.

"Love in Contemporary Christian Ethics." *Journal of Religious Ethics* 23 (1995): 167–97.

"The Order of Love, and Recent Catholic Ethics: A Constructive Proposal." *Theological Studies* 52 (1991): 255–88.

"The Preferential Option for the Poor: An Ethic for 'Saints and Heroes'"? *Irish Theological Quarterly* 59 (1993): 161–76.

"Proper and Improper Partiality and the Preferential Option for the Poor." *Theological Studies* 54 (1993): 242–71.

Post, Stephen G. "Love and the Order of Beneficence." *Soundings* 75 (1992): 499–516.

Review of Garth L. Hallett, *Christian Neighbor-Love: An Assessment of Six Rival Versions. Journal of Religious Ethics* 19 (1991): 196.

Spheres of Love: Toward a New Ethics of the Family. Dallas: Southern Methodist University Press, 1994.

A Theory of Agape: On the Meaning of Christian Love. Lewisburg, Pa.: Bucknell University Press, 1990.

Preiss, Théo. *Life in Christ.* Studies in Biblical Theology, 13. Trans. Harold Knight. Chicago: Alec R. Allenson, 1954.

Property: Its Duties and Rights. 2d edn. London: Macmillan, 1915.

Prümmer, Dominic M. *Manuale theologiae moralis.* 13th edn. Ed. Joachim Overbeck. 3 vols. Freiburg: Herder, 1958.

Quigley, Margaret, and Michael Garvey, eds., *The Dorothy Day Book.* Springfield, Ill.: Templegate, 1982.

Rachels, James. "Killing and Starving to Death." *Philosophy* 54 (1979): 159–71.

"Morality, Parents, and Children." In Graham and LaFollette, eds. *Person to Person,* 46–62.

Rahner, Karl. *Theological Investigations.* Vol. 6. Trans. Karl-H. and Boniface Kruger. Baltimore: Helicon; London: Darton, Longman, and Todd, 1969.

Ramsey, Boniface. "Almsgiving in the Latin Church: The Late Fourth and Early Fifth Centuries." *Theological Studies* 43 (1982): 226–59.

Ratschow, Carl Heinz. "Agape, Nächstenliebe und Bruderliebe." *Zeitschrift für systematische Theologie* 21 (1950): 160–82.

Raven, E. E. *The Heart of Christ's Religion.* London: Longmans, Green, 1933.

Reeder, John P., Jr. *Killing and Saving: Abortion, Hunger, and War.* University Park, Pa.: Pennsylvania State University Press, 1996.

Regis, Edward, Jr. "Rachels on Killing and Starving to Death." *Pacific Philosophical Quarterly* 62 (1981): 416–18.

Reiffenstuel, Anaklet. *Theologia moralis.* Venice: Sumptibus Jo. Baptistae Albritii, 1745.

Reisman, John M. *Anatomy of Friendship.* New York: Irvington, 1979.

Rescher, Nicholas. *Unselfishness: The Role of the Vicarious Affects in Moral Philosophy and Social Theory.* Pittsburgh: University of Pittsburgh Press, 1975.

Ridderbos, H. N. *Matthew.* Bible Student's Commentary. Trans. Ray Togtman. Grand Rapids, Mich.: Zondervan, 1987.

Riquet, Michel. *Le chrétien face à l'argent.* Paris: Éditions Spes, 1947.

Christian Charity in Action. Trans. P. J. Hepburne-Scott. Twentieth Century Encyclopedia of Catholicism, 105. New York: Hawthorn, 1961.

Robinson, J. A. T. "The 'Parable' of the Sheep and the Goats." *New Testament Studies* 2 (1955–6): 225–37.

Roey, Joseph Ernest van. *De virtute charitatis. Quaestiones selectae.* Mechlin: Dessain, 1929.

Roncaglia, Constantino. *Universa moralis theologia.* Vol. 1. Venice: Pitteri, 1753.

Rosenthal, Elisabeth. "The Fertility Market." *New York Times,* 10 January 1996: A1, C6.

Ross, W. D. *The Right and the Good.* Oxford: Clarendon, 1930.

Rouner, Leroy S., ed. *The Changing Face of Friendship.* Notre Dame: University of Notre Dame Press, 1994.

Sand, Alexander. *Das Evangelium nach Matthäus.* Regensburg: Friedrich Pustet, 1986.

Savonarola, Girolamo. *De simplicitate christianae vitae.* 1496. Ed. Pier Giorgio Ricci. Rome: Angelo Belardetti, 1959.

Schilling, Otto. *Handbuch der Moraltheologie.* Vol. 3. Stuttgart: Schwabenverlag, 1956.

Schüller, Bruno. *Die Begründung sittlicher Urteile: Typen ethischer Argumentation in der katholischen Moraltheologie.* Düsseldorf: Patmos, 1973.

"Neuere Beiträge zum Thema 'Begründung sittlicher Normen.' " *Theologische Berichte.* Vol. 4. Ed. Josef Pfammatter and Franz Furger. Zürich: Benziger, 1974. 109–81.

Schwartz, Aloysius. *Poverty: Sign of Our Times.* New York: Alba House, 1970.

The Starved and the Silent. Garden City, N.Y.: Doubleday, 1966.

Schwartz, Nancy L. *The Blue Guitar: Political Representation and Community.* Chicago: University of Chicago Press, 1988.

Schweizer, Eduard. *The Good News according to Matthew.* Trans. David E. Green. Atlanta: John Knox, 1975.

Sen, Amartya. "Population: Delusion and Reality." *The New York Review of Books,* 22 September 1994, 62–71.

Serafino da Lojano. *Institutiones theologiae moralis.* Vol. 2. Turin: Marietti, 1935.

Sharp, Frank Chapman. *Ethics.* New York: Century, 1928.

Sheedy, Charles E. *The Christian Virtues.* 2nd edn. Notre Dame: University of Notre Dame Press, 1951.

Sherlock, William. *The Nature and Measure of Charity.* London: Printed for W. Rogers, 1697.

Shewring, Walter, ed. *Rich and Poor in Christian Tradition.* London: Burns, Oates, and Washbourne, 1948.

Shue, Henry. *Basic Rights: Subsistence, Affluence, and U. S. Foreign Policy.* Princeton, NJ: Princeton University Press, 1980.

"The Burdens of Justice." *Journal of Philosophy* 80 (1983): 600–8.

"Mediating Duties." *Ethics* 98 (1987–8): 687–704.

Sider, Ronald J. *Rich Christians in an Age of Hunger: A Biblical Study.* New York: Paulist, 1978.

Sidgwick, Henry. *The Methods of Ethics.* 7th edn. London: Macmillan, 1907.

Simcox, Carroll E. *The First Gospel: Its Meaning and Message.* Greenwich, Conn.: Seabury, 1963.

Singer, Irving. *The Nature of Love: Plato to Luther.* New York: Random House, 1966.

Singer, Peter. *The Expanding Circle: Ethics and Sociobiology.* New York: Farrar, Straus and Giroux, 1981.

"Famine, Affluence, and Morality." *Philosophy and Public Affairs* 1 (1972): 229–43. Rpt. in Aiken and LaFollette, *World Hunger and Moral Obligation*, 22–36.

Practical Ethics. 2nd edn. Cambridge: Cambridge University Press, 1993.

"Reconsidering the Famine Relief Argument." In Brown and Shue, *Food Policy*, 36–53.

Smart, Ninian. "Friendship and Enmity among Nations." In Rouner, *The Changing Face of Friendship*, 155–67.

Smith, Adam. *The Theory of Moral Sentiments.* 1759. Ed. D. D. Raphael and A. L. Macfie. Indianapolis: Liberty Classics, 1982.

Smith, Brian H. *More than Altruism: The Politics of Private Foreign Aid.* Princeton: Princeton University Press, 1990.

Smith, Mary Ann. "The Haves and the Have Nots – Mending the Global Rift." *NETWORK Connection*, November/December 1995, 3–5.

Snarey, John. *How Fathers Care for the Next Generation: A Four-Decade Study.* Cambridge, Mass.: Harvard University Press, 1993.

Sneed, Joseph D. "A Utilitarian Framework for Policy Analysis in Food-Related Foreign Aid." In Brown and Shue, *Food Policy*, 103–28.

Snyder, Louis L. *Varieties of Nationalism: A Comparative Study.* New York: Holt, Rinehart and Winston, 1976.

Sommers, Christina Hoff. "Filial Morality." *Journal of Philosophy* 83 (1986): 439–56.

Soto, Domingo de. "Commentarium in II.II.q.32 De eleemosyna (anno 1539–40)." In Deuringer, *Probleme der Caritas in der Schule von Salamanca*, 143–58.

Spanneut, Michel. *Tertullien et les premiers moralistes africains.* Gembloux: J. Duculot; Paris: Lethielleux, 1969.

Sparshott, F. E. *An Enquiry into Goodness.* Chicago: University of Chicago Press, 1958.

Sporer, Patricius. *Theologia moralis super Decalogum*. Vol. 1. Salzburg: Mayr, 1722.

Steinbock, Bonnie, ed. *Killing and Letting Die*. Englewood Cliffs, NJ: Prentice-Hall, 1980.

Stone, Lawrence. "Class Divisions in England, 1540–1640." In Barber and Barber, *European Social Class*, 12–23.

Suarez, Francis. *Opera omnia*. Ed. C. Berton. Vol. 12. Paris: Vivès, 1858.

Summers, Ray. *Commentary on Luke*. Waco, Tex.: Word Books, 1972.

Tambasco, Anthony J. "Option for the Poor." In *The Deeper Meaning of Economic Life: Critical Essays on the U. S. Catholic Bishops' Pastoral Letter on the Economy*. Ed. R. Bruce Douglass. Washington: Georgetown University Press, 1986. 37–55.

Taylor, Jeremy. *The Great Exemplar of Sanctity and Holy Life*. Vol. 2, *The Whole Works*. London: Longman et al., 1847.

The Measures and Offices of Friendship. 1662. Delmar, New York: Scholars' Facsimiles and Reprints, 1984.

Taylor, Michael. *Good for the Poor: Christian Ethics and World Development*. London: Mowbray, 1990.

Tec, Nechamah. *When Light Pierced the Darkness: Christian Rescue of Jews in Nazi-Occupied Poland*. Oxford: Oxford University Press, 1986.

Telfer, Elizabeth. "Friendship." *Proceedings of the Aristotelian Society* 106 (1970–1): 223–41.

Temple, William. *Christianity and Social Order*. New York: Seabury, 1977.

Tenison, Thomas. *A Sermon Concerning Discretion in Giving Alms*. London: Printed for J. Macock for F. Tyton, 1681.

"The Oxford Declaration on Christian Faith and Economics." *Transformation* 7, no. 2 (1990):1–8.

Thouvenin, A. "Magnanimité." *Dictionnaire de théologie catholique*. Vol. 9:2. Paris, Letouzey, 1927. Col. 1550–3.

Toledo, Francisco de. *In Summam Theologiae S. Thomae Aquinatis enarratio*. Vol. 2. Turin: Marietti; Paris: Palmé, 1869.

Tooley, Michael. *Abortion and Infanticide*. Oxford: Clarendon, 1983.

"An Irrelevant Consideration: Killing versus Letting Die." In Steinbock, *Killing and Letting Die*, 56–62.

Torres, Luis de. *Disputationes in secundam secundae S.Thomae*. Lyons: Cardon, 1617.

Tournely, Honoré. *De universa theologia morali*. Vol. 3. Venice: Pezzana, 1756.

Toussaint, Stanley D. *Behold the King: A Study of Matthew*. Portland, Oregon: Multnomah, 1980.

Trammell, Richard L. "Saving Life and Taking Life." *Journal of Philosophy* 72 (1975): 131–7.

Tyndale, William. "The Parable of the Wicked Mammon." In idem, *Doctrinal Treatises*. Ed. Henry Walter. Cambridge: Cambridge University Press, 1848. 29–126.

Unger, Peter. *Living High and Letting Die: Our Illusion of Innocence*. New York: Oxford University Press, 1996.

Urmson, J. O. "Saints and Heroes." In *Essays in Moral Philosophy*. Ed. A. I. Melden. Seattle: University of Washington Press, 1958. 198–216.

Urwick, E. J. *Luxury and Waste of Life*. London: J. M. Dent, 1908.

Vacek, Edward Collins. *Love, Human and Divine: The Heart of Christian Ethics*. Washington: Georgetown University Press, 1994.

Valencia, Gregorio de. *Commentariorum theologicorum*. Vol. 3. Venice: Apud Iuntas, 1608.

Valuy, Benedict. *Fraternal Charity*. Authorized trans. 2nd edn. London: R. and T. Washbourne, 1908.

Vasquez, Gabriel. "Tractatus de eleemosyna." *Opuscula moralia*. Venice: Apud Petrum Mariam Bertanum, 1618. 1–21.

Vermeersch, Arthur. *Quaestiones de virtutibus religionis et pietatis ac vitiis contrariis*. Bruges: Beyaert, 1912.

Theologiae moralis principia – responsa – consilia. 3d edn. Vol. 2: *De virtutum exercitatione*. Rome: Università Gregoriana, 1937.

Vio, Tommaso de. *Commentaria in Summam theologicam sancti Thomae Aquinatis*. In St. Thomas Aquinas, *Opera omnia*, vols. 4–12. Rome: Typographia Polyglotta, 1888–1906.

"De eleemosynae praecepto." In idem, *Scripta philosophica: Opuscula oeconomico-socialia*. Ed. P. Zammit. Rome: Typographia Missionaria Dominicana, 1934. 1–37.

Vitoria, Francisco de. *De caritate et prudentia*. Vol. 2. *Comentarios a la Secunda secundae de Santo Tomás*. Ed. Vicente Beltrán de Heredia. Salamanca: Biblioteca de Téologos Españoles, 1932.

Vykopal, Adolfo. *Interpretazione della dottrina del superfluo in San Tommaso*. 2nd edn. Brescia: Morcelliana, 1962.

Wadell, Paul J. *Friendship and the Moral Life*. Notre Dame: University of Notre Dame Press, 1989.

Wallwork, Ernest. "Thou Shalt Love Thy Neighbor as Thyself: The Freudian Critique." *Journal of Religious Ethics* 10 (1982): 264–319.

Walsh, Terrance G. Review of Gustavo Gutiérrez, *Las Casas: In Search of the Poor of Jesus Christ*. *Theological Studies* 56 (1995): 367–9.

Walzer, Michael. *Spheres of Justice: A Defense of Pluralism and Equality*. New York: Basic Books, 1983.

Ward, Barbara. *Five Ideas That Change the World*. New York: Norton, 1959.

The Lopsided World. New York: Norton, 1968.

Nationalism and Ideology. New York: Norton, 1966.

The Rich Nations and the Poor Nations. New York: Norton, 1962.

Wasserstrom, Richard. "Lawyers as Professionals: Some Moral Issues." *Human Rights* 5 (1975–6): 1–24.

"Roles and Morality." In *The Good Lawyer: Lawyers' Roles and Lawyers' Ethics*, ed. David Luban. Totowa, NJ: Rowman and Allenheld, 1983. 25–37.

Wayland, Francis. *Elements of Moral Science.* Boston: Gould and Lincoln, 1853.

Welty, Eberhard. *A Handbook of Christian Social Ethics.* Vol. 1: *Man in Society.* Trans. Gregor Kirstein. New York: Herder and Herder, 1960.

Wesley, John. "The Danger of Riches." In *John Wesley's Sermons: An Anthology.* Ed. Albert C. Outler and Richard P. Heitzenrater. Nashville, Tenn.: Abingdon, 1991. 451–63.

"The Use of Money." *The Works of John Wesley.* Vol. 2: *Sermons II 34–70.* Ed. Albert C. Outler. Nashville, Tenn.: Abingdon, 1985. 266–80.

Westermarck, Edward A. *The Origin and Development of the Moral Ideas.* 2nd edn. 2 vols. London: Macmillan, 1912–17.

Whelan, John M., Jr. "Famine and Charity." *Southern Journal of Philosophy* 29 (1991): 149–66.

White, R. E. O. *The Insights of History.* Vol. 2: *The Changing Continuity of Christian Ethics.* Exeter: Paternoster, 1981.

Christian Ethics: The Historical Development. Atlanta: John Knox, 1981.

William of Auxerre. *Summa aurea.* 1500. Vol. 3, pt. 1. Ed. Jean Ribaillier. Paris: Centre National de la Recherche Scientifique; Rome: Editiones Collegii S. Bonaventurae ad Claras Aquas, 1986.

Williams, Daniel Day. *The Spirit and the Forms of Love.* New York: Harper and Row, 1968.

Winandy, Jacques. "La scène du Jugement Dernier." *Sciences Ecclésiastiques* 18 (1966): 169–86.

Winkler, Earl R. "Utilitarian Idealism and Personal Relations." *Canadian Journal of Philosophy* 12 (1982): 265–86.

Winslow, Donald F. "Gregory of Nazianzus and Love for the Poor." *Anglican Theological Review* 47 (1965): 348–59.

Wogaman, J. Philip. *A Christian Method of Moral Judgement.* Philadelphia: Westminster, 1976.

"Toward a Christian Definition of Justice." *Transformation* 7, no. 2 (1990): 18–23.

Zalba, Marcellinus. *Theologiae moralis summa.* 3 vols. Madrid: Biblioteca de autores cristianos, 1957.

Index